If Einstein Ran the Schools

If Einstein Ran the Schools

REVITALIZING U.S. EDUCATION

Thomas Armstrong, PhD

 PRAEGER®

An Imprint of ABC-CLIO, LLC
Santa Barbara, California • Denver, Colorado

Library of Congress Cataloging in Publication Control Number: 2019948980

ISBN: 978-1-4408-6977-8 (print)
      978-1-4408-6978-5 (ebook)

23 22 21 20 19   1 2 3 4 5

This book is also available as an eBook.

Praeger
An Imprint of ABC-CLIO, LLC

ABC-CLIO, LLC
147 Castilian Drive
Santa Barbara, California 93117
www.abc-clio.com

This book is printed on acid-free paper ∞

Manufactured in the United States of America

To my agent, Joëlle Delbourgo, without whose help this book never would have come into existence

Contents

CHAPTER ONE

The Purpose of Education: Introducing Incredible Kids to an Amazing World

It is nothing short of a miracle that modern methods of instruction have not yet entirely strangled the holy curiosity of inquiry.
—Albert Einstein[1]

OK, here's what I don't understand. On the one hand, you have the child, this incredible being who has been equipped by natural selection over the course of hundreds of thousands and even millions of years to be a curious, passionate learner. There's plenty of support for this view. Nuclear physicist J. Robert Oppenheimer once said, "There are children playing in the streets who could solve some of my top problems in physics, because they have modes of sensory perception that I lost long ago."[2] Neuroscientist Marian Diamond wrote, "The energy use in a two-year-old [brain] is equal to an adult's. And then, the levels keep right on rising until, by age three, the child's brain is twice as active as an adult's."[3] Harvard paleontologist Stephen Jay Gould believed that the key evolutionary advantage of *Homo sapiens* was *neoteny*, that is, the retention of childlike characteristics like flexibility and curiosity into adulthood.[4] Also keep in mind that children regularly learn the most complicated symbol system in the world, their own spoken language, without anyone directly teaching it to them. In some cases, they've created totally new languages![5] So I think I'm pretty safe in declaring that children are incredible learning beings superbly equipped to respond with excitement and understanding to the world around them.

On the other hand, there's this amazing world out there for children to learn about. Where do I start? There are the stars, the galaxies, and the possibility of multiple universes. There's nature, with its incredible diversity of plants, animals, birds, insects, and other living things. There's music of every conceivable type, from Mozart and Beethoven to jazz and blues, from the rhythms of Indonesian gamelan music to the ragas of Indian tradition. There's science, with its explorations of sub-atomic particles, its probes into the mysteries of the biological code, and its technological achievements in almost every aspect of modern life. There are numbers and mathematical systems, from the magic squares of the Cabalists to the Fibonacci sequence observable in the structure of chambered nautilus seashells. There are the histories of cultures: their conflicts and struggles as well as their achievements and triumphs. And books! There are books that provide a myriad of captivating stories and a treasure house of information about this remarkable world. Indeed, there's truly an amazing world out there for a child to encounter. As children's author Hans Christian Andersen once put it, "The whole world is a series of marvels, but we're so used to them that we call them everyday things!"[6]

THE MISEDUCATION OF AMERICA

So here's the part I don't understand. Education should be about introducing these incredible children to this amazing world. It should be the easiest thing in the world to do. It should be a slam dunk, something that educators could do in their sleep. And yet somehow we manage to muck it up. Michael Parker, program director of psychological services at the Fort Worth Independent School District, which serves eighty thousand students, writes, "I'm clearly seeing an increasing number of kindergartners and first-graders coming to our attention for aggressive behavior. We're talking about serious talking back to teachers, profanity, even biting, kicking and hitting adults, and we're seeing it in 5-year-olds" (please note that these *aren't* the kids diagnosed with emotional disturbances).[7] There are other troubling signs as well:

- One in ten preschoolers has had suicidal thoughts.[8]
- Doctors are increasingly seeing children in early elementary school suffering from migraine headaches and ulcers, and many physicians see a clear connection to school performance pressure.[9]

- The number of children diagnosed with attention deficit hyperactivity disorder (ADHD) has soared to 6.1 million, an increase of 1.7 million kids from 2003 to 2016.[10]

- Since 1990, creative thinking scores have significantly decreased, with the greatest decreases among children in kindergarten through third grade.[11]

- Nearly 10 percent of K–12 teachers report being threatened by a student, and 6 percent report being physically attacked.[12]

- A third of our adolescents report feeling depressed or overwhelmed because of stress, and their single biggest source of stress is school, according to the American Psychological Association.[13]

- Highly achieving teens are starting to refer to themselves as "robo-students," that is, students set on autopilot, going through the motions, getting high grades and test scores but not actually being engaged by the classroom material.[14]

- Over a third of U.S. college students report seriously considering attempting suicide.[15]

- Enrollment in teacher preparation programs has fallen some 35 percent over the past five years.[16]

Clearly, something has gone seriously, abnormally, atrociously wrong.

A large portion of the responsibility for these ills can and should be assigned to the miseducation that's been taking place over the past thirty-five years in our nation's schools. We've taken play out of preschools and kindergartens and replaced it with academic learning, a move that is not developmentally appropriate for young children. We've taken the joy of reading fiction out of elementary and high school curricula, and instead we're requiring students to read "informational texts" using "close reading" techniques more suited to university students studying literary criticism. We've cut back on physical education programs, recess, and the arts to give more time for sedentary academic "seat work." We've piled "rigorous" course and graduation requirements on students in middle school and high school just when they need to make their own decisions about learning topics and should be doing a lot of their learning out in the real world.[17]

We've forgotten about introducing incredible kids to an amazing world, and instead we're requiring them to master soulless objectives such as this third-grade academic standard from the country's national Common Core State Standards (adopted by thirty-six states and similar to standards in the other fourteen states): "Describe the relationship between a series of historical events, scientific ideas or concepts, or steps in technical procedures in a text, using language that pertains to time, sequence, and cause/

effect."[18] We've made standardized testing the primary way to determine a student's learning progress in school. We've increasingly dehumanized the learning process by using corporate, depersonalized learning systems that gather students' computer keystrokes and turn them into a collection of data points to be analyzed, stored, and even sold to the highest bidder. We've robbed public schools of badly needed funds by accelerating the transformation of our schools into for-profit academies and other choice-based institutions, where the bottom line is money, not student learning.

BAD MOON ON THE RISE: AMERICAN EDUCATION FROM 1983–2001

How did we ever get to this point? The answer to this question largely has to do with the machinations of politicians, CEOs of large corporations, and educational bureaucrats over the past thirty-five years. During this time, these power brokers have been engaged in a concerted attempt to turn our public (and private) schools into places where students are trained to become good corporate workers, cooperative team players, and skilled computer wonks content to toil docilely in cube farms and meeting rooms across America.

The initial kickoff to this "miseducation of America" came in April 1983, when the National Commission on Excellence in Education issued a report entitled "A Nation at Risk." This manifesto transformed education into a matter of national security, proclaiming, "The educational foundations of our society are presently being eroded by a rising tide of mediocrity that threatens our very future as a Nation and a people."[19] The commission called for standardized achievement tests to be administered at major transition points from one level of schooling to another. It proposed that textbooks be upgraded to include more "rigorous" content (this word *rigor* was to serve as a key rallying point in this campaign over the next three and a half decades, along with the word *accountability*). In addition, it recommended that students in high schools be assigned far more homework.

Two years after this declaration, the corporate world and business CEOs began to get involved, seeing their own financial interests threatened by this "rising tide of mediocrity." In 1985, the Carnegie Foundation for the Advancement of Teaching issued a report entitled "Corporate Classrooms: The Learning Business," where it revealed that nearly 75 percent of U.S. corporations were compelled to give their employees remedial classes in reading, writing, and computation because the schools had failed to adequately prepare their students for the workplace.[20] That same year, the Committee for Economic Development, an organization of two hundred business executives and educators, issued a report saying that the poor quality of American education was putting the economic future of the country in peril. They declared, "[E]ducation has a direct impact on employment, productivity, and growth, and on the nation's ability to compete in the world economy. . . . Therefore, we cannot fail to respond."[21]

Politics entered the scene in 1989, when President George H. W. Bush convened state governors at what became the first National Education Summit in Charlottesville, Virginia. Its aim was to establish broad educational goals for the nation. In his 1990 State of the Union message, Bush projected that by the year 2000, the nation would lead the world in mathematics and science achievement and every student would leave grades 4, 8, and 12 having demonstrated competency in English, mathematics, science, history, and geography (spoiler alert: this didn't even come *close* to happening).

In the 1990s, state governors and corporate CEOs began to work out the specifics of a national plan to establish standards for American students. One key figure in this effort was Louis V. Gerstner Jr., the chief executive officer of IBM, who told the National Governors Association at their annual meeting in 1995, "You are the CEOs of the organizations that fund and oversee the country's public schools. . . . That means you are responsible for their health. They are very sick at the moment."[22] Gerstner helped plan a second National Education Summit, in March 1996, where participants made a commitment to promote academic standards at the state and local levels. Also, significantly, they founded a nonprofit group, Achieve Inc., which two years later began the work of creating a set of national standards that would later be christened the Common Core State Standards.

HOW AMERICA LEFT KIDS BEHIND

The miseducation of America really began to take a firm grip (one might say a choke hold) on America's schools when Congress passed the No Child Left Behind Act (NCLB), which was signed into law by President George W. Bush on January 8, 2002. This law substantially increased the federal role in holding schools responsible for the academic progress of their students. Under the law, schools were charged with making what was called "adequate yearly progress" (AYP) on annual state standardized tests in reading and math. If a school missed its target for AYP, it began to suffer increasingly punitive measures from year to year, including having to allow students to transfer to a better-performing school in the district, having to provide free tutoring, or even having to let the government take over the school, close the school down, change it into a charter school, or enact other drastic measures to try turn things around academically.

NCLB turned out to be a disaster. As education critic Stan Karp observed, "By the time the first decade of NCLB was over, more than half the schools in the nation were on the lists of 'failing schools' and the rest were poised to follow. In Massachusetts, which is generally considered to have the toughest state standards in the nation, 80 percent of the schools were facing NCLB sanctions. . . . More than 4,000 public schools were closed across the country. Teachers and their unions were under siege. More than 300,000 teachers lost their jobs. The promised improvements in academic performance, even in narrow test score terms, never arrived."[23]

The results were so bad that in 2009, President Obama used a $4.25 billion grant to institute an initiative called "Race to the Top," which awarded incentive money to states who followed a standards-based program that evaluated teachers on the basis of their students' test scores. Furthermore, in 2011, President Obama began issuing waivers to states, exempting them from the more onerous features of NCLB, including the punitive sanctions for failure to make AYP. In return for these concessions, states had to agree to institute "college- and career-ready" academic standards using a program such as the Common Core State Standards, which Achieve Inc., with substantial support from the Bill and Melinda Gates Foundation, had created and unveiled to the public in 2010.[24] Finally, in 2015, Obama signed into law the Every Student Succeeds Act, which returned full responsibility for standards to the states while still requiring the standards to be approved by the federal government, and also mandated continued standardized testing of students.

With the election of Donald Trump as president in 2016, politics and corporate interests in education took a turn toward the privatization of America's schools. Campaigning on a platform of "school choice," Trump selected Betsy DeVos, the billionaire heiress of the Amway fortune, as U.S. secretary of education. DeVos, whose background in education was minimal and whose foundation had helped finance Michigan's poorly performing charter school movement, began immediately promoting the rapid expansion of private, for-profit charter schools where parents could use vouchers as an alternative to schooling their kids in local public schools. In the 2019 budget, President Trump proposed cutting $7.1 billion from the Department of Education and eliminating twenty-nine programs but providing $5 billion in tax credits for voucher programs and $500 million for federal charter school grants.[25] But as Diane Ravitch, former assistant U.S. secretary of Education and author of *Reign of Error: The Hoax of the Privatization Movement and the Danger to America's Public Schools*, put it, "Privately owned and managed charters do not improve public schools; they take funding away from public schools, thus disadvantaging them even further. In the name of 'choice' for the few, they weaken the schools that serve whoever arrives at the schoolhouse doors."[26]

THE CLOSING OF THE AMERICAN MIND

The upshot of this whole political and corporate-driven campaign is that after thirty-five years of summits, conferences, laws, and regulations, the United States still lags far behind most other developed countries in the world in academic achievement. In the most recent Programme for International Student Assessment (PISA) test results, which are given every three years to fifteen-year-olds around the world, the United States ranks twenty-fourth in reading, twenty-fourth in science, and thirty-eighth in math among participating nations.[27] According to the Brookings Institution, the United States' PISA scores have seen *no statistically significant change* from the first administration of the test in 2003 to the one in 2015.[28]

In addition, this corporatizing and politicizing of education have inflicted cultural wounds on our society that include declines in measures associated with an educated public. According to a 2016 Pew research survey, 26 percent of adult Americans reported not reading a book in whole or in part during the twelve months prior, up from 19 percent in 2011.[29] In response to a quiz administered by the International Center for the Advancement of Scientific Literacy, only 37 percent of adults agreed with the (true) statement "Human beings, as we know them today, developed from earlier species of animals," and 53 percent agreed with the (false) claim that "the earliest humans lived at the same time as the dinosaurs."[30] Attendance at events involving the arts (e.g., plays, musicals, musical concerts, art museums) has seen declines over the past two decades, according to surveys taken by the National Endowment for the Arts. Between 2002 and 2008 alone, there was a 12 percent drop in attendance at theatrical plays and a 9 percent drop in attendance at musicals. Ten years ago, more than one in four Americans visited art museums and galleries; now the figure is closer to one in five.[31]

TAKING SCHOOL REFORM TO A HIGHER LEVEL

Clearly politicians, corporate bigwigs, and school bureaucrats have failed in their attempt to transform American education. Who do we turn to next? I would like to suggest that we listen to what the greatest thinkers and creators of civilization have had to say about the best ways to educate children and adolescents. The people we should be consulting about how to make our schools better aren't the politicians or corporate executives who have political agendas or financial interests as motivating factors. Instead, we should be looking to the scientists, musicians, artists, writers, and other creative individuals whose discoveries, performances, and works have become part of the very fabric of our culture.

A good example of such an individual is Albert Einstein, the theoretical physicist whose ideas changed our views about space, time, and the universe itself. If Einstein ran our schools, he almost certainly would not include standardized tests. He himself flunked the botany, zoology, and language sections of the entrance exam he took to enter a polytechnic institute in Zurich (he was admitted the next year). Once he graduated from the polytechnic institute, he reflected: "The hitch in this was, of course, that one had to cram all this stuff into one's mind for the examinations, whether one liked it or not. This coercion had such a deterring effect that, after I had passed the final examination, I found the consideration of any scientific problems distasteful to me for an entire year."[32] Instead of tests and standards, Einstein would very likely put a strong emphasis on imagination, something schools do virtually nothing to develop (see chapter 2). Based on other statements he made throughout his life, it's also likely that he would emphasize curiosity, creativity, wonder, playfulness, and the nurturing of self-reliant individuals.

In the following chapters, I'll examine what Einstein and other eminent individuals have had to say about education, children, and learning. I'll describe how most of our schools fall far short of their ideals. Our illustrious board of education will include such creative figures as Leo Tolstoy, Jane Goodall, Pablo Casals, Rachel Carson, Doris Lessing, Rabindranath Tagore, Martin Luther King Jr., and the Dalai Lama. Their collective wisdom will serve as an exemplary template for a revitalization of education in the United States. I'll also provide examples of teachers and schools that have managed to embrace the ideas held by these and other eminent thinkers and creators while avoiding or blunting the effect of the standardized thinking and corporate reforms of the past thirty-five years.

This is a critical time for American education. We can continue to go along in our current trajectory toward more regimented learning, the exaltation of test scores, and an increasingly depersonalized approach to learning based upon computer algorithms. We can accelerate the development of privatized, for-profit charter schools that care far more about the financial bottom line than about the joy of learning. We can continue on our journey toward the datafication of learners and the increased participation of large corporations in education. Or, alternatively, we can wake up to a genuine vision of education, one that embraces creativity, curiosity, imagination, wonder, and other key learning capacities. We can reject the image of education that has been forged by politicians, corporate executives, and school bureaucrats and take up the suggestions of the world's true culture-makers for how best to create living schools that place natural, authentic learning as its highest goal. We can make the study of the joy of learning a top priority in educational research, developing schools that incorporate values based upon beauty, social justice, compassion, and reverence for all living things. It's only a matter of making a choice, both from the top down (e.g., education officials and administrators) and from the bottom up (individual parents, teachers, and students), a choice to say yes to the kind of education most of us started out with during the first few years of life, when learning came naturally and the world lay before us in all its incredible majesty.

CHAPTER TWO

Imagination: Unleashing Our Children's Ability to Mentally Soar

Knowledge is limited. Imagination encircles the world.

—Albert Einstein[1]

If Einstein ran today's schools, he almost certainly would give the imagination a prominent place in classroom instruction. After all, by using his imagination, he managed to change civilization's ideas about space, time, and the very structure of the universe. As a child, Einstein had enjoyed working with puzzles and three-dimensional models (he once made a card house fourteen stories high). In his midteens, having failed the natural science and language sections of the entrance examination to the Federal Polytechnic Institute in Zurich, he was told by the director to wait a year to take the tests again and to enroll in the meantime in the Kanton Schule in Aarau, thirty miles northwest of Zurich. This was a school based on the educational philosophy of Johann Heinrich Pestalozzi, an eighteenth-century Swiss educational reformer who thought that visual conceptualization (*Anschauung*) represented the very height of thought. He believed that images were more important than letters and numbers. This new school environment that placed a value on visual thinking was a far better fit for Einstein. Encouraged to use his imagination, at the age of sixteen Einstein did what he called "a thought experiment" (*Gedankenexperiment*), where he imagined himself racing beside a beam of light. He discovered that if he

11

were to do this in his mind, "I should observe such a beam of light as a spatially oscillating electromagnetic field at rest. . . . However, there seems to be no such thing."[2]

THE IMAGINATION OF THE SCIENTIST

Einstein's confrontation with this paradox set in motion further thought experiments involving railroad cars, lightning, and synchronized watches that led to his *special* theory of relativity, a view of the universe that posited time and space not as Newtonian absolutes but as entities that are relative to the position of the observer. Throughout the remainder of his life, Einstein would engage in picture-based thought experiments like these to work out theories related to gravitation, electromagnetic energy, quantum mechanics, and other scientific subjects.[3] Asked by a French mathematician to explain the nature of his thought processes, Einstein replied, "The words or the language, as they are written or spoken, do not seem to play any role in my mechanism of thought. The psychical entities which seem to serve as elements in thought are certain signs and more or less clear images which can be 'voluntarily' reproduced and combined. . . . The above-mentioned elements are, in my case, of visual and some of muscular type."[4] This "muscular" imagination may refer, at least in part, to a thought experiment Einstein did in his late twenties when he imagined standing in an accelerating closed container in open space. From his perspective inside the container, the physical sensation would feel like gravity. It was out of this positing of an equivalence between gravity and acceleration that he developed his *general* theory of relativity, which viewed gravity as the warping by matter or energy of the space-time continuum in the universe.

Einstein was by no means the only scientist to use the imagination in his work. The English scientist Michael Faraday discovered the phenomenon of electromagnetism by visualizing invisible lines of force as narrow tubes curving in the space around magnets and electric currents and, indeed, pervading the universe. Faraday did not use mathematics in explaining electromagnetism, and in fact, he never advanced beyond simple arithmetic (it was James Clerk Maxwell who eventually worked out the mathematics for electromagnetism, using equations that Faraday himself could not understand). The German chemist Friedrich A. Kekulé discovered the molecular structure for the ringlike organic chemical compound benzene through a dream he had about a snake swallowing its tail. The American inventor Elias Howe came up with the structure for the modern sewing machine after he had a dream about being attacked by people with spears that had holes through the points. Seymour Cray, who developed the fastest supercomputers of his day, built a "visual concept" of the whole machine in his head and then drew it.[5] Similarly, Nobel Prize–winning physicist Richard Feynman, "without ever writing down the equations. . . had a physical picture of the way things happen, and the picture gave him the solutions directly, with a minimum of calculation."[6] Finally, renowned scientist Stephen Hawking noted, "I tend to avoid equations as much as possible. I simply can't manage very complicated equations, so I have developed geometrical ways of thinking, instead."[7]

THE GREATEST UNTAPPED POTENTIAL IN EDUCATION

The imagination, of course, extends far beyond these scientific and technological achievements into literature, storytelling, music, dance, art, history, and in fact, to the whole enterprise of human achievement. My big question to the politicians, corporate executives, and school bureaucrats who have mismanaged education over the past thirty-five years is this: Why does education almost completely ignore the imagination?

Student imagination is, in my view, the most untapped resource in all of education. I'm reminded of a story told by the psychologist and researcher Mihaly Csikszentmihalyi about a study he did with adolescent learners. He supplied wireless pagers to a class of twenty-seven high school students. They were listening to a lecture about Genghis Khan's invasion of China in the thirteenth century. Csikszentmihalyi told them that whenever they received a random beep, they were to fill out a form he gave them and write down exactly what was going on in their minds at that moment in time. Csikszentmihalyi reflected on the outcome: "They mentioned their dates, their coming football game, how hungry they were, how sleepy they were etc. There were 2 who mentioned China; one of them said 'I always wondered why Chinese men wore their hair in pigtails' and the other one said, 'I was thinking about this great dinner we had with my family at the new Chinese restaurant.'"[8] No one was thinking about the lesson. All that student imagination was being deployed for other topics that were more personally compelling.

AMERICA'S NATIONAL CURRICULUM: ROTTEN TO THE CORE

The main reason the imagination is absent from nearly all classrooms today is that there is no room for it anywhere in the curriculum. As mentioned in the last chapter, a major component of the miseducation of America has been the institution of a set of uniform national standards, referred to as the Common Core State Standards (again, thirty-six states have adopted the standards, and the other fourteen use their own similar standards).[9] As mentioned in the previous chapter, the standards began to take shape in 1998, two years after a group of governors and CEOs founded Achieve Inc., a nonprofit, bipartisan effort to shepherd the process of setting and implementing standards at the state level. Over the next several years, Achieve Inc. released a series of reports emphasizing the need for uniform state standards, and in November 2009, the National Governors Association hired the organization to write curriculum standards in the areas of language arts and mathematics. On June 2, 2010, the final Common Core State Standards were released. In 2011–2012, two federally funded consortiums known as PARCC and Smarter Balanced began the development of standardized tests aligned directly to the Common Core (*align* is another key word used by the corporate reformers; it refers to making everything line up neatly in a row—another bow to uniformity). Finally, in 2014–2015, all participating states began to implement the new standardized tests for math and English language arts.

Although supporters of the Common Core claim that this is not a national curriculum, Peter W. Wood, president of the National Association of Scholars, begs to differ, saying that "[it] is, in fact, very much a curriculum. The sneakiness in this case is . . . aimed at getting around legal barriers that prohibit federal efforts to establish curricula, but the sneakiness is also aimed at diverting teachers and the public from the truth. . . . The Common Core standards are finely detailed, grade-by-grade specifications for what should be taught, how it should be taught, and when it should be taught."[10]

Perhaps the best way to get a sense of how unimaginative the Common Core and their aligned standardized tests are, is to view some examples of each. Here, for example, are a few language arts writing standards for the third through fifth grades:

- L.3.1f. Ensure subject-verb and pronoun-antecedent agreement.
- L.3.3a. Choose words and phrases for effect.
- L.4.1f. Produce complete sentences, recognizing and correcting inappropriate fragments and run-ons.
- L.4.1g. Correctly use frequently confused words (e.g., to/too/two; there/their).
- L.4.3a. Choose words and phrases to convey ideas precisely.
- L.4.3b. Choose punctuation for effect.
- L.5.1d. Recognize and correct inappropriate shifts in verb tense.[11]

Note how each standard is given a code name that conjures up memories of the Dewey decimal system or the Library of Congress classification system. More importantly, notice how each standard is decontextualized (e.g., "choose punctuation for effect"—in what context? a letter? a poem? an essay? a test item? and what kind of effect?). There is nothing in this list of standards that cries out for imaginative teaching. One might argue that a teacher could, in fact, craft teaching strategies that do activate students' imagination (e.g., "write a poem where you 'choose words and phrases for effect'"). Such a teacher, however, might well feel like a salmon swimming against the stream. The problem is, students won't be asked to write fanciful poems or do other imaginative things on the actual test, and in the vast majority of classrooms around the nation, teachers will be teaching to that unimaginative test. There are long lists of standards like the above that educators are responsible for teaching at each grade level (I counted sixty specific skills for third-grade language arts alone), and the quickest and most efficient way to prepare students for so many skills is to anticipate the form that the standards will take on the standardized tests and teach according to that format.

WHERE'S THE VALUE IN "VALUE-ADDED" EVALUATIONS?

As part of the so-called reform movement of the past thirty-five years, a method of evaluating teachers has been developed that bears the Orwellian-sounding name of "value-added measures." The term *value-added* comes from the corporate world and is used in its business context as a way of referring to augmenting value to a product or service by adding, for example, a free paring knife with that all-purpose cheese grater, or a wax job with every car wash. In the context of education, *value-added* has to do with evaluating teachers in whole or in part on the basis of the standardized test scores of their students. That's right. Teachers' effectiveness in many parts of the nation are being determined by student test results. I can't think of a better way to bludgeon a teacher's effectiveness than with a value-added evaluation system. With teachers' own job security and financial welfare on the line, it's unlikely that they will favor nurturing students' imaginations over test preparation. As award-winning veteran high school teacher Ron Maggiano put it, after resigning from his job in protest, "I can no longer cooperate with a testing regime that I believe is suffocating creativity and innovation in the classroom. We are not really educating our students anymore. We are merely teaching them to pass a test. This is wrong. Period."[12]

Part of the Common Core involves the use of what are called "exemplary texts," which are recommended readings from fiction and nonfiction that can be used in both practice tests and actual tests (the use of fiction texts is scaled back considerably at the high school level, dealing another blow to the imagination). One particular text for the seventh grade that is aligned to the Common Core is "The Capture of Father Time," by L. Frank Baum, the author of *The Wizard of Oz*. The story itself is actually quite imaginative in nature, telling the tale of a burgeoning young cowboy who accidentally lassos Father Time and freezes time throughout the world. It's a story that lends itself to imaginative possibilities in the curriculum. Some examples: Is there a Mother Time? Why not? How about a Father Space? How would our life be different if there were no time? (This reminds us of Einstein's thought experiment where, according to the special theory of relativity, anyone traveling the speed of light would experience time as stopped.) Plays could be enacted of the story, poems written, music composed, and dances choreographed using real lassos. In such a climate, the imagination of students could soar. But none of this is on the practice test provided by the Smarter Balanced consortium that cocreated the standardized tests that are aligned to the Common Core (by the way, speaking as a writer, there seems to be something grammatically peculiar about the name Smarter Balanced). Instead, students are asked to answer questions such as the following[13]:

- How does the author develop the relationship between Jim and Father Time? [choose one]

    A. Through their own points of view

    B. Through their dialogue with each other

    C. With description of each character

    D. With details about the setting

- What does the use of dialogue show about the relationship between Jim and Father Time? Select three options.

    o   The dialogue shows that Jim and Father Time are old friends.

    o   The dialogue signifies that they have a lot in common in their lives.

    o   The dialogue indicates that Jim and Father Time have different opinions.

    o   The dialogue demonstrates that Jim and Father Time reach a conclusion.

    o   The dialogue tells the reader that they do not understand each other's point of view.

    o   The dialogue helps the reader picture the scene between Father Time and Jim.

You get the idea. What is required from students are unimaginative paper and pencil answers that demonstrate what the Common Core people call "close reading." This is reading that sticks exclusively to the text and doesn't involve any subjective responses (including use of the imagination) or questions outside of the text, such as what might have motivated Baum to write the story in the first place.[14]

As noted above, standards are also applied to writing skills in the Common Core, where subjective feelings (e.g., the imagination) are to be avoided at all costs. Here's what the architect of the Common Core, Yale-educated Rhodes scholar David Coleman, famously told a group of New York state educators with regard to the teaching of writing: "As you grow up in this world you realize people really don't give as—about what you feel or what you think."[15] He's essentially saying no to the imagination, even though it took the imagination of L. Frank Baum to write the "exemplar" reading selection in the first place. And this is the kind of framework within which teachers across the country have to teach. Their own teaching strategies are not likely to stray very far from this text-based format, where students read stories and answer questions very much like the ones above or do writing assignments that are "aligned" to specific Common Core writing skills such as those mentioned earlier. In such an educational climate, the imagination of the student has no way to flourish.

We can see the same sort of imagination suppression going on in the Common Core mathematics standards. Here, for example, is Standard 7.EE.4a (seventh-grade math): "Solve word problems leading to equations of the form $px + q = r$ and $p(x + q) = r$, where p, q, and r are specific rational numbers. Solve equations of these forms fluently. Compare an algebraic solution to an arithmetic solution, identifying the sequence of the operations used in each approach. For example, the perimeter of a rectangle is 54 cm. Its length is 6 cm. What is its width?"[16] Clearly, the vast majority of teachers will prepare students to master this algebra standard by giving them problems to solve like the one above. Where's the imagination in that? You might argue that mathematics is different, that it doesn't lend itself to journeys through the imagination. If you thought that, you'd be wrong. Einstein's Uncle Jakob made mathematics come alive for little Albert by describing algebra as a "merry science." He compared algebra to a hunting expedition, saying to a young Einstein, "We go hunting for a little animal whose name we don't know, so we call it x. When we bag our game we pounce on it and give it its right name."[17] Imagination is alive mathematically in many other academic contexts as well, including the geometry and logic of Lewis Carroll's children's classic *Alice's Adventures in Wonderland*, the golden mean ratio of the Parthenon in Greece, Leonardo da Vinci's *The Vitruvian Man*, and the recursive structures of M. C. Escher's paintings.[18]

SCENARIOS OF SUCCESSFUL IMAGINATIVE TEACHING

Thankfully, there *are* imaginative teachers in our schools who have managed to buck this national trend toward unimaginative instruction.

Sometimes simply adopting an imaginative attitude is enough to make a huge difference in the lives of students. One early childhood educator used the five minutes between recess and lunch to play an imagination game out on the playground. The structure of the game involved selecting an inert object and then quickly brainstorming things it could possibly be. Kids decided, for example, that the playground slide might be Rapunzel's golden hair that they could slide down.[19]

Imagination can unlock the thinking of students who have had difficulty learning in the traditional way. Educational researchers recounted the story of Leo, a fourth-grade student who, unsuccessful in a standard learning environment, was being taught geology in an imaginative way. They wrote, "Leo found success in his ability to imagine the lives of rocks. Leo had no trouble imagining himself as a molecule swimming in molten lava, trying to form crystals . . . he 'swam' around the room with his eyes shut exclaiming, 'It's hard to swim in molten lava. If it cools too soon, I won't form crystals!'"[20]

At the high school level, a tenth-grade history teacher was charged with instructing her students about the Dutch resistance to the Nazi occupation during World War II. To do this, she calmly walked into her classroom and immediately assumed the role of a Dutch woman who had invited a group of non-Jewish citizens to a secret meeting. She thanked them for coming and then said, "'You are putting yourself in great risk but you are kind, generous people, and I knew you would come." The teacher recalled, "Slowly the students' eyes began to rise, small smiles began to appear on a few faces—they were hooked."[21] How different this scenario is from the more prevalent one where the teacher walks into the classroom and says, "Now class, turn your textbook to page 452, read the essay about the Dutch resistance meeting during World War II, and then answer the questions at the end."

Because the imagination is so vast—as broad and deep as our minds—there's no limit to the kinds of learning activities that can be structured around it. In one first-grade math class that was learning about measurement, students received a letter from the "Queen of the Giants" requesting that they locate the largest, heaviest, and longest objects in their classroom as well as the objects that covered the most space and held the most volume. Students then wrote letters to the Queen, in the form of blog posts, reporting on their investigations. They in turn received congratulatory responses back from the Queen (the teacher) herself![22]

In an Advanced Placement history class, Matt Levinson, head of school at University Prep in Seattle, Washington, engaged his students' imaginations in mock press conferences, trials, murder mysteries, dinner parties, spy dilemmas, and re-creations of reality TV shows. Also in Washington state, a husband-and-wife duo taught a science lesson on photosynthesis to seven-year-olds based on the question "Why are bananas green?" For part of the lesson, they asked this question: "So why do plants like the sun instead of fearing it?" One answer that teachers gave to the students was, "Thankfully, the plants have designed tiny devices—imagine them as green baseball mitts—to catch the balls of light and to use that power for good [chloroplasts]."[23] Such a fanciful explanation possesses more liveliness than a prosaic scientific explanation. Keep in mind that Einstein's own imagined sprint beside a beam of light was also fanciful (imagine if a teacher had come along and told the sixteen-year-old Albert, "Stop thinking nonsense! No one could ever run that fast!").

RESCUING IMAGINATION FROM THE DRAGON'S LAIR

Surprisingly, given the heavy emphasis placed in our schools on skill-based standards and standardized testing, the public at large generally supports efforts to make imaginative teaching and learning a more significant part of the educational scene. According to a national 2008 poll of one thousand likely voters, a whopping 89 percent said that using the imagination is important to innovation and success in a global, knowledge-based economy. Sixty-three percent of voters strongly believed that building capacities of the imagination that lead to innovation is just as important as the so-called basics for all students in the classroom. Eighty-eight percent of the respondents indicated that an education in and through the arts is essential to cultivating the imagination.[24]

Similarly, students who experience the imagination in their own learning almost always ask for more. In a British study of 1,700 students aged nine to thirteen, activities included viewing a visual work of art imaginatively and then making original pictures and doing creative writing based on that experience. Ninety-two percent of the students said they learned something new about their imagination. The researchers wrote,

> Hundreds of children reported that they had no idea that their imagination was so huge, wild, amazing, free and powerful; that they can now travel anywhere they want in their imagination; *that the imagination is even better than TV and video games* [emphasis is mine]; that their first picture surprised them because they didn't know they could draw so well; that they used to think art was dull and boring, but now it's "cool" and "more fun." The workshop changed positively the children's attitude to art.[25]

Seventy-six percent of the students indicated that they would like to take further courses in the arts, and a "surprising number" said that they would now like to pursue careers as artists.

A key ingredient in bringing the imagination into classrooms involves helping teachers get in touch with their own imagination. This may require them to remember their own early childhood activities or their current nighttime dreams, or it may require involving them in working with art media. Reading fiction is also helpful in activating the imagination. The fact that kids get more of their information from mass media these days may be one reason why our kids aren't as imaginative as they used to be (the media provides them with ready-made images, so they don't have to make their own).[26] But the biggest obstacle to using the imagination in learning is, as we've seen, the pressure on teachers to either deliver an unimaginative curriculum aligned to unimaginative tests or face the prospect of losing their jobs.

If Einstein ran our schools, our classrooms would be places where teachers would tell imaginative stories instead of delivering boring lectures, where they would have students work on imaginative scenarios and make-believe simulations rather than toiling in workbooks. They would be places where students' visual thinking would be taken seriously, and where the imagination would be integrated into every part of the curriculum. I like to think that our schools today are a little like the dragon Smaug from the J. R. R. Tolkien novel *The Lord of the Rings*, jealously sitting on a horde of precious jewels (the students' imagination). The big question is, What will it take to wrest these diamonds, gold, and rubies away from the fearsome beast so that they can be made available to every child in school? I leave it to your imagination to figure that one out.

CHAPTER THREE

Love of Learning: Affirming the Most Important Goal of Education

I have no special talent. I am only passionately curious.

—Albert Einstein[1]

Al Pacino turned me into a lifelong learner. At the age of forty-six, I happened to watch his movie *Looking for Richard* (1996), about his effort to mount a production of Shakespeare's play *Richard III*. I hadn't read much of substance since college, but Pacino's film inspired me to start reading Shakespeare's plays. I read the pocket-sized Folger Library editions that put Shakespeare's words on the right-hand side and the notes (including explanations of the meanings of Elizabethan words) on the left side. I loved them! Whoever said that Shakespeare is boring? After I'd read most of the plays, I decided to go back to the beginning of Western literature and read chronologically. I worked my way through Gilgamesh, the Iliad and Odyssey, the pre-Socratic philosophers, the major Greek tragedies, Plato and Aristotle, the Bible, and then I just kept on going until I reached the twenty-first century about ten years later (in the meantime, reading literature from non-Western cultures as well).

To support my reading, I listened to tapes offered by The Teaching Company (now called The Great Courses), which are lectures by college professors who receive high marks from their students for excellent teaching.[2] The tapes I listened to covered everything from the "History of

Ancient Egypt" and "A History of Hitler's Empire" to "Great World Religions" and "Classics of American Literature." Now, 1,200 books and 1,000 lectures later, I am less systematic in my reading, going for whatever strikes me as interesting (currently on my bedside table is Cormac McCarthy's *The Crossing*, Oliver Sacks's *Hallucinations*, and a book called *Lost Enlightenment* by S. Frederick Starr, about the rich intellectual tradition that flourished in Central Asia from 800 to 1200 CE). I'm also a film buff, having discovered The Criterion Channel, a streaming service of the greatest films in history, such as *Bicycle Thieves*, *The Rules of the Game*, and *Tokyo Story* (I watched 188 world-class movies in 2018).[3] Finally, I've been exploring classical music, having discovered fairly recently that you can listen to practically any great work of music on YouTube. This morning I listened to the *Enigma Variations* by Sir Edward Elgar (a work based upon a theme that you never hear, hence the enigma!).

It's hard to put into words the excitement I feel about studying literature, history, film, music, and other subjects. It's a little like trying to explain a headache to someone who's never had one, except that this is the reverse of a headache; it's a head-glow! I also feel it in the rest of my body as a sense of extreme well-being and as a voracious hunger, where I want to "eat" up all the learning in my immediate vicinity and keep on hunting for "learning fuel" wherever I can find it. *The love of learning is the single most important learning goal in all of education.* It's the first thing that student teachers should learn about in their college studies: what it is, how to discover it in themselves, and how to inspire it in their students. It's the topic that should be the most studied by education experts, the subject most researched by educational researchers, the factor most important in the evaluation of teachers (those who can't find it in themselves and evoke it in their students should quietly be referred to other careers), and the alpha and omega of every classroom lesson plan.

Needless to say, other than being used as a platitude in education books and articles, or as an inspirational theme to start the academic year, the love of learning is not taken very seriously in American education. Instead, joy takes a back seat to grades, test scores, deadlines, requirements, rubrics, standards, evidence-based teaching, and other passionless tools of the education trade. Even when the term is evoked in educational writings, it's often used in a way that leaves the impression that the writer had no fundamental idea of its intrinsic nature. One article is entitled "How Teachers Can Sell Love of Learning to Students," as if this love were a marketable commodity that could be sold to the highest bidder.[4] Another journal article asks the question, "Can Love of Learning Be Taught?" (the short answer is no, because every person is born with it; we'd be extinct if it wasn't part of our DNA; the better question would be, "Can Love of Learning Be Recovered?"). A website dedicated to "positive psychology" lists "love of learning" as one of twenty-four virtues and suggests that the love of learning can be developed through exercises such as the following: "Deliberately learn five new words, including their meaning and usage, at least twice a week" (this sounds more like a typical ho-hum classroom assignment than an invocation of a deeply rooted thirst for knowledge).[5] Even psychologist and Stanford education guru Carol Dweck falls into this pedagogical sinkhole when she writes, "Our work has shown that developing a growth mindset in your child, allowing them to understand how their effort and persistence build their intelligence, makes them love learning and gets them high grades."[6] How do you "make" someone love learning, since everyone is born with it?

THE HISTORY OF LOVING TO LEARN

The love of learning has deep historical roots. In fact, when we look at five of the greatest learning traditions in history—Confucian, Judaic, Ancient Greek, Islamic, and modern—we discover that they all have held the cultivation of the love of learning as one of the highest pursuits possible for human beings. Since the Middle Ages, the Jews have had a tradition of giving an alphabet board smothered in honey to a child who is starting to read so the child will always associate learning with sweetness.[7] In the religion of Islam, there's a hadith (saying of the prophet Muhammad), that goes, "The superiority of the learned man over the devout worshipper is like that of the full moon to the rest of the stars (i.e., in brightness)."[8] In his *Analects*, the Chinese sage Confucius wrote, "The love of humanity without the love of learning degenerates into silliness. The love of intelligence without the love of learning degenerates into frivolity. . . . The love of force without the love of learning degenerates into anarchy."[9]

The ancient Greeks also deeply revered learning and even had a name for the individual who loves to learn: *philomath*, from the Greek *philo-*, "loving," and *-math*, "to learn" (Benjamin Franklin used "Philomath" as an attribution of his in *Poor Richard's Almanack*). Plato, in his major work *The Republic*, quotes Socrates as saying that the guardian of his ideal city must possess a love of learning. He asks, "Aren't love of learning and love of wisdom the same? . . . [His interlocutor agrees.] So shall we be bold and assert that a human being . . . if he is going to be gentle to his own and those known to him, must by nature be a philosopher and a lover of learning?"[10]

If we look at modern philosophy, too, we find an understanding of the high priority that love of learning ought to assume in the educational process. Alfred North Whitehead, coauthor of one of the most important philosophical works of the twentieth century, *Principia Mathematica*, wrote an essay called "The Aims of Education," where he suggested that all educational efforts needed to go through a threefold process: romance, precision, and generalization. First, students need to become enamored of their studies (romance); second, they study the facts of their topic and receive a complete analysis of the structures involved (precision). Third, they can then return to romance, with the advantage of having new facts and techniques at hand (generalization). Whitehead describes the stage of romance as follows:

> The subject-matter has the vividness of novelty; it holds within itself unexplored connexions with possibilities half-disclosed by glimpses and half-concealed by the wealth of material . . . . Romantic emotion is essentially the excitement consequent on the transition from the bare facts to the first realisations of the import of their unexplored relationships. . . . Education must essentially be a setting in order of a ferment already stirring in the mind; you cannot educate mind in *vacuo*. In our concept of education we tend to confine it to the second stage of the cycle; namely, to the stage of precision. . . . *It is evident that a stage of precision is barren without a previous stage of romance* [emphasis is mine].[11]

VARIETIES OF "JOY OF LEARNING" EXPERIENCES

A real understanding of the love of learning comes from reports of peak experiences in learning, through first-hand accounts, case studies, anecdotes, memories, and other stories. This is an area of educational inquiry that cannot be researched quantitatively. (What could a researcher possibly measure—the width of the iris to get a sense of the "glow" in the eye of a joyful child?) We must somehow endeavor to capture the unique quality of each ecstatic learning experience on its own merits, for no one of them is like another. The stage of life most likely to reveal minibursts of this kind of joy is infancy. This makes sense, since we're evolutionarily programmed to have a passion to learn from the moment we're born. The ability to learn confers a large measure of adaptability to humans so that they can profit from life experiences and not keep making the same mistakes over and over again.[12] As an illustration, the Swiss genetic epistemologist Jean Piaget kept notes of his own infant son, Laurent, and observed him lying in his crib and exploring rattles hanging down from the hood of the crib by a chain:

> Laurent, by chance, strikes the chain while sucking his fingers. He grasps it and slowly displaces it while looking at the rattles. He then begins to swing it very gently, which produces a slight movement of the hanging rattles and an as yet faint sound inside them. Laurent then definitely increases by degrees his own movements. He shakes the chain more and more vigorously and laughs uproariously at the result obtained.[13]

At the sensorimotor level, Piaget's son was experiencing the visceral joy of learning. Passion for learning can also take the form of pure perception.

American child psychiatrist Daniel Stern writes about six-week-old Joey, who is attracted to a yellow patch of light on the wall:

> If something is only mildly intense (like a lamp lit in daylight), his attraction to it is weak. If too intense (like direct sunlight on him), he avoids it. But if it is moderately intense, like the patch of sunshine on the wall, he is spellbound. That just-tolerable intensity and contrast arouses him. He immediately alters in response to it. It increases his animation, activates his whole being. His attention is sharper. The patch of sunshine is a gentle "magnet" whose force he feels.[14]

These transient events can serve as starting points for a lifelong adventure in learning as infants mobilize all of their resources to make sense of the world around them.

As children grow, they begin to experience mental bursts of understanding during their explorations of their environment. Piaget tells the story of a mathematician friend of his who remembered one such event when he was five years old:

> He was seated on the ground in his garden and he was counting pebbles. Now to count these pebbles he put them in a row and he counted them one, two, three up to ten. Then he finished counting them and started to count them in the other direction. He began by the end and once again found he had ten. He found this marvelous. . . . So he put them in a circle and counted them that way and found ten once again.[15]

This discovery of what Piaget called "the conservation of number" (the recognition that number doesn't change with physical rearrangement) was a peak experience for this child. Similarly, in a British study of adult memories of religious experiences in childhood, a fifty-year-old woman recalled being three or four years old when she had a major aha moment concerning space:

> We were walking home along the pavement. I became spontaneously aware that each step I took decreased the way between me and my destination by precisely the same amount as it increased the distance between me and my point of departure. I had no sufficient command of language to tell anyone. It was perhaps the most thrilling and significant thing that has ever happened to me. There was something there to do with perfection, a perfect conjunction of increasing and decreasing. . . . And when I was 15, the formulation came, in a history lesson, and I let out a great shout of joy, and was duly reprimanded."[16]

In the same study, an adult reported a sudden insight about abstract nouns at the age of seven while attending a grammar lesson in school:

> I had an extraordinarily vivid insight which is absolutely beyond description but which has remained with me ever since as an abiding spiritual experience. The teacher was explaining that in addition to common nouns and proper

nouns there were also abstract nouns, which mostly ended in "-ness," such as goodness, badness, etc.; also a number of short but very important words such as love, hate, etc. It was at this point that I seemed to grow up mentally.[17]

Nowhere in the Common Core State Standards, in the standardized tests that accompany them, or, for that matter, in any of the teacher's manuals having to do with standards-based learning, are there any references to, or awareness of, these types of peak experiences. Yet they are the joyous, mind-bending events that people remember long after they've left their schoolbooks behind.[18]

THE MAGIC OF DESTINY EXPERIENCES

Many great thinkers and creators trace their own intellectual lives back to experiences like those cited above. David Henry Feldman, of Tufts University, and Howard Gardner, at Harvard University, have called these moments of intellectual or creative awakening "crystallizing experiences."[19] Helen Keller had such a crystallizing experience when as a child she made the connection between words and external objects at the water pump with her teacher Anne Sullivan:

> We walked down the path to the well-house, attracted by the fragrance of the honeysuckle with which it was covered. Someone was drawing water and my teacher placed my hand under the spout. As the cool stream gushed over one hand she spelled into the other the word water, first slowly, then rapidly. I stood still, my whole attention fixed upon the motions of her fingers. Suddenly I felt a misty consciousness as of something forgotten—a thrill of returning thought; and somehow the mystery of language was revealed to me. I knew then that "w-a-t-e-r" meant the wonderful cool something that was flowing over my hand. That living word awakened my soul, gave it light, hope, joy, set it free! There were barriers still, it is true, but barriers that could in time be swept away.[20]

Russian dancer Anna Pavlova had a crystallizing experience as an eight-year-old when she was taken as a special Christmas treat to see Tchaikovsky's *The Sleeping Beauty* performed by the Imperial Russian Ballet. She later wrote,

> I was spellbound. I gazed and gazed, and wild plans began to circulate in my brain. It was the second act and the corps de ballet were waltzing together. "Anna," said my mother, amazed at my excitement, "wouldn't you like to join these people and dance with them?" "No," I replied without hesitation, "I would rather dance by myself like the lovely Sleeping Beauty. One day I will and in this very theatre." My mother laughed, but I was lost in my dream and did not heed her. At eight years old I had found the one unchanging ambition of my life."[21]

Swedish film director Ingmar Bergman remembers as a child trading one hundred of his miniature soldiers to his brother for a cinematograph (an early motion picture projector). He writes in his autobiography, "I loaded the film. A picture of a meadow appeared on the wall. Asleep in the meadow was a young woman apparently wearing national costume. *Then I turned the handle!* It is impossible to describe this. I can't find words to express my excitement."[22] Russian artist Wassily Kandinsky remembered having acquired his first set of paints in early adolescence: "As a thirteen or fourteen-year-old boy, I bought a box of oil-colors with pennies slowly and painfully saved. To this very day I can still see these colors coming out of the tubes. One press of my fingers and jubilantly, festively, or grave and dreamy, or turned thoughtfully within themselves, the colors came forth . . . these curious, lovely things that are called colors."[23]

CHARTING LEARNING "EXPLOSIONS"

Another source of peak learning experiences comes from eminent teachers observing the passion for learning in their students. Early in his own career, the artist Marc Chagall noticed the fervor of his young students in learning to create art as he taught them at an orphanage in post-revolution Russia:

> Barefoot, lightly clad, each one shouted louder than the other: "Comrade Chagall, Comrade Chagall!" . . . The clamor came from every side. . . . I loved them. They drew pictures. They flung themselves at colors like wild beasts at meat. One of the boys seemed to be in a perpetual frenzy of creation. He painted, composed music and wrote verses. Another boy constructed his art calmly, like an engineer. Certain of them, devoted themselves to abstract art, approaching in this way the work of Cimabue and the art of stained-glass windows. I was entranced by their drawings, their inspired stammering and this lasted until the moment when I was obliged to give them up. What has become of you, my dear little ones? When I think of you, my heart bleeds.[24]

The Italian physician and educator Maria Montessori, developer of the world-renowned Montessori method of teaching, recalled being taken unawares when her five-year-old students suddenly "exploded" into writing on the terrace of her Casa dei Bambini ("Children's House") in a low-income area of Rome:

> On one winter day in December, a day full of sunshine, we climbed with the children to the terrace. They ran about freely, playing; some stayed round me. I was sitting near a chimneystack, and I said to a child of five who was near me, "Draw this chimney." He sat down on the ground obediently and

drew the pot on the floor, reproducing it so that it was quite recognizable. . . . [Then] the child looked at me, smiled, stood for a moment as if he would break into some joyous act and then shouted, "I write, I write!"; then, bending down, he wrote on the ground *'man'* (hand), then growing very enthusiastic, he wrote again *'camino'* (chimney), then *'tetto'* (roof). Whilst he was writing he continued to shout aloud "I am writing I can write," so that all others were attracted by his cries and made a circle round him staring in astonishment. Two or three of them in great excitement said to me, "Chalk, I will write too." And in fact they set about writing various words: *mamma, mano, gino, camino, ada*. . . . The first word written by my little ones fills them with an inexpressible joy.[25]

Teacher preparation manuals should be filled with examples of these passionate learning encounters so that educators know what to look for, what to value, and, most importantly, what to hope for in planning their daily lessons. I'd almost like to say that teachers should be evaluated by the number and quality of the peak learning experiences they evoke in their students rather than by test scores, but such a top-down requirement would easily degenerate into sheer nonsense. In such a system, I could see the emergence of "love of learning checklists," "love of learning stickers," "love of learning worksheets," and other bureaucratic monstrosities that would cut the joy of learning down cold in its tracks. Peak learning experiences have an almost mystical quality to them and could easily be (and in fact *are*) crushed by the pedagogical "bulldozers" of textbooks, objectives, agendas, schedules, and requirements. In their teacher-training programs, student teachers should be helped to discover their own love of learning and shown how to transmit this love to their students through interesting, novel, and rich learning experiences. All teachers should be taught to notice when this love occurs spontaneously in the course of a lesson, and how to acknowledge it, celebrate it, and reinforce it, so that it can occur again and again.

SCHOOLS' ONGOING CAMPAIGN TO "MOTIVATE" AND "ENGAGE" STUDENTS

To be fair, educators have been fumbling about in this area for decades, often focusing on the term *intrinsic motivation* as a key factor leading to success in school. Research links intrinsic motivation to a wide range of positive outcomes, including long-term achievement, conceptual understanding, lessened school-related anxiety, lower rates of skipping school, and lower high school dropout rates.[26] But love of learning is only one dimension of intrinsic motivation. Other components include personality traits such as perseverance, patience, resilience, and social conscience. The flip side of this inner drive is *extrinsic motivation,* or a student's dependence upon rewards, incentives, or reinforcements to learn. Teresa Amabile, a key researcher in the field of creative behavior, has found that offering children rewards to learn "decreases their motivation, undermines the globally assessed quality of their performance, and makes them much less likely to take risks or to approach a task with a playful or experimental attitude."[27] In one of her studies, children were informed that if they told a story, they would be allowed to use an instant camera. But children in another group were given the camera first, without any strings attached, and then they told a story. Results indicated that children in the no-reward condition told more creative stories than did students in the reward group.[28] Think about what we're doing to our kids when we grade them, test them, compare them, and reward them with smiley faces and stars!

In the 1990s, another term emerged that attempted to come to grips with this failure of schools to elicit students' natural love of learning: *student engagement*. Engagement covers an even broader range of attributes than intrinsic motivation does, including intellectual, emotional, behavioral, and social aspects of the learning process. Students can become engaged with learning at school because they view the work as a challenge, because they find it exciting, because they're curious about the material, because they want to learn with others, because they think the tasks are relevant to their lives, because they believe the work is socially important, and because of any number of other factors. The term has gained ascendancy over the past twenty years because so many students have become *disengaged* in their studies as a result of the onslaught of joyless academic learning and standardized testing that is such a key part of the miseducation of America.

The problem with the concept of student engagement is that the ulterior motives of educators attempting to address it are suspect. Rather than valuing and inspiring a genuine love for learning, it seems that many of the initiatives involved in student engagement are based on tricks to get students interested in the learning material so that they will do well on the tests. It's a little like putting chocolate on spinach.[29] I myself have been involved in this practice, exhorting teachers to get students engaged in learning academic material (e.g., reading, math, science) through such activities as role play, music, small-group discussion, field trips, and project-based learning.[30] While these strategies do work and do serve to get students more engaged in what they're learning, they avoid the bigger issue, which is how to elicit within students *the love of learning itself*, irrespective of the particular means used to study the material. The love of learning is such an inborn quality of being human that it seems demeaning to try to come up with lots of little tricks to make it happen.[31] As a way of engaging students, one source gives the following suggestion: "A teacher might ask students to walk up to the chalkboard and answer the question verbally while also writing the answer on the board."[32] How on earth will this strategy make some aspect of the world inherently exciting to a student? How will it help facilitate a lifelong passion for learning?

Cultivating a genuine love of learning requires that students engage with the essence of learning itself, that is, with the amazing world around us. One indication of how far away educators have strayed from this vital encounter is in the term they use to discuss this incredible world: *content* (as in a container's "contents"). Who could ever develop a love for "content"? My imagination conjures up a gray metal bottle containing an even grayer substance that represents its "content."[33] Instead of teaching "content," teachers need to engage students with real things, exciting stories, vivid histories, fascinating science ideas, intriguing math concepts, novel literary works, creative encounters with nature, and much more.

THE SPARK THAT IGNITES THE JOY OF LEARNING: PASSIONATE TEACHERS

Teachers reach students by contagion: students catch their teachers' excitement as if it were a blissful cold! I remember my seventh-grade geography teacher, Miss Arendes, as she taught us about the medieval Islamic traveler Ibn Battuta and the historian Ibn Khaldun (imagine how prescient she was, teaching Islamic history in Fargo, North Dakota, in 1962!). I can still see in my mind's eye and feel in my heart her enthusiasm; it spoke to me, saying, "There's something inherently fascinating about what I'm telling you." Not long ago, I read Ibn Battuta's account of his travels, inspired by what had happened to me in Miss Arendes's classroom more than fifty years ago. I also remember Miss Minnis, the principal of my elementary school, who shared the story of her summer trip to Australia in the late 1950s. The power of her experience informed my own excitement when I traveled to that country in 2000, and it captivates me still whenever I play "Waltzing Matilda" on the piano. When you think back to the teachers you loved decades ago, you usually don't remember the textbooks they used or the worksheets they made you fill out. You remember the vitality and aliveness of the teachers themselves. It's that enthusiasm that is the precious commodity here, one that, if we could bottle it up and distribute it to all our students, would make such a positive difference in their lives.

We need to place love of learning above everything else in education, make it a real research priority, regard it as a central organizing principle from which all other educational reforms emanate. Why is this so important? Because in the future, we don't know what people will need to learn. An unforeseen technology could make existing jobs obsolete overnight.

A sudden international incident could change the course of history, requiring entirely new insights and cognitive strategies to navigate the transition. By teaching our children to love learning above all, we are giving them the one thing they will need, no matter what happens in the future: the ability and passion to learn new things, to generate new ideas, to adapt to new ways of living in an uncertain world, and to master the unknown.

CHAPTER FOUR

Creativity: Teaching outside the Box

It is the supreme art of the teacher to awaken joy in creative expression and knowledge.

—Albert Einstein[1]

Leo Tolstoy, the author of *War and Peace* and *Anna Karenina,* was one of the world's greatest novelists, but he also had a keen interest in the education of children. He even started his own school for peasant children on his estate Yasnaya Polyana, 120 miles from Moscow, and published a local newspaper based on his experiences with the children. In this excerpt, the children have been working on their writing compositions while Tolstoy is at his desk writing his own story:

> Having finished his own composition, worse and faster than usual, Fedka climbed on the back of my chair and began to read over my shoulder. I could not go on; others came up to us and I read them what I had written. They did not like it and nobody praised it. I felt ashamed, and to soothe my literary ambitions I began to tell them of my plan for what was to follow. The further I got in the story, the more enthusiastic I became; I corrected myself and they kept helping me out. One student said the old man should turn out to be a magician; another remarked, "No, that won't do, he should just be a soldier . . . the best thing would be if he steals from him. . . . No, that wouldn't go with the proverb," and so on. All were exceedingly interested. It was obviously a new and exciting sensation for the students to be present at the process of creation, and to take part in it. The decisions they made were for the most part all the same, and were true to the plot as well as in the details

and characterizations. Almost all of them took part in the composing process, but from the start Semka and Fedka especially distinguished themselves, Semka by his perceptive, artistic descriptions, and Fedka by the
acuity of his poetic gifts, and especially by the glow and rapidity of his
imagination."[2]

What makes this passage so compelling is that it depicts the honoring
of children's creativity from one of the most creative individuals the world
has ever seen. While creativity is most often associated with the arts, it can
take place at any time and occur anywhere. Creativity researcher Ronald
Beghetto talks about how creativity can occur spontaneously in the
"micro-moments" of the classroom.[3] English teacher Karen Gallas provides an example of such a "micro-moment" with a six-year-old girl whom
she describes as a young naturalist. She writes, "Emily is sitting alone at a
table with one of her ants in her hand. She is talking to the ant, asking it
questions. EMILY: Do you have anything else to say? She puts her head
close to the ant and listens. Later she explains that the ant has been telling
her that she's [the ant] ten years old, and her birthday is August 2nd, and
it's a her."[4]

THE FANTASTIC NEUROPLASTIC BRAIN

The Russian psychologist Lev Vygotsky noted that "[a]ny human act
that gives rise to something new is referred to as a creative act, regardless
of whether what is created is a physical object or some mental or emotional construct that lives within the person who created it and is known
only to him."[5] He writes that "[t]he organic basis for such reproductive
activity or memory is the plasticity of our neural substance."[6] This pro-
nouncement in 1930 was remarkable inasmuch as scientists are only now
discovering the full extent of what is being referred to as the "neuroplasticity" of the brain, the ability of the brain to change its structure and
function over time in response to the environment.[7] The brain of a young
child has a surplus of dendrites or connections between brain cells that
are being "pruned" over time, depending in part upon the kind of experiences they have in life.[8] The magnitude of this surplus (said to be more
than twice as dense in a three-year-old compared with an adult) suggests
that many brain connections are present in childhood that will be eliminated by the time the child grows up. This seems to parallel the dynamic
capacity of the child's brain to come up with creative possibilities and
imaginative connections as she interacts with the world. What the child
needs under these circumstances is to have adults in her life who themselves have managed to retain some of this neural flexibility so that the
creative life is not lost.

DO SCHOOLS KILL CREATIVITY?

Unfortunately, the schools in the United States don't seem to be places where this kind of innate creative flexibility is being honored. Cultural anthropologist Jules Henry once wrote, "Classrooms—from kindergarten to graduate school . . . are not crucibles of creative activity and thought. . . . [W]ere young people truly creative the culture would fall apart, for originality, by definition, is different from what is given, and what is given is the culture itself. . . . Schools are the central conserving force of the culture . . . the function of education is to prevent the truly creative intellect from getting out of hand."[9] There are many reasons why creativity has been marginalized in classrooms in the United States. First, ever since a 1972 report delivered to the U.S. Congress by the educator Sidney Marland, creativity has tended to be largely associated with "gifted and talented" children and the programs that serve them rather than being seen as an intrinsic part of every child.[10] Second, creativity in U.S. schools has been closely linked to quantitatively based creativity tests, most commonly the Torrance Tests of Creative Thinking, as if any test could capture the whimsical, idiosyncratic, and subversively creative nature of an individual child.[11]

Third, creativity as a subject for the regular classroom, in the words of creativity experts James Kaufman and Ronald Beghetto, "is sometimes seen as a footnote, afterthought, or as an extra-curricular activity. . . . At worst, it can be seen as not relevant or even appropriate to educational practice."[12] In fact, research suggests that the majority of teachers do not generally incorporate creativity into their school assignments (particularly in schools with high proportions of minority and low-performing students), despite the findings that these practices lead to increased academic achievement.[13] Studies have also consistently demonstrated that teachers generally prefer noncreative, high academically achieving students over creative students. Researchers have shown, for example, that the qualities of the creative child (playful, open, critical of others, stubborn) are at odds with the qualities that teachers generally prefer to see in their students (studious, compliant, attentive, careful). As a result, students who are highly creative are more likely to be unpopular with their teachers and are more likely to get in trouble with them.[14] In fact, many creative students are likely to be diagnosed with attention deficit hyperactivity disorder and viewed as problems in the classroom.[15]

STANDARDIZATION: THE REAL CULPRIT IN "CREATICIDE"

To my mind, however, the biggest reason why creativity is not an integral part of every classroom has to do with standardized testing. It's curious to note that ever since the incorporation of a greater emphasis upon testing and accountability in education in the United States, measures of creativity in children have undergone a steady decline.[16] It's easy to see why this is the case. Standardized tests don't allow for creative answers. A student may be pondering a question on a test and have the thought, "I know what they *want* me to say here, but I've got a better answer, in fact, a *great* answer that I'm going to write here in the margins, and when they read it they're going to be really impressed with what I have to say!" The student, of course, doesn't realize that tests aren't scored by people. They're scored by computers, which are only looking for "right" answers. Creativity isn't about right answers. It's about lots of wrong, wild, crazy, treasonous, beautiful, horrible, unexpected, unconventional, and/or off-the-wall responses. And what about the student who might think, "I don't know the answer here, but if you ask me to sing it, dance it, or draw it, then I could tell you what I know"? Add to this the fact that 20 to 50 percent of teacher-effectiveness ratings are now being determined by their students' standardized test scores, and you can begin to understand why teachers aren't going to be taking any unnecessary risks when it comes to modifying the curriculum, trying out a novel teaching strategy, or catering to the "whims" of their creative students.[17]

Another key factor in this "creaticide" (the killing of creativity) has to do with the Common Core State Standards.[18] If you read through the standards (which you can do by going to http://www.corestandards.org), you'll find that they don't offer students much opportunity to be creative. Instead, even where students are asked to "write narratives to develop real or imagined experiences or events," (a third-grade language arts standard), they need to use "effective technique," "descriptive details," "clear event sequences," and "temporal words and phrases to signal order," and to "provide a sense of closure," among other requirements. And this is just one of scores of standards that teachers are required to teach to their students.

There's not much room here for the child who just wants to creatively express him- or herself or work on a creative problem without limits over an indeterminate amount of time and see where it leads. (Compare this to Stephen Hawking, who said, "It is no good getting furious if you get stuck. What I do is keep thinking about the problem but work on something else. Sometimes it is years before I see the way forward. In the case of information loss and black holes, it was 29 years."[19]) In addition, one of the "innovations" of the Common Core is to limit the fiction reading that students engage in and increase the amount of "informational texts" that are required, such as the Environmental Protection Agency's "Recommended Levels of Insulation" and the California Invasive Plant Council's invasive-plant inventory. As eighth-grade English teacher and Arkansas Teacher of the Year Jamie

Highfill, puts it, "I'm struggling with this, and my students are struggling. . . . With informational text, there isn't that human connection that you get with literature. And the kids are shutting down. They're getting bored. I'm seeing more behavior problems in my classroom than I've ever seen."[20]

WHITE DRESSES, MAZES, AND THE CREATIVE SPIRIT

Despite all of the above obstacles to creative learning and teaching in the schools, many brave educators have managed somehow to navigate the noncreative thickets of their own school settings to develop creative attitudes and activities in the classroom. Blackwell, Oklahoma, second-grade teacher Haley Curfman, for example, bought a completely white dress from Amazon and let her students draw, doodle, color, and write on it. She says that the project (which she's done more than once) takes from two weeks to a month to complete, and that "[m]y students were proud every time they saw it, and they should be because they put a lot of thought into their drawings and kind words."[21] In a similar vein, elementary school teacher (now Fordham University professor of education) David Rufo noticed his students drawing mazes in the margins of their math workbooks:

> I initially recall seeing the maze drawings in early October. At first, I didn't take much of an interest, but within a few weeks I began to notice how a few square inches of looping, spiraling, twisting parallel lines were slowly transformed into pulsating labyrinths that eventually covered whole pages. For me, the end result was a hypnotic, almost hallucinatory, experience. As I began to look more closely, I found that the drawings weren't mazes per se (containing starting points with single, hidden pathways leading to exits) as much as they were intricately woven fractals. [22]

Eventually a student asked if he could draw a maze on the classroom wall. Rufo wrote,

> With this simple, direct question, the basis of my philosophy as a teacher was put to the test. In my teaching experience, students were never allowed to draw on the classroom walls; however, as I considered this appeal I found that I couldn't think of a good enough reason to preclude my students from drawing maze designs on the walls of our classroom. In fact, I thought these beautiful and intriguing works of art could only serve to improve the appearance of our scuffed, white washed walls, and so I gave my consent. It wasn't long before the idea of drawing maze designs on the walls grew in popularity, and by December there were 10 different maze drawings in progress. During these times it was exhilarating to witness the arts-based learning that transpired. Some students wanted to be the sole creator of

their drawings whereas others sought out partners to help them generate their complex, large-scale pieces. Two of the students even wrote a "How To" book that delineated their particular style and approach.[23]

AWAKENING GENIUS IN THE CLASSROOM

One short-term project that offers students the chance to dip into the wellsprings of their own creativity is National Novel Writing Month, which, during the month of November, challenges adults and students alike to write a complete novel of a designated number of words (it's suggested that first graders produce a novel of a few hundred words, fifth graders about five thousand, middle school students ten thousand; high school students twenty thousand to fifty thousand words). There are no conditions or requirements. Students' spelling or grammar is not graded. Teachers are not looking for "effective technique," "descriptive details," "clear event sequences," or other Common Core requirements. The only measure of success is that the student complete the novel and meet a self-imposed word length. Battle Creek, Michigan, middle school teacher Luke Perry received permission from his principal to temporarily set aside the regular curriculum, and a third of the middle school population embarked on this writing adventure. Eventually, Perry was having students read from their novels over the school's PA system. "I can't gush enough about it," Perry said. "I'll never teach the same way again."[24] (Those wishing for information about participating in National Novel Writing Month can go to https://nanowrimo.org.)

Another ongoing opportunity that provides a foundation for the realization of creative potential is the "Genius Hour." Initially inspired by tech giant Google's invitation to its software engineers to devote 20 percent of their time to a project of great interest, the Genius Hour enjoins teachers to free up an hour per day (more or less) to let students engage in "passion projects." While students may choose relatively noncreative pursuits, such as learning a foreign language, they often use their time to come up with novel inventions, writings, or other creative projects. At Douglas Park Elementary School in Regina, Saskatchewan, seventh grader Isaac used his passion for video games to build one of his own. He started out knowing a little bit about coding but eventually mastered a more complex programming language and ultimately developed a chase game where characters jumped and leaped across a background of houses, trees, and a terrain that continually changed as they moved along. (For information about setting up a Genius Hour, go to http://geniushour.com.[25])

A program that focuses more explicitly on technology is the Maker Movement, which emerged about fifteen years ago when a group of inventors, tinkerers, computer geeks, hobbyists, and artisans began to promote a do-it-yourself ethos for the digital age, using recycled materials, electronics, 3-D printers, open source computer programs, and various odds and ends to create interesting and useful products. At Analy High School, in Sebastopol, California, curriculum coordinator Casey Shea manages the school's "maker room," which consists of a laser cutter, a 3-D printer, computers, computer parts, circuit breakers, and other high- and low-tech gadgets and tools, where students create their own robots, rockets, catapults, and other projects that combine science, technology, engineering, math, and art and design skills.[26] A related initiative in education, called "design thinking," uses the methods of professional designers to help students engage in thought-provoking projects that have practical uses. Students at Catlin Gabel School, an independent K–12 school in Portland, Oregon, for example, are set with the problem of collaboratively designing a user-friendly shoe. They go out into the community to interview strangers about their shoe needs, consult with shoe-making entrepreneurs, and research, brainstorm, and create prototypes that meet their requirements.[27]

CREATIVITY AS A BASIC HUMAN NEED

Recently, there's been an increase in the public call to make our schools more responsive to the creativity of its students. Creativity gurus such as Yong Zhao and Ken Robinson have received a great deal of publicity in promoting creativity in education (Robinson's TED talk "Do Schools Kill Creativity?" is the most popular TED talk of all time, with more than fifty-five million views).[28] One thing I've noticed, though, is that these injunctions for greater creativity in education are often couched in economic terms. Robinson, for example, writes that "the fact is if America wants to remain competitive in the global markets of the 21st century, creativity is not a luxury. America needs a workforce that is flexible, adaptable and highly creative; and it needs an education system that can develop these qualities in everyone."[29] The problem with this assessment is that creativity is being made to serve the needs of business, and in particular the needs of corporations, which allow for innovation only so long as it fits their bottom line (Google, for example, no longer promotes its 20 percent Genius time initiative). Creativity is desirable for the schools not because it will lead to a better iPhone or smart speaker but because it's a basic human need. Speaking for the artist in each one of us, pioneer of modern dance Martha Graham writes about this deeper well of creativity that we should tap into while helping our students reclaim their natural-born right to be creative human beings:

> There is a vitality, a life force, an energy, a quickening that is translated through you into action, and because there is only one of you in all of time,

this expression is unique. And if you block it, it will never exist through any other medium and it will be lost. The world will not have it. It is not your business to determine how good it is nor how valuable nor how it compares with other expressions. It is your business to keep it yours clearly and directly, to keep the channel open. You do not even have to believe in yourself or your work. You have to keep yourself open and aware to the urges that motivate you. Keep the channel open. . . . No artist is pleased. [There is] no satisfaction whatever at any time. There is only a queer divine dissatisfaction, a blessed unrest that keeps us marching.[30]

CHAPTER FIVE

Playfulness: Restoring Childhood to Preschool and Kindergarten

The desire to arrive finally at logically connected concepts is the emotional basis of a vague play with basic ideas. . . . . This combinatory or associative play seems to be the essential feature in productive thought.

—Albert Einstein[1]

One of life's most refreshing occupations is watching children at play. I'm not talking about formal competitions, such as soccer, or technological pursuits, such as video games. I'm referring to free, unstructured play where children develop their own imaginative journeys (e.g., playing house, building a rocket ship from blocks), fashion self-directed challenges and experiences of the world (e.g., climbing trees, building forts), create intrinsically valuable products (e.g., mud pies, sand castles), and operate within ever-changing limits and rules set by the children themselves, not by adults. While many people regard children's play as incidental to the process of learning, the truth is that it serves as a core activity that promotes the child's development in a number of ways. In the process of running, jumping, crawling, skipping, building, and crafting, the child improves sensorimotor control. In the dynamic give-and-take of children's play, there are ample opportunities to develop important social skills. In the active process of matching, counting, comparing, measuring, sizing, weighing, shaping, and constructing play objects, children acquire cognitive abilities. In the encountering of life challenges, mastering of skills, and responding to interesting encounters with the world, the child matures emotionally.[2] Just in terms of language skills, alone, one educator observed in children's play the "spontaneous use of complex rhythms and phonological patterning, use of alliteration and assonance, the handling of sophisticated narrative structures and rhyme."[3]

PLAY: THE CRUCIBLE OF CIVILIZATION

Perhaps the most important argument in favor of play, though, is that it promotes creativity. When children play, they take what "is" in the world (e.g., a cardboard box), combine it with what is "possible" in their imagination (e.g., a trip to Mars), and from this mysterious alchemical transformation create something new (e.g., a rocket ship to Mars made from the cardboard box). Child psychiatrist D. W. Winnicott talks about the significance of the child's "play space." He writes, "This area of playing is not inner psychic reality. It is outside the individual, but it is not the external world. Into this play area the child gathers objects or phenomena from external reality and uses these in the service of some sample derived from inner or personal reality. . . . The child puts out a sample of dream potential and lives with this sample in a chosen setting of fragments from external reality."[4] In essence, the child participates in the same sort of creative process that underscores the work of highly accomplished adult innovators.

In fact, many of the greatest thinkers and creators in the world have characterized their basic working style as playful in nature. Isaac Newton, for example, wrote, "I do not know what I may appear to the world; but to myself I seem to have been only like a boy playing on the sea shore and diverting himself and then finding a smoother pebble or a prettier shell than ordinary while the greater ocean of truth lay all undiscovered before me."[5] Alexander Fleming, the Scottish bacteriologist who discovered penicillin, said, "I play with microbes. It is very pleasant to break the rules."[6] Frank Lloyd Wright traced his architectural gifts back to play with plain wooden blocks in kindergarten. He wrote about, "[t]he smooth shapely maple blocks with which to build, the sense of which never afterwards leaves the fingers."[7] Futurist Buckminster Fuller displayed his geometric genius early in life, creating in his kindergarten class an octet truss made of toothpicks and dried peas—the first geodesic dome—a design that he patented in 1961.[8] The great German composer Gustave Mahler compared composing music to playing with building blocks gathered in childhood.[9]

There is something about play that strikes at the very heart of civilization. Cultural historian Johan Huizinga wrote that playfulness "as a social impulse [is] older than culture itself. . . . Ritual grew up in sacred play; poetry was born in play and nourished on play; music and dancing were pure play. . . . We have to conclude that civilization is, in its earliest phases, played."[10] Evolutionary thinkers believe that play evolved by conferring advantages on human beings related to creativity, flexibility, and the ability to adapt to changing circumstances. One group of evolutionary psychologists wrote, "Arguably, child play is among the most important means of deferred adaptation . . . a reflection of the adaptive value of immaturity. . . . We learn through trial and error (no less than through guidance and education) what our physical and social environments require, and we acquire the competencies that are useful or necessary within our respective environment—the rules of surviving (e.g., getting food, avoiding predators, infections, or poisonous fruits) as well as the rules of social life (e.g., cooperation, competition, getting accepted by peers)."[11]

HOW PLAY ENRICHES THE BRAIN

Scientists are only now beginning to understand the important role that play has in the maturation of the brain. While most of this research has been conducted on rats and thus cannot be directly applied to human children, there is much that is suggestive here about the ability of play to literally "grow" a brain. The dendritic length, complexity, and spine density of the medial prefrontal cortex (an area of the brain important for executive functioning skills such as memory and decision making) are refined by play.[12] Play stimulates the production of brain-derived neurotrophic factor (BDNF) in the amygdala, dorsolateral frontal cortex, hippocampus, and pons. BDNF is a chemical that supports the survival of existing neurons (brain cells) and encourages the growth and differentiation of new neurons and synapses (junctions between brain cells).[13] Play even has an important role in gene expression (the turning on or off of a gene's ability to make proteins or RNA). Gene expression analyses indicate that the activities of approximately one-third of the 1,200 genes in the frontal and posterior cortical regions of the brain were significantly modified by play *within an hour after a thirty-minute play session.*[14]

At the same time, play deprivation can have negative consequences for brain development. In one study, rats that were deprived of play as pups (raised in cages without toys), had more immature medial prefrontal cortices compared with rats that played, suggesting that play deprivation interfered with the process of synaptogenesis (creation of new brain connections) and pruning (clearing out of excess brain connections to make way for more efficient brain functioning).[15] According to a recent clinical report in the prestigious journal *Pediatrics*, "The absence of the play experience leads to anatomically measurable changes in the neurons of the PFC [pre-frontal cortex]."[16] Play also has an important role in stress management. Rats previously induced to be anxious became relaxed and calm after rough-and-tumble play with a nonanxious, playful rat.[17] In a study with hamsters, deprivation of social play in juvenile hamsters disrupted neuronal development in the ventromedial prefrontal cortex (an area of the brain important for planning, personality expression, and moderation of social behavior) and increased vulnerability to the effects of social stress in adulthood."[18] There are also indications that the rise of attention deficit hyperactivity disorder over the past three decades may be tied to a decline in children's play and a rise in the consumption of mass media.[19]

THE DISAPPEARANCE OF PLAY IN OUR TIME

Given the powerful advantages of play, and the dire consequences of not playing, it is truly alarming to observe that children's play is disappearing in our culture. A national survey of 8,950 preschool children and parents found that only 51 percent of children went outside to walk or play once per day with either parent.[20] In an analysis of the use of children's time from 1981 to 1997, researchers found that children's playtime decreased by 25 percent.[21] The same researchers discovered an additional 4 percent loss of play from 1997 to 2003, and a 37 percent decline in outdoor activities during that same time period.[22] A further study revealed that young children spent 70–83 percent of their time being sedentary in childcare—even when excluding time spent in naps and meals—and *only spent 2–3 percent of the time in vigorous activities*.[23] These statistics stand in stark contrast to the guidelines of the U.S. Department of Health and Human Services, which recommends that preschool-aged children (ages three through five years) should be physically active throughout the day, and older children and adolescents should engage in moderate to vigorous activity for at least an hour a day.[24] Experts have linked the decline in physical activity with a steep rise in obesity and type 2 diabetes among children and adolescents, another powerful reason to support frequent play experiences for kids of all ages.[25]

A good measure of the blame for these declines rests with the schools. Since the increase in standardized testing and the adoption of the Common Core State Standards (and other states' individual standards), recess has declined. Only three states laws require daily recess for all age levels.[26] Only one state requires classroom-based physical activity breaks.[27] And the free, unstructured play that was traditionally so much a part of pre-schools and kindergartens (keep in mind that *kindergarten* is German for "children's garden") has given way to developmentally inappropriate teacher-directed academic instruction. In one study at the University of Virginia, researchers interviewed kindergarten teachers in 1998 and then again in 2010 on how their instruction had changed over those years. The percentage of teachers who felt that kindergartners should learn to read increased sharply from 31 percent to 80 percent. The percentage of teachers who reported that knowing the letters of the alphabet was very important or essential more than doubled from 19 percent in 1998 to 48 percent in 2010. At the same time, the provision of time, space, and materials for play declined significantly. The percentage of teachers who had a dramatic play area in their classrooms declined from 87 percent to 58 percent, and those who had an art area decreased from 92 percent to 71 percent.[28]

FROM CHILDREN'S GARDENS TO WORKSHEET WASTELANDS

The human costs of this shift from developmental kindergartens (disparagingly called "pablum kindergartens") to "academically rigorous" ones (which we might dub "straightjacket kindergartens") are enormous. As one kindergarten teacher reports, "I teach kindergarten. The five-year-olds have an incredibly tight schedule to keep in our county: an hour of math, hour of science, 2 hours of language arts, half hour of social studies. We kindergarten teachers have had to sneak in rest time and social centers (such as puppets, blocks, housekeeping, playdough) which are so critical to their development. . . . My poor babies turned in papers with sentences made of fragments from our fact chart we had made, but they hung their heads because they couldn't read the sentences they'd managed to write."[29] Meghan Lynch, a postdoctoral fellow at the University of Toronto, shares comments on kindergarten teachers' encounters with their academically minded principals:

> One recounted, "If the principal walks into one of our K classrooms and sees the children 'playing' instead of working at their seats, the teacher receives discipline." Likewise, another teacher detailed how she "had the kids on the floor in a circle and they were singing 'Farmer in the Dell.' The superintendent walked by and said, 'You are going to stop singing and start teaching, right?'" In another discussion, a teacher described a time when she was moving to a new classroom only to find her entire closet full of play-based kindergarten teaching supplies had been thrown away: "My principal said to throw everything away. I was shocked, then extremely upset. I talked to her, and told her I was disrespected. She said, sorry, but told me I could not bring anything into my classroom, that I had too much in there already."[30]

"The changes to kindergarten make me sick," says a veteran teacher in Arkansas. "Think about what you did in first grade—that's what my 5-year-old babies are expected to do."[31]

Meanwhile, preschoolers are having to learn in classes that are more like academic kindergartens so that they can prepare for the hundred-plus standards the Common Core specifies each kindergartner must meet. One Common Core reading standard for kindergarten requires students to "know and apply grade-level phonics and word analysis skills in decoding words." A writing standard reads, "Use a combination of drawing, dictating, and writing to narrate a single event or several loosely linked events, tell about the events in the order in which they occurred, and provide a reaction to what happened."[32] A Common Core math standard for kindergartners that involves algebraic thinking reads, "Decompose numbers less than or equal to 10 into pairs in more than one way, e.g., by using objects or drawings, and record each decomposition by a drawing or equation (e.g., $5 = 2 + 3$ and $5 = 4 + 1$)."[33] That means time must be taken to practice the standards and then test kids to ensure that the standards have been met. Children's playtime is effectively squeezed out (30 percent of U.S. kindergarten classes don't even have recess).[34] It is perhaps not surprising then that a research study suggested that children who had preschool experiences that were academically directed received lower grades six years later, when compared with kids who were exposed to more active, child-initiated early learning experiences in preschool.[35]

REGGIO EMILIA AND WALDORF EDUCATION AS PLAY HAVENS

The good news is that there are many examples of early childhood education programs that do promote play at the core of their curriculum, and these schools serve as beacons in the midst of the academic grind that is increasingly becoming a part of the preschool and kindergarten scene. The Reggio Emilia schools, for example, emerged from a small town in northern Italy in the wake of World War II to become a movement adopted by many schools around the world, including in the United States. In Reggio Emilia schools, there is a profound respect for the integrity and insight of young children. The teachers treat their young charges as cocreators of the curriculum. They look for cues from the children as they engage in free play as to what the next steps in the curriculum might be. In one instance, teachers noticed that many of the five- and six-year-old children were bringing dinosaur toys to school, and the children's play sometimes spontaneously turned to dinosaurs. They began to initiate an investigation into the world of dinosaurs with a small group of interested children. The kids drew dinosaurs, made them in clay, shared ideas about them, decided to visit a local library to learn more about them, and invited friends and relatives to the school to share what they'd been learning. One group of four boys who were making dinosaurs in clay wondered aloud about how they could make a really huge dinosaur. After working with three-dimensional models and voting on which dinosaur they would create, the children drew to scale a two-dimensional representation of a Diplodocus that was twenty-seven meters long, on their school field.[36]

Waldorf education represents another school approach that is fully play-based at the kindergarten level. It was developed by Austrian philosopher, social reformer, architect, and mystic Rudolf Steiner, who named it after the Waldorf-Astoria cigarette factory in Stuttgart, Germany, where the workers' children were the first students enrolled in his small school in 1919. In preschool and kindergarten, academics are nowhere to be found. Instead, the kids interact with simple natural non-mass-market toys and materials (like wooden blocks, wooden trucks, and silk scarves) as they engage in imaginative play. Sara Baldwin, a kindergarten teacher at Ashwood Waldorf School in Rockport, Maine, says, "Free play is the heart of the morning in a Waldorf kindergarten, and the children waste no time. A trio dons silk capes and crowns, the leader declares, 'I'm the king, you're the knight, and you're the bishop!' They're off to slay dragons. . . . Another pair pulls out two wooden play stands, and begin draping them with silks and play cloths, fastening them with chunky wooden clips to create a cozy little home."[37] Waldorf early childhood education eschews formal reading and math lessons and also keeps hi-tech devices out of the classroom (and parents are encouraged to go along with this at home).

PLAYFUL PRESCHOOLS

Besides these two international school movements, there are many wonderful developmental preschools and kindergartens scattered across the United States. A great example is the Roseville Community Preschool in Roseville, California, founded in the 1970s by the early childhood educator Bev Bos. One can get a sense of the ethos of the school by reading the school rules, which enjoin students to "run, jump, dig, explore, talk, build, tear down, pour, yell, saw, hammer, paint, ride, imagine, sing, wonder, measure, ponder, play, be alone, examine, experiment, express, daydream."[38] There are numerous centers for experimentation, including a place for stones, sand, pipettes, food color, and water to combine and explore, pour, mold and change. There is a dress-up room, an art area, and a child-sized room containing miniature beds, a stove, a refrigerator, a table, chairs, dolls, books, and cooking utensils. As Bev Bos put it, "There is no teacher's voice controlling and directing here, just the occasional word of encouragement and the sharing of an idea, a dialogue, a conversation, a scribed story, or a song."[39] Wander around the school and you will see children painting, digging in sand, make-believe fishing in a puddle of water, building with blocks, putting on plays, planting seeds, hanging from trees, swinging on swings, playing hide-and-go-seek, exploring the natural surroundings, cooking with Play-Doh, experimenting with simple science materials, singing, and living.

Another independent early childhood center that promotes play and hands-on learning is Habibis Hutch, a preschool in Austin, Texas, that calls itself a "natural childlife preserve." Children spend most of their day playing on swing sets, in sand piles, in playhouses, and with art materials and toys.[40] They perform their own plays and participate in a cooking class. The preschool's website explains, "We follow no themes, have no units or formalized lessons, and are never found with children sitting before a looming teacher. We learn together, side by side with our hands and our hearts."[41] This is what early childhood education should look like for all students: no formal lessons, no workbooks, no standardized testing. Clearly, the scientific evidence shows that play nurtures all levels of a child's development and that to deprive children of play has serious consequences for their physical, mental, emotional, and cognitive health. Such deprivation also bodes ill for society in general. For what happens to a civilization that has lost its urge to play? It simply ceases to exist as a vital force—and to think that this loss could be going on right now, in front of us, without our even knowing it. A greater tragedy could scarcely be envisioned.

CHAPTER SIX

Curiosity: Feeding Our Children's Hunger for Knowledge

The important thing is not to stop questioning. Curiosity has its own reason for existence. One cannot help but be in awe when he contemplates the mysteries of eternity, of life, of the marvelous structure of reality. It is enough if one tries merely to comprehend a little of this mystery each day. Never lose a holy curiosity.

—Albert Einstein[1]

In 1999, an educational technologist named Sugata Mitra and a few of his colleagues set up a computer literally in a "hole in the wall" in a slum area of New Delhi, India. It had online capability and a number of programs, but no instructions were provided. Without any prompting from adults, children began to gather around the computer and interact with it. After only a few hours, the children were surfing the internet. "Within six months," says Mitra, "the children of the neighborhood had learned all the mouse operations, could open and close programs, and were going online to download games, music and videos."[2] While subsequent experiences with Mitra's "minimally invasive education" approach have been mixed, this remarkable case history gives us a window into the insatiable curiosity of children and how that curiosity sparks learning.[3]

As the father of American psychology William James wrote in 1899, "Young children are possessed by curiosity about every new impression

49

that assails them."[4] If curiosity had not been hard-wired into our genes, it's likely that we'd be fossils now in an antediluvian lake bed. To be curious is to deploy all five senses in investigating the surrounding environment. If that environment contains food, shelter, or other rewards, then the curious organism will be more likely to find these resources and survive, thus replicating its DNA for future generations.[5] The chronically bored, on the other hand, will be left in the dust and become yesterday's evolutionary leftovers. This helps explain why even newborn babies display curiosity and get bored with the same old same old.[6] Everyone is familiar with the curiosity of toddlers who investigate everything in sight, using their teeth, fingers, nose, ears, and eyes to "devour" whatever strikes them as interesting (and it's a testament to the curiosity of young children that parents have to childproof a house as soon as a baby learns to crawl). When children learn to speak, they are constantly asking "Why?" questions about the world around them. Child development researcher Michele Chouinard analyzed the questions of four children ranging in age from fourteen months to five years and came up with 24,741 questions in 229.5 hours of conversation. That's 107 questions per hour![7]

SCHOOL: FROM QUESTION MARKS TO PERIODS

But something happens to that curiosity as the child grows up. It shuts down. As English poet William Wordsworth put it, "Shades of the prison-house begin to close / Upon the growing Boy."[8] Not surprisingly, a lot of this dampening of the child's instinct to be curious about the world happens in school. Researchers Barbara Tizard and Martin Hughes recorded conversations of young children at home and at school. They found that the children asked an average of twenty-six questions per hour at home and two or three questions per hour at school.[9] Educational pioneer Neil Postman put it this way: "All children enter school as question marks and leave as periods."[10] Poll numbers seem to back him up. The Gallup organization asked teens to select, from a list of fourteen adjectives, the top three words that described how they felt at school. *Bored* was chosen most often (by half the students), followed by *tired* (43 percent). Only 2 percent said they were never bored at school.[11]

According to educational psychologist Ronald Beghetto, in the course of their schooling, students learn that there is a set routine that relies heavily on teacher lectures: "[B]y the time most students have completed their first years of formal schooling they come to learn their 'role' in this pattern of talk: Wait for the teacher to ask a question, quickly raise your hand, quietly wait until the teacher calls on you, (or calls on someone who raised their hand before you), share your response (usually by trying to match your response with what you think the teacher expects to hear) and wait for the teacher to tell you if your answer is appropriate, correct, or acceptable."[12]

There's clearly no room in this model for curiosity. And this sort of pattern gets set up as early as preschool. In one study, researchers showed four-year-olds a toy made up of four tubes sticking out in different directions. Each tube did something interesting: if you pulled on one tube, it squeaked; another tube concealed a mirror; and pressing a pad in a third tube made music play. In the "teacher-directed" scenario, the experimenter told a child, "This is my toy; I'm going to show you how my toy works. Watch this!" And then she pulled on the tube to make it squeak. The experimenter then said, "Wow, see that? This is how my toy works!" Then she pulled the tube again to make it squeak. In the "open-ended" scenario, the experimenter said, "I just found this new toy! See this toy?" Then she seemingly pulled a tube by accident and made it squeak. Expressing surprise, she said, "Huh! Did you see that? Let me try to do that!" and she again pulled on the squeaking tube. The researchers then left each child alone to play with the toy. The results indicated that the kids in the open-ended scenario tended to engage in more exploratory play and investigated the functions of all the tubes, while the kids in the teacher-directed scenario ("this is how my toy works") were less curious about the toy and focused mainly on the one tube that squeaked.[13] This study suggests that there is something in the tenor of teacher-directed instruction that seems to suppress curiosity.

In another study, researchers recorded students and teachers in kindergarten and fifth-grade classrooms over a period of several months at different times of the day. The key researcher, Susan Engel, concluded, "We found almost no signs of curiosity in either age group, in any activity or part of the room. There was little exploration of objects, little exploratory gazing of any kind. But most remarkably, to us, children asked very few questions, except about rules or the social dynamics. Children wanted to know how long they had to finish a task, whether they could or could not use a certain toy, and where the line was for snack. They also asked one another questions about friendships and allegiances (Did Molly go with you to practice? Are you going to eat lunch with Jack?). They almost never asked another child, or the teacher, questions about anything they were studying or working with in the classroom."[14]

The reasons for such low levels of curiosity are varied. One set of researchers suggested that when teachers may not know the answers, they are reluctant to field questions from students.[15] George Loewenstein, a professor of economics and psychology at Carnegie Mellon University, points out that the traits of a curious student clash with the goal-directed, outcomes-oriented, orderly ethos of the typical American teacher.

He points out, "Curiosity tends to be associated with impulsive behavior. People who are curious not only desire information intensely, but desire it immediately and even seek it out against their better judgement."[16] It is rather telling that the number one "disorder" of childhood is ADHD, one of whose symptoms is "impulsivity" (see chapter 9 for more on the novelty-seeking behaviors of kids with ADHD). As developmental and cognitive psychologist Wendy L. Ostroff explains in her book *Cultivating Curiosity in K-12 Classrooms*, "Curiosity is by nature subversive to the traditional, top-down classroom. When order in the classroom is desired most of all, curiosity can become a liability."[17]

STANDARDIZATION AND THE DEATH OF CURIOSITY

The implementation of standardized testing, the Common Core and other state standards over the past decade or two in America, has added to teachers' reluctance to take the extra time needed to explore students' "off-task" questions and feed their curiosity. One teacher writing in the *Washington Post* (she wrote anonymously for fear of "retaliation") said, "I can't do projects with my students anymore because I have to teach the curriculum word-for-word, and I am only allowed to use standards-based assessments (which I must create myself). It doesn't matter how my students learn best. It doesn't matter that the Common Core State Standards and other states' standards assume a steady progression of skills that my students have not been formerly taught."[18] This is from a teacher who, previous to this new demand for accountability, had done amazing things with her classes: "My students have owned and managed their own businesses, written children's books and read them to younger students, done year-long literature studies on specialized topics, hosted project fairs, and an array of other student-created, choice-driven projects. They have designed, researched, written and read beyond their peers. My high school students were required to read 25 novels per year . . . yes, even the ones with learning disabilities could meet this goal with the help of assistive technology."[19]

CURIOUS MINDS CREATED CIVILIZATION

The fact that curiosity is given so little attention in our schools is tragic, especially since, like creativity and playfulness, it is one of the foundational attributes of civilization (without curiosity there would be no civilization). It's interesting that while curiosity tends to get driven out of us as we go through school, some people manage to hold onto theirs, and many of these individuals are the geniuses of our culture, several of whom have credited curiosity with helping them in their discoveries and creations. Referring to Francis Crick, codiscoverer of the DNA molecule, British neuroscientist Colin Blakemore once said, "He simply had one of the most penetrating minds I've ever encountered. . . . He was childlike in his curiosity."[20] Another famous scientist, Stephen Hawking, said, "Remember to look up at the stars and not down at your feet. Try to make sense of what you see and wonder about what makes the universe exist. Be curious."[21] And Nobel Prize–winning physicist Richard Feynman was famous for dropping his usual lab work to try for hours to discover where the ants on his floor were coming from, how they communicated with each other, how they knew where the food was, how he could affect their movement, and so on.[22] He also credited his Nobel Prize–winning discovery to an incident where he watched a dinner plate go wobbling through the air.[23]

THE NEUROSCIENCE BEHIND CURIOSITY

The fact that curiosity is driven by specific brain mechanisms is only now beginning to be discovered through functional magnetic resonance imaging (fMRI) technology. In one study, subjects were presented with blurred and clear images of common objects. Experimenters found that initially the presentation of ambiguous (blurry) visual input activated the anterior insula and the anterior cingulate gyrus, brain regions sensitive to conflict and arousal. Once the nature of the ambiguous object was revealed (through a clear picture), areas of the brain were activated in the striatal region, which is involved in reward processing. Finally, the relief of perceptual curiosity was associated with enhanced hippocampal activation, which is involved with perceptual memory and new learning.[24]

In another study, subjects were queried as to their curiosity about several trivia questions. Then their brains were scanned while viewing the answers to these questions. In addition, they were shown incidental photos of neutral faces. The results of fMRI scanning revealed that activity in the midbrain and the nucleus accumbens was enhanced during states of high curiosity (part of the dopaminergic circuit associated with reward seeking, learning, and memory). Participants showed improved memory for things they were interested in, and, perhaps more surprisingly, they also showed enhanced memory for incidental stimuli viewed while they were in a state of high curiosity. There was something about the state of curiosity that enhanced even their memory of things they weren't particularly curious about. "Curiosity may put the brain in a state that allows it to learn and retain any kind of information, like a vortex that sucks in what you are motivated to learn, and also everything around it," explained lead researcher Dr. Matthias J. Gruber.[25]

CURIOSITY AND SCHOOL ACHIEVEMENT

These brain studies suggest that students will more easily learn things that they are curious about, and this is what the evidence suggests from looking at students' curiosity levels and their academic achievement. In one study conducted at the University of Michigan with 6,200 kindergartners, researchers found that children with the greatest amount of curiosity had the highest achievement levels in math and reading. Interestingly, the connection between curiosity and academic achievement was greater for children with low socioeconomic status (SES). In fact, curious students from poor backgrounds did as well academically as students with high SES.[26] In another study, three-year-old children with greater curiosity and exploratory tendencies demonstrated greater intelligence at age eleven.[27] In a meta-analysis of more than two hundred studies involving fifty thousand children, researchers also found a link between curiosity and academic performance.[28] "I'm a strong believer in the importance of a hungry mind for achievement," said lead author Sophie von Stumm, "so I was just glad to finally have a good piece of evidence. . . . Teachers have a great opportunity to inspire curiosity in their students, to make them engaged and independent learners. That is very important."[29] Perhaps most importantly, curiosity has been seen as independent of self-control. That means that a child with high levels of curiosity can succeed in school academically even if he has low self-control.[30]

CLASSROOMS FOR QUESTION-HUNGRY KIDS

Despite the poor record of U.S. schools in cultivating curiosity in the classroom, there are several classrooms and programs that recognize its value and integrate it into the curriculum. One classic primary-school activity that many teachers still use is some form of show-and-tell, which gives students the opportunity to bring in curious objects and answer questions from their inquisitive classmates. Kristin Wideen, a teacher with the Greater Essex County District School Board in Windsor, Ontario, set up a science table in her third-grade classroom and invited her students to bring in things they had questions about or natural treasures they wanted to share with the rest of the class. Students filled up "bug jars," with bugs gathered during recess. They grew crystals in a jar, and two students brought in birds' nests (unoccupied) found near their homes.[31] Liz DesLauriers, a French teacher at Mounds Park Academy in St. Paul, Minnesota, listens to the students for clues as to what comes next in the schedule: "If a particular group seems curious about something I will change up my plan and tailor it to what they are interested in. For example, I have a group right now that seems particularly interested in the geography of France.

It was only mentioned briefly in a lesson, but they showed curiosity and interest in it so I'm going to head in that direction. We are now making maps and discussing different cities and landmarks."[32]

Artifacts that teachers bring in can also serve as a stimulant for curiosity in school. Oakland, California, high school teacher Courtney Couvreur, for example, brought in a rock with shells embedded in it and kept it on her desk. Students would ask about it, and express shock that it was found on a beach in Santa Cruz. "Once a student knew that I hadn't made it," she relates, "these same students became endless founts of questions: How did it get this way? Did someone make it? What were those white marks? Were they shells? How did they get inside the rock? When did the shells become part of the rock?"[33] Couvreur gathered other natural objects including a pinecone, a sand dollar, a quartz geode, a large cross-section of a colorful stone, a bivalve shell, a small animal vertebrate bone, and a spider-plant clipping. Then she had students work in groups, assigned each group to one of the artifacts, and had them write down as many questions as they could in five minutes. After the time was up, the groups shifted to another artifact and repeated the process. "During their exploration," says Couvreur, "I resisted the urge to answer most questions, as the goal wasn't to understand pinecones or bivalve shells deeply. The goal was to practice generating questions, so that their brains would be primed to learn how to pursue their own evidence."[34]

School partnerships with art or science museums can also help to spark curiosity. The Long Beach (California) Museum of Art, for example, sponsored an exhibition entitled "Exploring the Self through Cabinets of Curiosity," where fifty-one students from the Long Beach Unified School District created artful collections of objects that fascinated them. Curiosity cabinets or *Wunderkammer* were once a colorful part of European history; well-traveled individuals would fill their cabinets with odd and idiosyncratic objects found, made, or borrowed during the era of world exploration, from the sixteenth to the eighteenth century.[35] Wilson High School junior Quincy Irving mixed tiny toy cars, plastic army men, spoons, and keys in plaster and then painted a self-portrait over it.[36] Millikan High School junior Sara Von Epp made her curiosity cabinet using a key, a tin, and a swallow bird. "I'm just attracted to them. I love the way they look," Von Epp said. "They're my obsessions."[37]

THE WORLD OF CURIOSITY MACHINES

Now that we live in a technological world, the computer and the Internet serve as a powerful conduit to a person's curiosity. In fact, I've taken to calling computers "curiosity machines" because we can look up anything, get answers about nearly everything, and encounter many other things that stimulate our curiosity to know more and more about the world around us. Here's a list of one week's worth of my curiosity quest on the internet: audio tracks for Linda Ronstadt's first album with the Stone Poneys, Norman Rockwell's painting of Bertrand Russell, a definition of the term *economies of scale*, an account of Sylvia Plath's last days before her suicide, and the definition of the word *kraal* (South African term for a village of huts formed in a circle). Curiosity expert Susan Williams, a professor at Williams College, sees the value of the internet being used this way in the classroom: "One easy starting place is urging students to use the internet to ask any question that occurs to them—or arises in class discussion or work. Google can be a curious person's best friend. For instance, today I used Google to answer the following unexpected questions: Which of Henry VIII's wives came after Anne Boleyn, what kind of milk is mozzarella made of, and what does the city Hyderabad look like? The ease with which we can look things up online is exhilarating—and it makes the urge to know feel good more often."[38] However, whether the internet or other curiosity-inspiring activities are used in classrooms depends upon having curious teachers to begin with. While this may represent the biggest challenge, it is also the greatest opportunity for educators to make a major difference in the lives of their innately curious students.

CHAPTER SEVEN

Wonder: Reawakening Our Children's Sense of Awe for the Mystery of Life

---

The most beautiful emotion we can experience is the mysterious. It is the fundamental emotion that stands at the cradle of all true art and science. He to whom this emotion is a stranger, who can no longer wonder and stand rapt in awe, is as good as dead, . . .

—Albert Einstein[1]

When Einstein was four or five years old and ill in bed, his father showed him a magnetic compass. Observing the mysterious attraction of the iron needle to the north, regardless of where the compass was pointed, Einstein became very excited and later, as an adult, wrote, "That this needle behaved in such a determined way did not at all fit into the nature of events. . . . I can still remember—or at least I believe I can remember—that this experience made a deep and lasting impression on me. . . . Something deeply hidden had to be behind things."[2] This may have been Einstein's first conscious experience of wonder.

THE ARCHAEOLOGY OF WONDER

A high priority has been placed on wonder by the world's poets, scientists, and philosophers. In his *Metaphysics*, Aristotle said, "It was because of wonder that men both now and originally began to philosophize."[3] In Plato's dialogue *Theaetetus*, Socrates praised wonder as the origin of wisdom and said, "The man who said Iris [messenger of the heavens] was the daughter of Thaumas [wonder] seems to have been doing his genealogy not at all badly."[4] Blake rhapsodized it in his poetry: "To see a World in a Grain of Sand / And a Heaven in a Wild-flower / Hold Infinity in the palm of your hand / And Eternity in an hour."[5] And the contemporary biologist Richard Dawkins described the having of an "appetite for wonder" as the beginning of scientific inquiry.[6]

The wonder that Einstein and these other eminent individuals speak of is an emotion that is often neglected in contemporary discussions of the human emotions, yet the French philosopher Rene Descartes suggested it is one of the six basic passions.[7] For little children, wide-eyed wonder is an inborn instinct they have regarding the marvels encountered every day of their young lives: a flower blooming, a glorious sunset, a strong gust of wind in the trees. Having a sense of wonder means being surprised about things in the world that are not easily assimilated into one's existing frame of reference. Since children haven't yet acquired many sophisticated cognitive schemas for making sense out of the world, they have many more "wonder" experiences than adults (and I should state here that I'm referring to *wonder* as a noun ["the world is filled with wonder"], rather than a verb ["I wonder where birds go when it's cold"], which is more akin to *curiosity*; see chapter 6).

While experiences of wonder may be as simple as a rainbow seen in a spray of water or a bubble floating in the air, and while it may be quickly forgotten, children's encounter with wonder may stay with them for the rest of their lives. In a study conducted at Manchester College in Oxford, England, a fifty-two-year-old woman remembering back to childhood reported her own experience with wonder:

> The most profound experience of my life came to me when I was very young—between four and five years old. . . . My mother and I were walking on a stretch of land . . . known locally as "the moors." As the sun declined and the slight chill of evening came on, a pearly mist formed over the ground. . . . Suddenly I seemed to see the mist as a shimmering gossamer tissue and the harebells [flowers], appearing here and there, seemed to shine with a brilliant fire. Somehow, I understood that this was the living tissue of life itself, in which that which we call consciousness was embedded. . . . The vision has never left me. It is as clear today as fifty years ago, and with it the same intense feeling of love of the world and the certainty of ultimate good.[8]

In the same study, a seventy-five-year-old man remembered being seven years old and preparing to go out on a walk when he had the following thought: "'Here am I, a little boy of seven; I wonder where I was eight years ago.' At that tremendous thought I stood rooted to the carpet . . . with a wave of tremendous feeling sweeping over me. I suddenly felt old and aware of being somebody very ancient. . . . Eight years ago, thought I, why not eighty or eight hundred?"[9]

Sadly, the experience of wonder, whether short-lived or life-changing, begins to fade as we grow older. Environmentalist Rachel Carson wrote:

> A child's world is fresh and new and beautiful, full of wonder and excitement. It is our misfortune that for most of us that clear-eyed vision, that true instinct for what is beautiful and awe-inspiring, is dimmed and even lost before we reach adulthood. If I had influence with the good fairy who is supposed to preside over the christening of all children, I should ask that her gift to each child in the world would be a sense of wonder so indestructible that it would last throughout life, as an unfailing antidote against the boredom and disenchantment of later years, the sterile preoccupation with things that are artificial, the alienation from the sources of our strength.[10]

Wonder seems to be a rarer occurrence in this technological world of ours, where people are apt to spend more time looking down at their phones than looking up at the stars (although virtual reality does hold a promise of taking viewers into wondrous and awe-inspiring scenarios).[11]

WONDER: MISSING IN ACTION FROM OUR SCHOOLS

It goes almost without saying that the emotion of wonder is given very little consideration in most U.S. schools. Although school administrators may start the first teacher meeting of the year with a rallying cry for them to spark wonder in their students, there is precious little follow-up on this inspirational theme. Instead, kids lose their sense of wonder during their school encounters with grades, test scores, schedules, deadlines, standards, tasks, assignments, homework, workbooks, and textbooks. Consider, for example, the Common Core of State Standards. Here is an example of one standard for third-grade language arts that is focused on reading informational texts: "Describe the relationship between a series of historical events, scientific ideas or concepts, or steps in technical procedures in a text, using language that pertains to time, sequence, and cause/effect."[12] Not much there to provoke wonder, is there? In fact, in the whole of the state standards, the word *wonder* is mentioned only three times in the language arts section (once as a verb [e.g., a state of mind], once in a science book title, and once in the use of *Alice in Wonderland* as an exemplary text).[13] It is not mentioned at all in the mathematics standards. In part to make room for more instructional time on these standards, schools have cut back on time spent outside in nature, a virtual seedbed of wonder, and have reduced or eliminated courses in the arts, which again provide greater opportunities for wonder to flourish.

There's a deeper reason for wonder's absence from the K–12 classroom. Educational researcher Philip W. Jackson makes a distinction between two styles of teaching. One is the *mimetic* style, which seeks to provide information or procedures to students through imitation of what is to be learned. In this style of teaching, the educator is a specialist in content who passes along information to the student, who is lacking this knowledge. The process is judged as successful when the student can reproduce (imitate) the knowledge given. There is, however, another style of teaching that Jackson calls *transformative*, which is not concerned with transmitting units of information to students but instead focuses on influencing a fundamental change in the moral, philosophical, or psychological outlook of the student. It lacks a distinctive methodology or curriculum but rather, as Jackson notes, aims toward "a qualitative change often of dramatic proportion, a metamorphosis, so to speak [of the student]. Such changes would include all those traits of character and of personality most highly prized by the society at large."[14] The difficulty here is that most teachers practice the *mimetic* style of teaching, while it is the *transformative* style that needs to be adopted so that wonder can be considered important enough to integrate into the classroom.

WONDER AS THE KEY TO LEARNING

If wonder were simply an emotional thrill that was tangential to the process of learning, then it might be understandable why it receives short shrift in American education. However, wonder is inextricably bound up with the deeper processes of thinking and learning. Awe and wonder happen when we encounter an experience that, first, provokes a sense of vastness, and second, reflects the difficulty that we have in assimilating it into our existing comprehension of the world.[15] As the French genetic epistemologist Jean Piaget pointed out, learning is really a tightrope act (he called it equilibration) between two processes: assimilation and accommodation. We assimilate when we fit things in the world into our preexisting cognitive schemas. Children who see a zebra for the first time may call it a horse, because they're familiar with horses and are assimilating the zebra to their existing knowledge of horses. Conversely, we accommodate when we adjust our thinking processes to a new and unfamiliar experience. Another way of saying this is that *we learn*. The children who see the zebra begin to modify their existing knowledge;

initially they see, perhaps, a horse with stripes, and then eventually they accommodate their existing knowledge of animals to include a zebra. The experience of awe or wonder is just a more intense version of this learning process, where we feel the creative tension between the urge to assimilate and the need to accommodate. That's why so many eminent figures in history have seen wonder as something very special, because it stimulates this back-and-forth action between assimilation and accommodation and thus serves as the spark that initiates a desire to learn more about the world.

There are additional benefits to experiencing wonder. Some researchers have found, for example, that awe (a special version of wonder) tends to promote altruism and kindness toward other people. In one experiment, a group of undergraduates (the awe group) were asked to stand and look up at a giant eucalyptus tree for one minute while a control group standing just a few yards away looked at a tall building. Then the experimenter walked toward the two groups with a questionnaire and a box of pens that he proceeded to spill, ostensibly by accident. The awe group was more likely to help the experimenter pick up the pens.[16] Another study suggested that subjects who experienced awe are less likely to be aggressive toward others.[17]

One evolutionary explanation for these results is that people in prehistoric times needed to band together in order to meet the demands of a hostile environment. Those capable of experiencing awe, and thus more prosocial, were in a better position to accomplish what needed to be done and thus pass their genes onto the next generation. In addition, the capacity to embrace a wider view of a clan's surroundings through awe experiences can also be an adaptive evolutionary trait leading to higher survival benefits. Moreover, there are distinct biological benefits to awe and wonder. In one study, immersive videos that provoked awe led to higher activation of the parasympathetic system, that part of our nervous system that helps to calm down the stress response of the sympathetic nervous system.[18] In another study, experiences of awe and wonder were seen to lower levels of interleukin-6, a molecule associated with inflammation and poor health outcomes.[19]

While the studies cited above were largely done with adults, there is emerging research that awe and wonder have a positive impact on learning in children and adolescents. In one study, a teacher gave wonder-inspiring lessons to a class of ninth-grade science students, while to a second classroom, serving as a control group. a traditional science curriculum was delivered. An analysis of students' comments provided evidence that wonder, experienced as astonishment and the shock of awareness, helped students change their outlook on natural phenomena compared with students in the control classroom. In addition, exposure to a "wonder-full" curriculum led to students asking more questions and having a better memory of scientific phenomena such as the speed of light, the independence of the speed of an object and its mass or weight, and Newton's third law of motion (for every action there is an equal and opposite reaction).[20] Another study suggested that the experience of awe positively affected key creative thinking components, including fluency, flexibility, and elaboration, as measured by the Torrance Tests of Creative Thinking.[21]

SCHOOL ENCOUNTERS WITH WONDER

Italian educator Marisa Musaio writes, "Educating to wonder cannot be reduced to a simple question of methods and projects: it implies a complete re-interpretation of the very concept of education, if we don't want it to lose its significance."[22] Nevertheless, we can point to certain systems and practices in schools that make room for wonder amid the lesson plans and workbooks. One approach that does this is Waldorf education. In one seventh-grade English class, Waldorf teacher Betty Staley had students keeping journals like Henry Thoreau's, and then spending twenty minutes a day for a week sitting on logs, lying under trees or berry bushes, camouflaged in tall grasses, next to a bog near the school. She writes, "Day by day the experiences deepened. The young people's conversations changed radically. They became very sensitive to the differences in their spot of bog because of the change in clouds or temperature. . . . As a class, we were deeply changed by the experience. A sense of stillness and reverence settled over our otherwise active, bustling group of twenty-five."[23] Similarly, at Newcomers High School in Long Island City, New York, Julie Mann takes her students on "awe walks" to connect with nature or art. When they write about these experiences and share them in the classroom, she says, kids who never talk in class or pay attention come to life. "It helps them feel less marginalized, with a sense that life is still good," she says.[24]

Another major strand of progressive child-centered learning, Montessori education, weaves wonder into its curriculum through something Maria Montessori called "cosmic education." This begins with a study of the whole universe and then works its way toward the parts (including individual cultures, life forms, history, and geography). Having a sense of the whole to begin with, the child is then able to understand the parts in relation to the whole. As is the case with Montessori education in general, children aren't directed toward a specific area of study but instead study what interests them within this cosmic scheme. For one child (or group of children), this may involve assembling an electric circuit from simple materials. For another child, it may include putting together a colorful puzzle of the map of the world. For a third child, it may involve forming a whole city or village at a sand table. Or the topic of study may involve learning that early invertebrates during the Paleozoic Era cleaned the sea by eating the calcium carbonate, thus enabling new forms of life to evolve. As Maria Montessori wrote,

> A global vision of cosmic events fascinates children and their interest will soon remain fixed on one particular part as a starting point for more intensive studies. Thus, the way leads from the whole, via the parts, back to the whole. The children will develop a kind of philosophy that teaches them the unity of the universe. This is the very thing to organize their intelligence and to give them a better insight into their own place and task in the world, at the same time presenting a chance for the development of their creative energy.[25]

Students in science classes at Lennox Memorial High School in Lennox, Massachusetts, watch the video "Powers of Ten" as a way of learning about the mathematical idea of scale. This nine-minute video takes students on an awe-inspiring journey, by powers of ten, from the farthest edges of the universe to deep inside the atom.[26] Middle school teacher Pam Schmidt shares her interest and wonder about snakes by keeping fifty snakes of all shapes and sizes in her classroom. The kids love it. "At my school, we have the GREATEST mad scientist teacher EVER!!! Ms. Schmidt is mad about snakes," says one student with a ball python wrapped around her arm.[27] Author Greg Levoy writes, "Growing your sense of wonder is often about simply getting out from behind the desk and the chores from time to time, the habits and routines that define and confine your everyday life, and creating opportunities to encounter wonder, put yourself in its path, and deliberately create a little estrangement from business as usual."[28]

CREATING YOUR OWN "WONDERS OF THE WORLD" LIST

Ultimately, then, wonder in the classroom begins with teachers who themselves are filled with wonder at the universe's marvels. Ecology pioneer Rachel Carson wrote, "If a child is to keep alive his inborn sense of wonder, he needs the companionship of at least one adult who can share it, rediscovering with him the joy, excitement and mystery of the world we live in."[29] I have my own list of "wonder-filled" things that includes facts such as these:

1. Each one of us started out life as a one-celled organism.
2. A man named Philip Pettit walked on a tightrope between the Twin Towers in New York.

3. A blood cell travels twelve thousand miles through our bodies in the course of a day.

Wonder also connects me to experiences I've had standing before the Grand Canyon, visiting Machu Picchu in Peru, and looking up at the glow-worms in the dark caves of Waitomo in New Zealand. Oh, and you can throw in the book *Finnegan's Wake*, the paintings of Vermeer, the music of Mozart, and certain colors and formations of clouds at sunrise or sunset. Now, what's on your own list of wonders?

CHAPTER EIGHT

Individuality: Resisting Standardization, Datafication, and Depersonalization in Education

The development of general ability for independent thinking and judgment should always be placed foremost, not the acquisition of special knowledge.

—Albert Einstein[1]

In 1934, Albert Einstein, responding to a young girl's letter about how she'd been having difficulties at school with her teachers, wrote, "I suffered at the hands of my teachers a similar treatment; they disliked me for my independence and passed me over when they wanted assistants."[2] Depending on the source, Einstein was either thrown out of the Luitpold Gymnasium (high school) in Munich, Germany, or was encouraged to leave on his own. One teacher in particular seemed to have it in for him. When Einstein defended himself by saying that he had committed no offense, the teacher replied, "Yes, that is true, but you sit there in the back row and smile; and your mere presence here spoils the respect of the class for me."[3] If Einstein ran the schools, he almost certainly would have never created a school system based on uniform standards. In an essay entitled "On Education," he wrote: "A community of standardized individuals without personal originality and personal aims would be a poor community without possibilities for development. On the contrary, the aim must be the

65

training of independently acting and thinking individuals, who, however, see in the service of the community their highest life problem."[4] Elsewhere, Einstein stated, "Only the individual can think, and thereby create new values for society—nay, even set up new moral standards to which the life of the community conforms. Without creative, independently thinking and judging personalities the upward development of society is as unthinkable as the development of the individual personality without the nourishing soil of the community."[5]

THE MARVEL OF INDIVIDUALITY

Each one of us, all seven and a half billion of us, is a unique and unrepeatable miracle. Even identical twins do not have the same genes.[6] Moreover, we are much more than our genes. We know now that the environment has a powerful impact upon how the genes we are given at conception are expressed, whether they are turned on or off (a process referred to as epigenetics). And each person has a unique history with variable parenting, exposure to or protection from disease, presence or absence of trauma or other adverse childhood experiences, access to or isolation from rich cultural resources, few or manifold relationships with siblings and/or peers, and vibrant or dispirited community involvement. Each individual is also situated somewhere on a spectrum with respect to a wide range of traits, including cognitive flexibility, attention, working memory, resilience to adversity, self-regulation, language development, creative expression, sociability, and a hundred other factors. Probably this amazing singularity that is each one of us is what prompted Spanish musician Pablo Casals to write, "Each second we live is a new and unique moment of the universe, a moment that will never be again. And what do we teach our children? We teach them that two and two make four, and that Paris is the capital of France. When will we also teach them what they are? We should say to each of them: Do you know what you are? You are a marvel. You are unique. In all the years that have passed, there has never been another child like you. Your legs, your arms, your clever fingers, the way you move. You may become a Shakespeare, a Michelangelo, a Beethoven. You have the capacity for anything. Yes, you are a marvel."[7]

INDOCTRINATION IN THE CLASSROOM

As Casals intimates, this view of each child as a unique, unrepeatable marvel contrasts sharply with the instrumental values inherent in conventional schooling. Nobel Prize–winning author Doris Lessing offers a blunt characterization of how this regimentation occurs from the very start of a child's school experience:

> It starts when the child is as young as five or six, when he arrives at school. It starts with marks, rewards, "places," "streams," stars—and still in many places, stripes. . . . From the very beginning the child is trained to think in this way: always in terms of comparison, of success, and of failure. It is a weeding-out system; the weaker get discouraged and fall out; a system designed to produce a few winners who are always in competition with each other. It is my belief—though this is not the place to develop this—that the talents every child has, regardless of his official "I.Q.", could stay with him through life, to enrich him and everybody else, if these talents were not regarded as commodities with a value in the success-stakes. . . . The other thing taught from the start is to distrust one's own judgement. Children are taught submission to authority, how to search for other people's opinions and decisions, and how to quote and comply.[8]

The irony is that this indoctrination is happening in a nation that is proud of its rugged individualism. We have plenty of American heroes who have proclaimed nonconformity as one of our highest ideals. Ralph Waldo Emerson wrote in his essay "Self-Reliance," "Insist on yourself, never imitate. Your own gift you can offer with the cumulative force of a whole life's cultivation, but of the adopted talent of another, you have only an extemporaneous, half possession."[9] Henry David Thoreau said, "I was not born to be forced. I will breathe after my own fashion. Let us see who is the strongest."[10] However, our schools appeared to have lost touch with this ideal beginning in the early part of the twentieth century, when the assembly line ideas of efficiency expert Frederick Winslow Taylor were transplanted from the industrial world into the American classroom.[11] Now, in the twenty-first century, it seems our values have shifted from the factory model of learning to a more contemporary corporate perspective; we've traded in the assembly line for the cube farm. However, in both cases, there's an emphasis on conformity (in the meeting room corporate atmosphere of today, this is referred to as "collaboration"). "What we're teaching today is obedience, conformity, following orders," says education historian Diane Ravitch, author of *The Death and Life of the Great American School System*.[12]

THE MOVEMENT TOWARD BLAND UNIFORMITY

The threat to students' individuality comes from many quarters. In the United States, school uniforms are increasingly becoming mandatory in the public schools, from 13.8 percent of schools in 2006 to 21.5 percent in 2016, even though a majority of students don't want to wear them.[13] Social and emotional development programs have become more common in the schools. These programs seek to promote what Val Gillies, a professor of social and policy studies at London South Bank University, characterizes as a "calm, emotionally flat ideal," and they tend to regard individualistic emotions such as aggressiveness, rebelliousness, skepticism, and passion as less than desirable feelings for the classroom.[14] The Common Core State Standards (and other states' standards) have wrapped their conformist tentacles around American classrooms, requiring all students in each grade to meet hundreds of specific standards such as these (for fifth graders and high schoolers, respectively): "Form and use the perfect (e.g., I had walked; I have walked; I will have walked) verb tenses"; and "understand radian measure of an angle as the length of the arc on the unit circle subtended by the angle."[15]

Most importantly, the Common Core has been "aligned to" (a code phrase suggesting uniformity) standardized testing. As Jack Hassard, former high school science teacher and professor emeritus of science education at Georgia State University, has put it, "We think that Common Standards and Assessments are the antithesis of the progressive values upon which this nation was founded. The idea of having a single set of standards and associated assessments appears to remove individuality, creativity and innovation from American classrooms."[16] Educator Justin Tarte put it more bluntly: "Asking all 6th-grade kids to master the same concept at the same time is like asking all 35-year-olds to wear the same size shirt."[17] Or, more tellingly, as one higher schooler noted, "'I attend one of the top high schools in my state, yet they still shatter the individuality of students. We are taught to go to school, learn what the teachers tell us, and get good grades. We are not told to find out what we truly enjoy doing. We are not told to find something to be passionate about. We are told it is bad to stand out. Teachers show us this, administrators show us this, and our peers show us this."[18]

DEPERSONALIZED LEARNING

One name for this standard-by-standard approach to learning is "competency-based instruction." Students begin work on one of the Common Core standards such as this: "Understand division as an unknown-factor problem. For example, find 32 ÷ 8 by finding the number that makes 32 when multiplied by 8." And once they have mastered that standard, they go on to the next one and the one after that and the one after that . . . ad infinitum (or at least it feels that way!). This Orwellian, "competency-based" approach to learning has also been called "personalized learning." In point of fact, personalized learning has become a big business in education, with companies like Google and Microsoft pouring billions of dollars into computerized programs that "personalize" instruction by giving each student material delivered via computer that is "at their own level" with respect to math, language, or science standards.[19] Actually, as education historian Diane Ravitch points out, this is really "*de*personalized learning." The computer programs use impersonal algorithms to translate students' responses into a new set of problems that are neither too easy nor too difficult for them. Students study the material while sitting at their computer work stations and are tested based on the material they have ostensibly mastered (and like standardized testing in general, the material to be tested on and the test itself are essentially the same).

Computers are even scoring students' essays. In order to make this work, the instructions for writing the essay need to include material that will be called upon in the essay, thus giving no credit for any background knowledge the student may wish to interject into the essay. Anthony Cody, cofounder of the Network for Public Education, writes, "Here we are beginning to see the ways in which grading technology may be shaping the tests, and the very way we ask students to show how they are applying the skills they have learned. If this is the 'Smarter' test [this is a reference to the Smarter Balance consortium, one of two nationwide testing agencies grounded in the Common Core], it seems far less intelligent than a qualified teacher, capable of challenging students with an open-ended question. And if we are sacrificing intelligence, creativity and critical thinking for the sake of the efficiency and standardization provided by a computer, this seems a very poor trade."[20] One teacher who used this "robo-grading" system commented, "My brightest students who did not follow the directions to a t were marked down. They often developed very complicated analyses, but were marked down because they did not regurgitate the expected words and organization. Those who did best on the scoring tended to be those who were willing to regurgitate the obvious."[21] In the Columbus City Schools, which had just started to use machine scoring, nearly half of the third graders earned a zero in the writing portion, even students who were considered "accelerated" because of their performance on the rest of the test.[22]

THE DATAFICATION OF REALITY

Add to this litany of soul-destroying practices another dimension of uniformity: the growing use of "data" to profile every aspect of a student's life at school. As students sit in front of computers engaged with these so-called "personalized" learning systems, algorithms record every keystroke and turn them into pieces of data. Jose Ferreira, CEO of Knewton, an edutech company, said in a 2012 speech that his "adaptive learning" platform, used by ten million students globally, collects *five to ten million data points per student per day*, down to how many seconds it takes a student to answer an algebra problem. Advanced technologies enable schools and edu-businesses to collect, analyze, and sell this data. This can result in a massive invasion of the students' privacy. For example, a high school student profiled in a National Education Policy Center report often consulted commercial programs like dictionary.com and SparkNotes. "Once when she had been looking at shoes [online]," says NPR correspondent Anya Kamenetz, "an ad for shoes appeared in the middle of a SparkNotes chapter summary."[23] Kamenetz reports on the difficulties posed by computerized instruction with regard to the complexities of human life and the idiosyncratic nature of student learning: "Computer systems are most comfortable recording and analyzing quantifiable, structured data. The number of absences in a semester, say; or a three-digit score on a multiple-choice test that can be graded by machine, where every question has just one right answer. But what about a semester-long group project where one student overcame her natural tendency to procrastinate, excelled in the design and construction of Odysseus's ship out of cardboard, but then plagiarized part of the explanatory text? What about a student who manages 'only' 10 absences despite changing living situations three times during the semester? Can dashboards reflect these complexities?"[24]

As a result of these dehumanizing computer programs, educators are losing touch with students' individuality—their hopes, dreams, fears, and ambitions. Instead, teachers can ascertain a student's future through what is called "predictive analysis," another number-crunching set of algorithms that a computer uses, which will predict at grade nine, for example, the chances of a student's likely on-time graduation from high school.[25] Administrators have even set up "data walls," where students can see each other's test results and be humiliated in front of their peers.[26]

DISEMPOWERING TEACHERS

A further way in which technology has interfered with how teachers teach students can be seen in the rise of evidence-based practices in education. Good teachers have always created lesson plans and curriculum materials based on what would work best for students' individual needs. One student may need to be engaged with videos, another with books, a third with a pep-talk boost to the student's self-confidence, a fourth with competitive games that teach skills, a fifth with opportunities to speak in front of the class. All of that is out the window now, because teachers are being told that in order to qualify for federal funding, schools must use teaching techniques that are on a list of research- or evidence-based, approved methods. To attain this status, a teaching strategy must be evaluated in an experimental classroom, and the results (as measured on a standardized test), must be significantly higher than those attained in a control group classroom that did not receive the benefit of that teaching strategy. Never mind the fact that there are too many variables in each classroom to be able to isolate the benefit of any specific teaching strategy.

Nevertheless, the results of this analysis are reflected in what's called an "effect size." This is the difference between the experimental and the control groups' pre- and postintervention test scores, measured as the difference between their standard deviations (a statistic that represents the degree of deviation from the mean, or average, score). New Zealand educator John Hattie has given effect sizes for hundreds of teaching strategies and concluded that an effect size of 0.4 or above represents a "thumbs-up" for that technique.[27] A 0 would mean there were no differences between groups, and a 1 would mean that a person in the experimental group who scored at the mean would be doing as well as a person in the control group who scored 1 standard deviation or 34.1 percent above the mean. Thus, an effect size of 0.4 would be somewhere between these two numbers (about 13 percent above the mean). To bolster his case, Hattie has looked at "meta-analyses," which take several similar studies and number-crunch them together to attain a single evaluative measure. You've perhaps noticed, by the way, that we've stopped talking about real human beings here and are awash in statistics. The crux of my argument about evidence-based teaching is that we're no longer letting teachers dip into their own rich fount of training and experience to individualize for students. We've turned that task over to bean-counting educational researchers.

Albert Einstein had something to say about this: "The teacher should be given extensive liberty in the selection of the material to be taught and the methods of teaching employed by him. For it is true also of him that pleasure in the shaping of his work is killed by force and exterior pressure."[28] In this brave new world of testing, accountability, quantification, and scientism (the misplaced belief that science is capable of ascertaining the truth of all things), the teacher is disempowered and must choose from a menu of "approved" teaching methods. Since the teacher sets the tenor for the classroom, this practice of "evidence-based" teaching serves to disempower students as well.

To be fair, many educators have sought to move against the tide of opinion and address the issue of individualism in their schools. I've seen several instances online of classroom teachers (usually primary level) who have engaged in projects where students paint their own unique images on small stones or other objects as a way of expressing their individuality.[29] But is that about individuality or the uniformity of small stones? On a much larger scale, two very popular movements in education, "differentiated learning" and "universal design for learning," help teachers tweak their lessons in such a way that kids from different backgrounds or kids who learn differently or those who have specific obstacles to learning can gain access to the material.[30] The problem with these programs is that, while they can be used to promote individual projects and self-directed learning, they are mostly used to help students adapt to an existing curriculum that itself is largely based on standardized learning goals and standardized tests. Similarly, other innovations such as "blended learning" and "the flipped classroom," while allowing students to individually regulate the time they spend on a learning task, still require the task to be aligned to the Common Core Standards and standardized testing.

AUTHENTIC PERSONALIZATION IN SCHOOLS

To truly individualize student learning, the student himself must be the initiator and the prime monitor of his own learning. The Avalon School in St. Paul, Minnesota, for example, is a seventh- to twelfth-grade charter school entirely structured around student-initiated projects. One senior at Avalon did his senior project on theater production. He analyzed several plays, took a course in stagecraft at nearby Hamline University, and produced, directed, performed in, and built stage sets for plays performed before the Avalon community. Another student at Avalon spent over eight hundred hours in her senior year working with a nonprofit educational advocacy group to help pass legislation in Minnesota expanding opportunities for individualized learning programs in the state.[31] At Monument Mountain Regional High School in Barrington, Massachusetts, students participated in a program called the Independent Project where they created their own curriculum and engaged in learning activities of their choice, including traditional academic pursuits as well as projects like taking flight lessons, writing a novel, and building a kayak.[32]

Sudbury Valley School in Framingham, Massachusetts, may represent the ultimate example of a school that allows students to express themselves fully as individuals. There are no formal courses, although students can request them and find a teacher to teach them. One alumna of Sudbury, Harvard-educated Debra Sivia Sadofsky, remembers, "Throughout the years I participated in a variety of academic learning—sometimes in classes, but some self-study. Not all of the classes I took were academic—one favorite seminar stands out. It was the sandwich seminar—which coincidentally was taught by the same staff member as the history courses! It was a cooking class in which we discussed the components of the best sandwich, e.g., type of bread, spreads, enough but not too many fillings, etc. Not only did we have fun, but I still make a mean sandwich!"[33] There are no tests or evaluations at Sudbury. Students have an equal say in the governance of the school, meeting once a week to decide on everything from budgets and hiring teachers to dealing with discipline issues. Four-year-olds at the school have the same vote as do older students and adult staff members. Students are free every day to do whatever they wish to do, as long as it doesn't violate any of the school's rules. The school has computers, a fully equipped kitchen, a woodworking shop, an art room, playground equipment, toys and games of various sorts, and many books. Students also have access to a pond, a field, and a nearby forest for outdoor play and exploration. There are at least twenty-five other schools around the world that are based on Sudbury's educational principles.[34]

THE DANGER OF TOO MUCH UNIFORMITY

These exemplary schools show us what is possible in providing students with learning environments that allow them to shape their own individual lives. True, not every public school in the United States is currently able to extend this amount of freedom to its students, but these schools give educators an ideal to pursue. In addition, they model what real individuality in schools looks like and how schools that promote individuality can be administered. It's time for American schools to reassert the nation's long tradition of standing up for the individualist and the nonconformist. We face a critical moment in our nation's history when the forces of standardization could overwhelm these locally inspired movements toward championing the rights and needs of children and adolescents in expressing their uniqueness.

I fear that many parents and educators do not actually realize how much danger we may be in when it comes to flirting with what is increasingly looking like a totalitarian system of education. Lawrence Baines, a professor of education at the University of Toronto, writing in the prestigious journal *Teachers College Record*, goes so far as to make comparisons between American education's move toward a standardized system in the past decade and efforts by Joseph Stalin in the 1930s to nationalize Russia's schools.[35] He writes, "Soviet teachers in the 1930s had little leeway to veer from the newly revised Soviet curriculum, despite the composition of the children who might be sitting in their classrooms. Similarly, in most states in America today, the same curriculum must be delivered to all students—whether they happen to be poor immigrants from Somalia sitting in an urban classroom in Minneapolis or a group of profoundly gifted savants sitting in a classroom in a wealthy suburb of Atlanta."[36] Furthermore, there are ominous resonances between the standardization of American education and the educational ideals of Nazi Germany. In May 1933, Wilhelm

Frick, the minister of the Interior in the Third Reich, stated that "the individualistic concept of education has been the main contributor to the destruction of national life within society and state and above all in its unrestrained application in the post-war era has shown its total inadequacy as a guiding principle for German education."[37] To some, these comparisons may seem far-fetched and alarmist. But only by standing guard against the creeping standardization in our schools, and standing firm in the promotion of an authentic education geared to the needs of individual learners, can we forestall any possibility of this type of nightmare scenario being enacted on American soil.

CHAPTER NINE

Neurodiversity: Emphasizing the Strengths of Kids with Special Needs

[Einstein] was . . . considered backward by his teachers. He told me that his teachers reported to his father that he was mentally slow, unsociable and adrift forever in his foolish dreams.
—Albert Einstein Jr.[1]

In 1962, psychologist Victor Goertzel and his wife, Mildred Goertzel, published a book called *Cradles of Eminence: A Provocative Study of the Childhoods of Over 400 Famous Twentieth-Century Men and Women.* They selected individuals who had at least two biographies written about them and who had made a positive contribution to society. According to the Goertzels, 60 percent of the four hundred had experienced serious school problems. Thomas Edison reported, "I remember that I was never able to get along at school. I was always at the foot of the class. I used to feel that the teachers did not sympathize with me, and that my father thought I was stupid."[2] Teachers regarded the French writer Marcel Proust's writing compositions as disorganized.[3] Norwegian composer Edvard Grieg would stand under a rainspout at school so he'd get wet and be sent home for a change of clothes. He wrote, "The only excuse I will make for myself is that school was in the last degree unsympathetic to me, its materialism, its coarseness, its coldness were so abhorrent to my nature that I thought of the most incredible ways of escaping from it, if only for a short time. . . . I have not the least doubt that school developed in me nothing but what was evil and left the good untouched."[4] Norwegian writer Sigrid Undset shared Grieg's feelings: "I hated school so intensely. It interfered with my freedom. I avoided the discipline by an elaborate technique of being absent-minded during classes."[5]

Other such misfits include Winston Churchill, Henry Ford, Ludwig van Beethoven, Charles Darwin, Leonardo da Vinci (see Appendix B), and Pablo Picasso. It's important to keep in mind that these eminent individuals were not yet famous. As far as their parents and teachers were concerned, they were poor students, and it's very likely that if they were growing up in today's American education system, they would have been tested, diagnosed with one or more labels such as learning disabilities, ADHD, dysgraphia, or oppositional defiant disorder and, finally, sent off to a special education class where they would engage in intensive remediation tailored to their shortcomings as students.

A CULTURE OF DEFICIT, DISORDER, AND DYSFUNCTION

Today there are over six and a half million children in the United States receiving special education services (13 percent of all public school students).[6] We don't know whether there are future inventors, composers, novelists, or scientists toiling away over their special education worksheets and workbooks in these programs, but the answer is, "very likely." Whether or not they'll be able to rise to prominence in the world is an open question. Moreover, many of the other kids in special education likewise possess abilities, talents, and capacities, which, while perhaps not reaching the Einstein or Edison level, would nevertheless help to propel them into successful careers as entrepreneurs, physicians, data analysts, caregivers, biologists, ecologists, photographers, cooks, and artists, among others. The biggest problem for them very probably isn't their academic deficiencies or behaviors. It's having to counter the negative expectations that parents and teachers have of them.

What I'm talking about here is a system that is based upon identifying disabilities, not strengths. A look at the pioneers of the U.S. special education movement in the twentieth century reveals a history steeped in deficit, disorder, and dysfunction. They include eugenicist Henry H. Goddard, who coined the diagnostic term *moron* in 1910; neuropathologist Samuel Orton, who, in 1925, asked teachers to refer students to him "who were considered defective or who were retarded or failing in their school work"; neuropsychiatrist Alfred A. Strauss, who in the 1940s at Wayne County Training School in Michigan worked out the psychopathology of the "minimally brain injured child"; and psychologists Samuel Kirk and William Cruickshank, who began using the term *learning disability* in 1963.[7]

These and other thinkers created the foundations upon which our current special education system is based. In my own experience as a special educator in the 1970s and 1980s in the United States and Canada, I was charged with administering diagnostic tests, filling out behavioral checklists, and helping students meet hundreds of instructional objectives based on their deficits. Instead of celebrating the playfulness, imagination, inventiveness, and curiosity that these students possessed, I confronted a long list of soulless requirements, including the need to improve students' auditory sequential memory, visual-spatial perception, short-term memory, and sensory-motor skills. The whole child in all his, depth, profundity, and dignity, had somehow become dismembered.

The situation for special education students is not much different today than it was thirty years ago. In fact, in some ways, it's actually worse. With the advent of the Common Core State Standards and similar state standards over the past decade, kids are confronted with the requirement to not only meet the special instructional goals that teachers set for them as part of their individualized education plans but also to cope with the academic standards mandated for *all* students at the state and federal levels. In some cases, we're talking about students having to demonstrate competency in understanding Shakespeare and *Huckleberry Finn* when they are still reading at the first-grade level, or needing to write essays "in which the development and organization are appropriate to task, purpose, and audience," (a fifth-grade standard) when they can't even write their own name!

A few years back, a group of nine New York principals wrote a letter to their special education students' parents about the effects of standardized testing on them: "We know that many children cried during or after testing, and others vomited or lost control of their bowels or bladders. Others simply gave up. One teacher reported that a student kept banging his head on the desk, and wrote, 'This is too hard,' and 'I can't do this,' throughout his test booklet."[8] While the Common Core and other state standards provide limited support and accommodation for students with special needs, there still isn't much budge room on the standards themselves. Katharine Beals, a lecturer at the University of Pennsylvania School of Education, reports that while the texts used in meeting Common Core standards may be supplemented with support structures such as glossaries and storyboards, "one can't adjust the text itself to match the student's reading level."[9]

A PARADIGM SHIFT FROM DISABILITY TO DIVERSITY

Not only are these students pressured to achieve at levels beyond their capacity but, with all the emphasis on their disabilities, their real strengths and abilities—where they could experience far more success and meaning— lay undiscovered or ignored. What the field of special education requires is a fundamental paradigm shift from an emphasis on deficit and dysfunction to one that accentuates strengths and diversity. Fortunately, there is a concept that could assist in this shift. Starting in the 1990s a new movement began to emerge from the autism-rights community promoting the idea of "neurodiversity," the notion that neurological differences are to be recognized and respected as any other human variation such as race, gender, sexual preference, or cultural background.

With the concept of neurodiversity, people with autism signaled to the world that they wanted to be liberated from the prison of negative expectations. Instead, they wished to be seen in a more positive way—as "differently wired" individuals. The first use of the word "neurodiversity" in print was by journalist Harvey Blume, who declared in the *Atlantic* in 1998 that "[n]eurodiversity may be every bit as crucial for the human race as biodiversity is for life in general. Who can say what form of wiring will prove best at any given moment?"[10] Since that time, the concept has grown to encompass other diagnostic categories besides autism and has also been applied to higher education, business, and medicine. Regrettably, it has been very slow to take off in the field where it is needed most, public school special education programs.[11]

What makes the neurodiversity movement so compelling is that it is backed by two decades of research highlighting the strengths and abilities of individuals with a wide range of diagnostic labels. People on the autism spectrum, for example, have special gifts in detecting small details in more complex patterns, and are systemizers rather than empathizers (e.g., are good in systems that have fixed inputs and outputs like machines, computer programs, and mathematical subjects). They score 30 to 70 percent higher on the Raven's Progressive Matrices IQ test than on the more social Wechsler Scales.[12] Individuals diagnosed with dyslexia often possess special three-dimensional spatial abilities, talent in the perception of wide and diffuse images, and proclivities in entrepreneurship.[13] Those diagnosed with ADHD frequently display greater levels of novelty-seeking and creativity than matched controls.[14] For those diagnosed with intellectual disabilities, there are links to enhanced social and emotional expressiveness (especially with Down syndrome) and special musical abilities (for Williams syndrome).[15] Those diagnosed with emotional and behavioral difficulties such as bipolar disorder display a range of creative behaviors in drama, writing, music, and dance, as well as generalized creative behavior.[16] Deaf individuals have been reported to have enhanced visual imagery abilities.[17] Both early- and late-onset blind individuals show supranormal auditory abilities in both near and far space.[18]

The fact that the DNA for these neurological differences is still in the gene pool suggests that it conferred advantages on the development of *Homo sapiens*. Evolutionary psychobiologists, for example, have suggested that the traits associated with ADHD may have been favorable in a hunting and gathering society where the ability to move fast (hyperactivity), respond quickly to stimuli (impulsivity), and attend to multiple stimuli out in the wild (distractibility) could have led to improved chances for survival in that environment.[19] The systemizing abilities of people on the autistic spectrum may have been useful in fashioning tools. As autism activist Temple Grandin once put it, "Some guy with high-functioning Asperger's developed the first stone spear; it wasn't developed by the social ones yakking around the campfire."[20] The bipolar individual may have been graced with extra dynamism in the manic phase of a mood cycle to provide the energy for hunting or for the sexual or aggressive drive needed to procreate and pass on one's genes.[21] Similarly, the three-dimensional thinking seen in some people with dyslexia may have been highly adaptive in preliterate cultures for designing tools, plotting out hunting routes, and constructing shelters.[22]

TRANSFORMING SPECIAL EDUCATION

Clearly, these new insights into old disorders require a complete restructuring of special education programs in the United States. Rather than testing for deficits, disorders, and dysfunctions, special educators need to build an entirely new assessment strategy focused on strengths, talents, and abilities. Instead of spending most of their time remediating weaknesses, special educators need to shift to an approach that favors building on strengths and using them to help overcome difficulties. Instead of explaining children's disorders to them using metaphors based on machines (e.g., for ADHD children: your "motor" runs too fast), children should be introduced to the idea of the brain as a "rain forest" with tremendous diversity and capacity for change.[23] Instead of counseling individuals with neurological disorders on how to "learn to live with your disability," special educators (and parents) should teach kids practical ways of maximizing their strengths and minimizing their difficulties.

I've used the concept of "niche construction" from evolutionary biology to help illustrate the kind of approach I have in mind.[24] When a bird builds a nest or a beaver builds a dam, they are engaged in niche construction, or the construction of an environment that will enhance their chances for survival in the natural world. Similarly, rather than putting all the emphasis in special education on trying to get the child to fit into the status quo, we should consider engaging in niche construction, where we change the environment to fit the child's unique ways of being and knowing. Some of the components of niche construction for kids with special needs include:

1. Helping them discover their own strengths.

2. Developing teaching strategies based on those strengths (e.g., having a highly mobile student diagnosed with ADHD learn his vocabulary words by acting them out).

3. Inspiring students by exposing them to role models with disabilities who succeeded in life.

4. Employing assistive technology and Universal Design for Learning tools to help them "work around" difficult tasks (e.g., speech-to-text apps for children who have difficulty getting their ideas down on paper).

5. Creating a rich social network of individuals who will support them in realizing their potential (e.g., tutors, paraprofessionals, peer teachers, and collaborative groups).

6. Making modifications to the learning environment (e.g., for a child diagnosed with ADHD, providing furniture that allows for movement in school such as a stand-up desk or a stability ball rather than a straight chair).[25]

7. Envisioning positive futures for neurodiverse kids by exposing them to careers that make the most of their gifts and abilities (e.g., for a highly visual student diagnosed with dyslexia, careers such as architecture, graphic design, or biochemistry).

8. Teaching concepts that help cultivate the inner resources necessary to succeed such as growth mind-set, mindfulness, resilience, and self-determination.

NEURODIVERSITY IN ACTION

While the concept of neurodiversity has been slow to catch on in special education classrooms in America, there are a few examples to point to where its principles and practices have been successfully carried out. Former middle school/high school teacher Patrick Waters recognizes the strengths of neurodiverse students as he helps them navigate "maker spaces," where they create novel inventions from cast-off computer parts and electronic gadgets. He writes, "Students with ADHD are project butterflies, generating idea after idea after idea, bouncing between and contributing to team after team. . . . Students on the autism spectrum who have an affinity for making will bring a questioning and curiosity about conventional thinking and a strong recall of factual information."[26] Educators at Stevenson School in Carmel, California, promote neurodiversity as a method of achieving equity, which they define as "getting what you need, not getting the same as everyone else. This is as true for the student-genius with debilitating social-emotional glitches as it is for the dyslexic/ADHD child with academic learning challenges. Within this operating philosophy, we look at equity from a different point of view and provide a broad range of options."[27] At the sixth-grade level, for example, teachers supplement a history textbook with photographs, videos, annotations, key vocabulary, and other structural supports to enable neurodiverse students to more easily access the text.

One key factor in the success of neurodiversity is the inclusion of kids with special needs in classrooms with typically developing students. A stellar example of this practice is the William W. Henderson Inclusion Elementary School, a K–5 school in Dorchester, Massachusetts that serves 230 students. About one-third of the school population consists of students with special needs who are for the most part fully included in the regular classroom program. While visiting the school, I met Richard, a ten-year-old who read for me a marvelously imaginative and well-developed science fiction story. Only later, as I observed his "stimming" out on the playground (making his fingers dance in front of his eyes) did I realize that he was on the autism spectrum. I saw Rachel, who had significant physical and intellectual disabilities, smiling away as she worked industriously on a school project with the help of a paraprofessional. I heard students cheer when one of their peers achieved a significant learning goal. This is how the whole day went, seeing children diagnosed with disabilities flourishing in both academic and nonacademic ways alongside their neurotypical peers.

For many years, the school's principal was William Henderson (they named the school after him on his retirement), who is himself neurodiverse, having become blind as a young adult. In his book *The Blind Advantage: How Going Blind Made Me a Stronger Principal and How Including Children with Disabilities Made the School Better for Everyone*, he recounts many examples of teachers who celebrated the gifts of their neurodiverse students, including "the English teacher who depicts Johnny (who has learning disabilities) as a kid who writes great stories using that special computer program; the teacher aide who brags about how terrific Chuck (a boy with cognitive delays) has been combining geometric shapes; the music specialist who relates how fantastic Ashley (who has autism) sings during music performances . . . the special education teacher who points out to the physics teacher how Willy (who has ADHD) can fix all kinds of car problems."[28] It is this prizing of diversity—recognizing strengths as well as challenges—that should be foundational for any special education program.

THE FUTURE BELONGS TO THE NEURODIVERSE

Championing neurodiversity for kids with special needs is critical for their own future. Too often, both parents and teachers wring their hands in despair over worries about what will happen to their children and adolescents when they reach adulthood. Yet it is now becoming clear that the future can be bright for many students with special needs as long as educators keep their eye on the prize and recognize the many new careers are opening up that require the gifts and abilities that these kids possess. Nowhere is this more remarkable than with individuals on the autism spectrum. Several years ago, a company in Denmark called *Specialisterne* (Danish for "Specialists"), began hiring individuals on the spectrum because they did the work better than anyone else. Among other services, this information technology company looks for glitches in computer code for programs developed by firms such as Microsoft and Oracle. It's very boring work for neurotypicals, but for people on the spectrum who are good at spotting small details in a larger array of figures and who enjoy working with systems like computer programs, it's a dream job (Specialisterne's motto is "Passion for Detail"). Three-quarters of the employees at Specialisterne are on the spectrum, and the success of this company has led to other computer firms recruiting individuals with autism.[29] Similarly, the 3-D spatial gifts and global vision of people diagnosed with dyslexia are well suited to careers in biochemistry, business, genetics, and astronomy.[30] The high-stimulation, novelty-seeking abilities of people diagnosed with ADHD suit them for careers in firefighting, emergency room medicine, forest management, land surveying, and building construction.[31] The emotional warmth and friendliness of many people with intellectual disabilities can make them wonderful caregivers. By discarding the deficit mindset and embracing a diversity mindset based on strengths, talents, and abilities, educators can learn to celebrate the joys and challenges of neurodiversity in their students' lives.

CHAPTER TEN

Compassion: Educating the Heart in the "Selfie" Generation

Our task must be to free ourselves from our prison by widening our circle of compassion to embrace all humanity and the whole of nature in its beauty.

—Albert Einstein[1]

First-grade teacher Mrs. Prest told her class of six- and seven-year-olds that children in Africa were dying because of a lack of clean water. One student, Ryan Hreljac, was so moved by this that he began to do extra work around the house to earn money for wells in these communities. Over time, this led to the establishment of Ryan's Well Foundation, a nonprofit organization that has brought safe water and sanitation services to almost a million people as of 2019.[2] In today's world, where violence and apathy are increasingly becoming a part of our daily experience, there has never been a greater need for the kind of compassion that moved Ryan to action.

The schools are ideally positioned to become places where students can learn how to be kind to one another, since lessons learned in early development will have a huge impact on whether such values are incorporated into society at large when these kids reach adulthood. His Holiness the 14th Dalai Lama, the foremost spiritual leader of the Gelug School of Tibetan Buddhism, has criticized modern education because of its materialistic basis and its failure to develop inner qualities of peace. He writes, "Our modern education system would be improved if it included training in how to deal with mind and emotions. . . . In addition to basic education, we need to encourage warm-heartedness, concern for others and compassion."[3] Too much attention has been given to the training of the mind at the cost of not educating the heart. The Dalai Lama points out that "one problem with our current society is that we have an attitude towards education as if it is there to simply make you more clever, make you more ingenious. . . . The most important use of knowledge and education is to help us understand the importance of engaging in more wholesome actions and bringing about discipline within our minds. The proper utilization of our intelligence and knowledge is to effect changes from within to develop a good heart."[4]

KINDNESS IS IN OUR GENES

Compassion represents an intrinsic part of the human condition. The word *kind* is etymologically related to the words *kin* and *kindred*, suggesting that there is a natural relationship of kindness between members of the same family, group, or species (the *Oxford English Dictionary*'s first definition of *kindly* is "exists or takes place according to natural laws"). Yale psychologist Paul Bloom writes, "Babies, notably, cry more to the cries of other babies than to tape recordings of their own crying, suggesting that they are responding to their awareness of someone else's pain, not merely to a certain pitch of sound. Babies also seem to want to assuage the pain of others: once they have enough physical competence (starting at about 1 year old), they soothe others in distress by stroking and touching or by handing over a bottle or toy."[5] This instinctual response appears to have been selected for by evolution to ensure that members of a group would support each other in the wild and thus have greater chances for survival than uncompassionate groups. Even chimpanzees will return favors to nonkin members at a cost to themselves if these outsiders have previously assisted them in finding food, and especially if the nonkin member incurred a risk in providing the favor.[6]

WELCOME TO THE "SELFIE" WORLD

While kindness seems to be embedded in our genes, it requires support and encouragement from the environment in order to flourish. In our contemporary society, however, and especially among our children and adolescents, compassion seems to be in short supply or at least is not valued nearly as much as it should be. According to a study by the Harvard Graduate School of Education, almost 80 percent of middle and high school students reported that their parents are more concerned about their happiness or achievement than about their caring for others. The students were three times more likely to agree than disagree with this statement: "My parents are prouder if I get good grades in my classes than if I'm a caring community member in class and school."[7]

These results were similar to those in a study commissioned by the children's magazine *Highlights*, where 44 percent of the respondents (ages six to twelve) said their parents most wanted them to be happy, 33 percent said their parents' priority was that they should do well in school, and 23 percent said their parents most wanted them to be kind.[8] This was despite the results of another survey conducted by the creators of *Sesame Street*, reporting that nearly 80 percent of parents agreed with the statement that "it's more important that my children are kind to others than academically successful."[9] It's possible that this latter statistic differed from the first two surveys because it presumably came largely from preschool parents who were not yet as concerned with school academics and achievement levels. Three-quarters of these parents said that they often worried that "the world is an unkind place for children."

By the time students reach college, their attitudes seem to have crystallized into a primarily self-centered focus. Two studies have demonstrated significant increases in narcissism in college students over the past thirty years (as measured by the Narcissistic Personality Inventory), with the biggest increases occurring since the year 2000.[10] Another research effort that did a meta-analysis of studies measuring empathy and perspective taking among college students (the ability to see another person's point of view) revealed a sharp decline over time in what they termed empathic concern, followed by perspective taking.[11]

One consequence of the above findings may be the incidence of bullying that occurs each year in America's schools. In 2017, almost 20 percent of students reported having been bullied at school.[12] Eighty-eight percent of teenage social media users have witnessed other people be mean or cruel on social network sites.[13] According to Williams College professors Susan Engel and Marlene Sandstrom,

> in American curriculums, a growing emphasis on standardized test scores as the primary measure of "successful" schools has crowded out what should be an essential criterion for well-educated students: a sense of responsibility for the well-being of others. What's more, the danger of anti-bullying laws, which have now been passed by all but six states, is that they may subtly encourage schools to address this complicated problem quickly and superficially. Many schools are buying expensive anti-bullying curriculum packages, big glossy binders that look reassuring on the bookshelf and technically place schools closer to compliance with the new laws. But our research on child development makes it clear that there is only one way to truly combat

bullying. As an essential part of the school curriculum, we have to teach children how to be good to one another, how to cooperate, how to defend someone who is being picked on and how to stand up for what is right.[14]

THE PERKS OF PRACTICING KINDNESS

There are many benefits to practicing compassion in the schools that go beyond bullying prevention. In one study, nine- to eleven-year-olds were assigned to one of two groups. One group was assigned the task of doing three acts of kindness, while the other group did an alternative activity not related to kindness (they mapped locations of places they had visited). Results indicated that the children in the kindness group had improved well-being and increased peer popularity compared with the control group.[15] Another study looked at the effectiveness of a program called cognitively-based compassion training (CBCT) with a group of at-risk adolescents and found improvements in feelings of hopefulness and a trend toward a decrease in generalized anxiety.[16] As a third set of researchers put it, "Acts of kindness can build trust and acceptance between people, encourage social bonds, provide givers and receivers with the benefits of positive social interaction, and enable helpers to use and develop personal skills and thus themselves."[17]

Unfortunately, our schools still lag far behind in letting these research findings affect their policies and priorities. The emphasis on standards and standardized testing creates an environment where students feel pressured to perform. The words *kindness, compassion,* and *empathy* are nowhere to be found in the Common Core State Standards. Even in kindergarten, it's more important for children to count to 100 by ones and tens than to share a favorite toy with a classmate. And sometimes the impact of these standards undercuts students' compassion in subtler ways. One feature of the Common Core standards, for example, has been an increase in the number of "informational texts" (nonfiction) that students are assigned to read, thereby resulting in a decline in required fiction. From grades 3 to 5, the guidelines, which previously had included a preponderance of fictional texts, shifted to an even mix of 50 percent fiction and 50 percent informational texts. By grade 12, this ratio increases to 70 percent of informational texts and only 30 percent of fiction. This is significant because research has revealed that reading literary fiction actually promotes an increase in empathy, social perception, and emotional intelligence, even after only a few minutes of reading.[18]

SCHOOLS THAT CELEBRATE COMPASSION

The good news is that some schools and school districts are beginning to see the benefits of what are called "noncognitive skills" (motivation, integrity, social competence) and are recognizing the importance of teaching students to be kind to one another.[19] One of the most comprehensive examples of this kind of change is the Compassionate Schools Project. As noted on its website (http://www.compassionateschools.org), "the project interweaves support in academic achievement, mental fitness, health, and compassionate character."[20] The project is a collaboration between the Curry School of Education at the University of Virginia and the Jefferson Public Schools in Louisville, Kentucky. Twenty-five elementary schools in the district are part of a seven-year, eleven-million-dollar effort to research the impact of teaching kindness, mindfulness (an awareness of each present moment in time), and compassion for self and others. Students have compassion class for fifty minutes twice a week; they are taught, for example, to respond to the anger they feel toward another student not by insulting or fighting but by pausing, finding their "anchor" (placing one hand on the chest and the other hand on the stomach), and taking three deep breaths. Students also engage in mindful movement exercises, learn how to recognize physical signs that they're stressed or upset, and practice different ways of being kind toward their classmates. The project is a randomized controlled study that is using twenty-one other schools as a control group to see if its curriculum really makes a difference in both academic and nonacademic skills. The control group will engage in the program at the conclusion of the study.

Another important project is the "kindness curriculum" for preschool students, which was created by the Center for Healthy Minds at the University of Wisconsin, Madison. (A free copy of the curriculum is available at https://centerhealthyminds.org/join-the-movement/sign-up-to-receive -the-kindness-curriculum.) It was adapted by *Sesame Street* as part of their 2017 season-long theme, "K is for Kindness." The curriculum is a twelve-week program (two sessions per week) where students practice mindfulness (awareness of the present moment) and keep track of their acts of kindness on a "Kindness Garden" poster in the classroom. Project supervisors Lisa Flook and Laura Pinger write, "The idea is that friendship is like a seed—it needs to be nurtured and taken care of in order to grow. Through that exercise, we got students talking about how kindness feels good and how we might grow more friendship in the classroom."[21] Kids learn to communicate compassionately with each other, for example, by having one person "speak from the heart," holding a "peace wand" with a heart on it, while another student holds a wand with a star, listens to what the first child has said, and then repeats it back to their partner.

The curriculum also contains books on the theme of kindness, kindness songs, movement activities, and discussions on what kindness is all about. They read, for example, the book *Sumi's First Day of School Ever,* which is the story of an immigrant student who struggles with English. After reading it, they brainstorm ways they could help Sumi adjust to her new environment, including practicing something as simple as a smile. "At the heart of the discussion is empowering young children to begin to feel how positive qualities such as kindness and gratitude feel in their bodies, physically," says Flook. "This is where a mindful approach comes in—the skills build on paying attention to the body and extend to offering kind attention to ourselves and the world around us."[22] A randomized controlled study evaluating the curriculum found that students displayed improvements in social competence and earned higher report card grades in the domains of learning, health, and social-emotional development, whereas the control group exhibited more selfish behavior over time.[23]

KINDNESS PROJECTS ACROSS THE UNITED STATES

Other schools and districts have found different ways of incorporating kindness and compassion into their programs. Frank Wagner Elementary School, in Monroe, Washington, observes Kindness Week around Valentine's Day. The Denver-based Random Acts of Kindness Foundation supports the weeklong event every February to celebrate the idea of expressing selfless love. Frank Wagner staff and students write kind notes to classmates, sign posters to thank local agencies for keeping the community safe, and recognize the children who have gone above and beyond the norm to be caring, during a school-wide assembly. They also decorate rocks with positive wishes and plant them around the school and community for others to find.[24]

Students at Reed Intermediate School in Newtown, Connecticut, work individually and in small groups to create "kindness carts." Each cart has a different theme and sells a specific product to fund a third-world community project, such as building a new well in West Africa. One stand sells lemonade, another tacos, a third sells dog treats (e.g., "Happy Jack's Gourmet Dog Treats").[25] Students in the Worcester (Massachusetts) Technical High School carpentry department have built "buddy benches" for three elementary schools in the area. Erin Dobson, principal of one of those schools, Tatnuck Magnet, stated, "The buddy bench has been a success at Tatnuck. Younger children use the bench when they are feeling lonely and want a friend to play with. Students use the buddy bench as a strategy in their tool kit to initiate friendships and support other students in need of a friend. The buddy bench has been successful, especially in the primary grades."[26]

A NEGLECTED SKILL: BEING KIND TO YOURSELF

In addition to being kind to others, an emerging focus of research is self-compassion. One of the pioneers in the field, Kristin Neff, points out that self-compassion is not to be confused with self-esteem. She writes, "Continually feeding our need for positive self-evaluation is a bit like stuffing ourselves with candy. We get a brief sugar high, then a crash. And right after the crash comes a pendulum swing to despair as we realize that . . . [w]e can't always feel special and above average."[27] Self-compassion, on the other hand is about stopping the process of self-judgment. Neff points out that "self-compassion is a powerful way to achieve emotional well-being and contentment in our lives, helping us avoid destructive patterns of fear, negativity, and isolation. More so than self-esteem, the nurturing quality of self-compassion allows us to flourish, to appreciate the beauty and richness of life, even in hard times. When we soothe our agitated minds with self-compassion, we're better able to notice what's right as well as what's wrong, so that we can orient ourselves toward that which gives us joy."[28]

At a local elementary school in Northampton, Massachusetts, author and girls' advocate Rachel Simmons teaches self-compassion as a volunteer to children as young as five. She has the youngsters share embarrassing moments ("I fell off the monkey bars in front of my friends") and practice hugging themselves as a form of self-soothing.[29] Mindfulness practices, which involve a nonjudgmental monitoring of one's present-moment experience, serve as an ideal means of helping to foster self-compassion. Austin, Texas, high school junior Xavier Zamarron comments, "A lot of things can stack up on you, so it's nice to take a breath once in a while. And also in high school you kind of feel like a crappy person all the time because of just society, and like you wonder if you're cool or not, but none of that really matters. When we practice mindfulness, we're only worried about what we think about ourselves."[30] In a meta-analysis of nineteen studies on self-compassion in adolescents, researchers found an inverse relationship between self-compassion and psychological distress indexed by anxiety, depression, and stress.[31] Another study revealed that self-compassion can overcome the negative effects of low self-esteem (in other words, you can have low self-esteem and still function at a high level if you have self-compassion).[32] Finally, a study revealed that self-compassion can even mobilize the immune system of the body to counteract the toxic effects of stress.[33]

As we read about the latest school or workplace shootings, watch or hear about violence in the media, or learn about the latest violent crimes in our community on the local news, we should try to remember the vital importance of efforts to integrate kindness into the curriculum of schools from preschool to high school. As a quote attributed to Frederick Douglass says, "It is easier to build strong children than to repair broken men." Perhaps the greatest intervention of all is for us as adults to model kindness to children and teens. According to the *Highlights* survey noted above, 68 percent of children reported having seen their parents or adults acting unkindly or saying mean things. As *Education Week* staff writer Evie Blad points out, "Children notice if Mom follows her talk on loving your neighbor with a fit of road rage on the way to soccer practice. And they also notice school environments that feel chaotic or unsupportive and disharmony among adults. It's not just about teaching children about kindness and cooperation . . . it's also about creating a school environment that is conducive to their development in those areas."[34] As we've seen in this chapter, some schools are starting to wake up to this need. Harvard researcher Nicholas Christakis and University of California, San Diego, social scientist James Fowler have demonstrated that behavior for the social good is contagious and can spread quickly from person to person in a larger social network.[35] Let's hope that this contagion of kindness spreads throughout our schools. Since it's instinctual within the human species, an epidemic of kindness in our culture could actually be possible. As one little boy said to his preschool teacher after a lesson emphasizing compassion, "Miss Lisa, I was born to be kind."[36]

CHAPTER ELEVEN

Care for Nature: Cultivating a Reverence for All Living Things

---

In every true searcher of Nature there is a kind of religious reverence.
—Albert Einstein[1]

Rabindranath Tagore was an Indian poet, essayist, and novelist (the first non-European to win the Nobel Prize in Literature) who started his own school for children and adolescents in 1901. He boldly revealed his contempt for traditional methods of education in one of his short stories, entitled "The Parrot's Training," where a bird is caged and force-fed pages of a school textbook until it dies.[2] Tagore placed a strong emphasis on learning from nature. He observed, "The mind of the child is always on the alert, restless and eager to receive firsthand knowledge from mother nature. Children should be surrounded with the things of nature which have their own educational value."[3] Like Albert Einstein, Tagore had a great antipathy toward standardization and wrote, "The regular type of school is a manufactory and is a mere method of discipline specially designed for grinding out uniform results."[4] He noted that a nature-focused pathway to learning was part of an old tradition in his country: "[I]n . . . ancient India the school was where life itself was. There the students were brought up, not in the academic atmosphere of scholarship and learning, or in the maimed life of monastic seclusion, but in the atmosphere of living aspiration. They took the cattle to pasture, collected firewood, gathered fruit, cultivated kindness to all creatures, and grew in their spirit with their teachers' own spiritual growth."[5]

OUR ENDANGERED PLANET

Rather than dismissing Tagore's educational philosophy as simply a quaint reflection of life in an agrarian country, we should be fervently embracing his message in a world that is rapidly destroying its natural inheritance. The number of animals living on Earth has plunged by half since 1970.[6] It's estimated that in the last four decades, we've lost more than 50 percent of the planet's biodiversity.[7] These losses are primarily due to the activities of human beings and their livestock and include deforestation; the introduction of invasive species into ecosystems; industrialization and the pollution it causes to the air, water, and land; warfare; overfishing; overhunting; overpopulation; and overconsumption. The World Wildlife Federation reports that all economic activity in the world depends upon the estimated $125 trillion a year in services that nature provides to us free of charge.[8] Things have gotten so bad that scientists are now beginning to talk about a "sixth extinction" of all life forms on Earth if nothing dramatic is done to undo the effects of humanity's predations.[9] While third-world countries are a big source of biodiversity degradation, the United States has a major share of the responsibility, representing only 5 percent of the world's population, but consuming about 25 percent of the world's natural resources.[10] A recent UN report found that humanity has until 2040 to achieve "rapid and far-reaching" transformation of society if we wish to avoid the dire environmental consequences of climate change signaled by a warming of 1.5 degrees Celsius above preindustrial levels.[11]

THE EPIDEMIC OF "NATURE DEFICIT DISORDER"

American biologist E. O. Wilson believes that human beings are born with a natural affiliation for nature, a phenomenon he calls "biophilia."[12] We see biophilia at work in the lives of very young children who love to check under rocks for bugs; climb trees; stare at spiders spinning their webs; collect pine cones, leaves, and flowers; and engage with nature in so many other ways. What we're confronted with today, however, is the emergence of a whole new generation of children who suffer from what author and journalist Richard Louv calls "nature deficit disorder."[13] Children and adolescents have become estranged from nature as a result of increased urbanization, parental worries about "stranger danger," increased homework in an age of school accountability, after-school activities, and, perhaps most significantly, the rapid surge in the use of technology including computers, smartphones, tablets, video games, cruising the internet, and engaging with social media platforms such as Facebook and Instagram. According to polling data (as incredible as it seems), kids devote an average of only four to seven minutes a day in unstructured outdoor play, whereas they spend an average of seven and a half hours on electronic media.[14] And most of that media time is spent indoors. As one suburban fifth grader related to Louv, "I like to play indoors better 'cause that's where all the electrical outlets are."[15]

This level of disengagement with nature not only puts the entire planet at risk but also appears to be at least partly responsible for many of the ailments from which youth are increasingly suffering. Perhaps the biggest of these ills is obesity—caused in large part by a poor diet and a sedentary lifestyle—which exposes the sufferer to a wide range of health problems including diabetes, cardiovascular diseases, and cancer. The prevalence of childhood obesity has increased dramatically among all age groups since 1988 and is especially severe among children aged two to five years and adolescent females aged sixteen to nineteen years.[16] Young children living in areas with less green exposure have significantly higher odds of being overweight/obese.[17]

Similarly, it seems that the prevalence of children and adolescents diagnosed with ADHD (6.1 million in the United States in 2016) may be due in part to the absence of experiences in nature.[18] Research suggests that exposure to a "green" environment lessens the symptoms of ADHD and that the wilder the natural environment is, the more the symptoms decline.[19] Still another epidemic, this one of mood disorders among adolescents (an estimated 14.3 percent of adolescents have mood disorders), appears to be ameliorated by exposure to nature.[20] Other benefits of time spent in nature include better school achievement, higher levels of fitness, better cognitive performance, improved eyesight, better sleep, stronger bones, a longer life span, and better health as an adult.[21]

Given all these advantages, there are limited opportunities for students to spend time outdoors while in school. A decline in recess first began in the early 1990s, and it further declined with the enactment of the federal No Child Left Behind law in 2001, which emphasized standardized testing in English language arts and mathematics. To focus on these core academic skills, many districts reduced the time for recess, art, music, physical education, and even lunch.[22] While 80 percent of school districts claim to provide daily recess, research conducted by the Centers for Disease Control and Prevention revealed that 60 percent of school districts have no policy regarding daily recess for elementary schools and only 20 percent mandate daily recess.[23] In addition, teachers are reluctant to let kids go outside during regular classroom sessions for fear that they will come back all hyped up and distracted, despite research evidence that outdoor time actually increases student engagement and attention once they're back in the classroom.[24] Furthermore, the subject of environmental studies is not included in the Common Core standards that structure so much of education today, and even when it is included, much of the curriculum is involved with indoor academic studies (books, lectures, making posters, class discussion, etc.) with few opportunities to actually get out and directly experience nature.[25]

NATURE PRESCHOOLS AND FOREST KINDERGARTENS

While these and other factors serve to keep students indoors most of the time, there are a growing number of schools in the United States that make it a priority to connect students with the great outdoors. One encouraging trend is the recent growth of "nature" or "forest" preschools and kindergartens in the United States. Children in these schools spend 70 to 100 percent of their time out in nature, in an immersive environment where the curriculum develops out of the experiences the children have as they play. Popular in Germany, where there are an estimated 1,500 forest schools, or *Waldkindergärten*, their numbers have increased in the United States from only 20 schools in 2008 to around 250 today.

In a sense, these schools are a reaction to the increasingly academic kindergartens cited in chapter 5, and a throwback to the original *kindergärten* (German for "children's' garden") developed by Friedrich Froebel in Germany in the nineteenth century. Fiddleheads Forest School in Seattle, Washington, for example, is an outdoor school nestled in the trees of the University of Washington Botanic Gardens. There are no buildings associated with the school, so children spend all of their time outdoors, going on "listening walks" where they stand in a circle in silence and listen to the sounds of the forest, cart loads of rocks around in a wheelbarrow, play at being pirates, examine trees hit by lightning, search for seeds, run up and down hills, and closely observe the wildlife and plant life in the surrounding area.[26] "Some days we're setting up and we hear eagles calling to each other, and we run out and look up," cofounder Kit Harrington said. "Kids are the best at sharing in joy and wonder."[27]

Spending 100 percent of their time outdoors is not as easily negotiated by elementary schools (although in Norway, many elementary schools have a *gapahuk*, or rough-and-ready wooden structure near the school, in which to engage in *uteskole* or "outdoor education"). However, some U.S. elementary schools have managed to increased access to nature for their students in innovative ways. At Leo Politi Elementary School in Los Angeles, California, volunteer environmental education students from Dorsey High School ripped out five thousand square feet of concrete and Bermuda grass and planted native bushes, flowers, plants, and trees, including six live oaks. The plants, bushes, and trees attract insects, which attract birds, which provide students with many opportunities to explore the environment. "Questions about why some birds flocked to one plant and not another led to discussions about soil composition and water cycles, weather patterns and seasons, avian migration and the tilt of the Earth in its orbit around the sun," said principal Brad Rumble.[28] As part of one project, students compiled an online, illustrated survey of every species documented in their urban bird sanctuary. At Oak Forest Elementary School in Humble, Texas, a reading teacher asked a bird-loving friend to put up a few bird feeders to attract her "reluctant readers." Not only did the bird-tenders do better in reading but this project led to the formation of a nature club, which gave rise to a vegetable garden, additional planting around the school yard, and the creation of butterfly and hummingbird gardens.[29]

FROM BLUE-TONGUED SKINKS TO AQUAPONICS

Animals are the attraction at Seth Low Intermediate School 96 in Brooklyn, New York. Science and zoology teacher Dominica Fiume is wild about them and makes sure they're an integral part of the curriculum. Her classroom includes chinchillas, guinea pigs, rabbits, some bearded dragons, a two-foot-long blue-tongued skink, a ball python, an albino corn snake, parakeets and doves, leopard geckos, six aquatic turtles, and an African clawed frog. "You learn new things here," said Antonella Bassini, an eighth grader who is part of Ms. Fiume's Zoo Crew, a group that comes to school early to feed the animals. "Like, you have to put vitamins on the mouse before you feed it to the snake."[30] A teacher at Christ Church Episcopal [Middle] School in Greenville, South Carolina, transformed a detention pond (a body of water that catches runoff from nearby streams) behind the school into a "wetlands laboratory." Students used dip nets to capture crawfish, tadpoles, dragonfly larvae, and aquatic spiders. Then, after observing and identifying the creatures, they created a live food web, depicting the ecosystem's network of interconnected feeding patterns.[31]

Students at Lansing High School, in Leavenworth, Kansas, engage in aquaponics, which is a combination of aquaculture (raising fish) and hydroponics (soilless growing of plants). They stocked their three-hundred-gallon tank with tilapia and are in the process of germinating seeds that will grow basil, lettuce, tomatoes, and green beans. Once the fish and produce are ready to be harvested, students will coordinate with the school's culinary department to begin a farm-to-table pilot program.[32] In Seattle, Washington, the Seattle Aquarium works with several area high schools that each "adopt" a nearby marine reserve-beach. Students study and monitor twenty-four species, from starfish to sea slugs, that are strong indicators of the health of a beach's environment. They also engage in marine biology by going a couple miles out to sea on a floating lab, a seventy-foot-long motorized vessel, casting nets and helping count, measure, and identify bottom fish as well as sharks, skates, and stingrays. Maine high school students monitored the waters around Mount Desert Island, an hour southeast of Bangor, by regularly testing phytoplankton for toxic species, particularly the most prevalent one, Alexandrium, which is known to trigger red tide events—toxic discoloration of ocean waters—that can result in poisoning shellfish.[33]

The Roots & Shoots program is an important environmental initiative for kids founded by British primatologist Jane Goodall. Goodall is perhaps the world's leading expert on chimpanzees, someone who has marshaled her knowledge and expertise concerning nature to teach others how to respect animals, protect endangered species from human predators, and live in harmony with nature. In a 2013 keynote speech she delivered at New York University, she shared some of her own ideas about education: "Children I think are born with an immense desire to learn. . . . [They] are made to spend too long sitting in class and not enough time going out and learning the way that we learn best, which is by exploring. It's by touching. It's by feeling."[34] In Goodall's Roots & Shoots program, students find or create their own group and then design their own project to address needs that they care most about. Projects include planting gardens, creating a nature camp, cleaning up trash in a local forest, creating a pollination program by planting flora that attract butterflies, initiating a "save the wolves" campaign, tree planting, and creek restoration.[35]

MAKING IT REAL IN NATURE CLASS

The activities and programs described above clearly have a positive impact on students' lives. But the question remains how this activism can translate into a lifelong stewardship of the environment and a proactive attitude toward saving the world from environmental disaster. Research indicates that people are much more likely to be concerned with environmental issues if they feel like they are a part of nature.[36] A Swedish study indicated that schools that are closer to urban green spaces had children who were more empathetic and concerned for other life-forms and more aware of human–nature interdependence.[37] Perhaps most significantly for educators is the finding that school-related exposure mechanisms to nature did not significantly predict environmental literacy and were only marginally predictive of environmental stewardship. What really counted was giving students the opportunity to choose on their own to engage in free, hands-on experiences in nature. The study's authors point out: "Our findings may be suggesting that free choice learning, through self-exposure to nature, might be the most effective approach to fostering not only environmental literacy but also political-ecological

citizenship."[38]   Another   study   concluded   that   young   children's
environmental education needs to be immersive and open-ended rather
than structured and scripted.[39] Essentially, kids just need time in nature to
explore freely all the delights that are there to be had. As the poet and
essayist Mary Oliver put it,

> Teach the children. We don't matter so much, but children do. Show them
> daisies and the pale hepatica. Teach them the taste of sassafras and winter-
> green. The lives of the blue quarters, blueberries. And the aromatic ones—
> rosemary, oregano. Give them peppermints to put in their pockets when
> they go to school. Give them the fields and the woods and the possibility of
> the world salvaged from the lords of profit. Stand them in the stream, head
> them upstream, rejoice as they learn to love this green space they live in, its
> sticks and leaves and then the silent beautiful blossom. . . . Attention is the
> beginning of devotion.[40]

CHAPTER TWELVE

Tolerance: Nurturing a Deep Respect for Human Differences

Laws alone cannot secure freedom of expression; in order that every man present his views without penalty there must be spirit of tolerance in the entire population.

—Albert Einstein[1]

Martin Luther King Jr. helped to propel the civil rights movement in the United States toward a new era of legislation that brought greater freedoms and rights to people of color. When he was a student at Morehouse College, in Atlanta, Georgia, in 1947, he wrote a college term paper that contained the seeds of his ideas about education and learning. In this paper, King wrote that schools must prepare students to think broadly, without bias, prejudice, or bigotry. He wrote, "[E]ven the press, the classroom, the platform, and the pulpit in many instances do not give us objective and unbiased truths. To save man from the morass of propaganda, in my opinion, is one of the chief aims of education."[2]

In an MLK-inspired school, a high priority would be placed on challenging narrow beliefs and developing tolerance for a wide range of differences. Students would be urged to question the daily newspaper, television broadcasts, internet web pages, blog posts, and social media. They would be empowered to confront the bully, the bigot, and the blowhard. But King said that the development of these critical thinking abilities was not enough, that we must also educate for character. He wrote, "The most dangerous criminal may be the man gifted with reason, but with no morals. The late Eugene Talmadge [former governor of Georgia], in my opinion, possessed one of the better minds of Georgia, or even America. Moreover, he wore the Phi Beta Kappa key. By all measuring rods, Mr. Talmadge could think critically and intensively; yet he contends that I am an inferior being. Are those the types of men we call educated?"[3] Students in an MLK-inspired classroom would be encouraged to develop qualities of empathy for one's fellow beings and tolerance for diversity of race, religion, ethnicity, gender identity, sexual orientation and disability status. They would be encouraged to engage in political and social activities designed to raise awareness about tolerating differences, exposing inequalities, and crusading for social justice.

INTOLERANCE ON THE RISE

King's words have never been more relevant than they are today. The United States has become increasingly polarized over the past three decades, fueled in part by the growth of the internet, where people can isolate themselves on websites and social networking platforms that share their views, no matter how extreme or vitriolic. The number of hate groups in the country has surged to an all-time high of 1,020 as of 2019, the fourth straight year there has been an increase.[4] Gun deaths are on the rise, bucking a ten-year decline.[5] Every day, forty-seven children and teens are shot in murders, assaults, suicides and suicide attempts, unintentional shootings, and police interventions.[6] One in five immigrant children under the age of thirteen have been "detained" by the government as a result of "zero tolerance" border policies.[7] Nine out of ten LGBTQ teens have been bullied in school, and more than one-third of gay youths have missed a day of school because they felt unsafe.[8] More than 25 percent of U.S. students report seeing hate-related graffiti in their schools.[9] "Hate has become mainstream," said Robert Trestan, the regional director of the Anti-Defamation League in New England: "Students have access to this vitriol. Whether it's on their phones, television, social media, or they hear people saying it, everyone has the same access to the same information and images in today's world."[10]

THE NATURE OF PREJUDICE

While it's often said that prejudice is learned and not inborn, it may be closer to the truth to say that we come into life primed for bias, but that culture has a major role in whether that bias solidifies into intolerance or is transformed instead into a more accepting attitude toward others who are perceived as different. From an evolutionary point of view, the ability to discriminate between "us" and "them" may have offered survival benefits, inasmuch as in a hunting and gathering society, knowing who your friends are (e.g., your clan) and who your enemies are may have made the difference between being protected and nurtured versus being attacked or endangered, the latter of which would interfere with the ability to pass one's genes on to future generations.[11]

Research suggests that prelinguistic infants prefer those who share even trivial similarities with themselves, and these preferences appear to reflect a cognitive comparison process ("like me"/"not like me").[12] Young children's brains are highly neuroplastic and extremely vulnerable to racist influences as they are growing up.[13] Gordon Allport, a pioneer in the psychology of prejudice, relates the story of a six-year-old girl running home from school and asking a question to her parent: "Mother, what is the name of the children I am supposed to hate?"[14] Harvard researcher Mahzarin Banaji points out, "We have known for a very long time that children process information differently than adults. That is a given. . . . But what has changed, where racism and other prejudice are concerned, is that we had far over-calculated how long it takes for these traits to become imbedded in a child's brain. It's quite shocking really, but the gist of it is that 3- and 4-year-olds demonstrate the same level and type of bias as adults. This tells us that children 'get it' very, very quickly, and that it doesn't require a mature level of cognition to form negative biases."[15] Other studies have shown that explicitly racist beliefs go "underground" starting around age ten ("Who me? I'm not biased!"), while implicit (subconscious) racism remains and becomes automatized around the age of twelve or thirteen.[16]

THE SCHOOLS TACKLE INTOLERANCE (OR NOT)

The schools, which should represent places where racism, sexism, and other forms of prejudice are closely examined and effectively unlearned, may in some ways be exacerbating the problem of intolerance in children and adolescents. School policies, for example, that enforce "zero tolerance" of disruptive school acts (including acts as innocuous as wearing hats inside the school), have been seen to affect a disproportionate number of African American boys. Black students are suspended and expelled from school at three times the rate of white students.[17] This statistic squares with findings that implicit bias in teachers was found to explain the differing ethnic achievement gap as a result of teachers having lower expectations for black students. And these findings, coupled with the increasing involvement of law enforcement personnel in school discipline cases, have been seen by many to fuel the "school-to-prison" pipeline (blacks are incarcerated in state prisons in the United States at more than five times the rate of whites).[18]

The explosion in the use of private school vouchers over the past fifteen years likewise presents problems, since most civil rights protections that students enjoy when they attend public schools do not apply to private schools. While some states provide minimal protections, even the most protective laws include no safeguards against LGBTQ discrimination and no requirement to address the needs of students not fluent in English.[19] School textbooks, especially in history, often fail to candidly express the realities of discrimination, slavery, and prejudice. A survey conducted by the Southern Poverty Law Center in 2017, for example, revealed that only 8 percent of high school seniors were able identify slavery as the central cause of the Civil War.[20] And even when schools try to teach tolerance, they sometimes end up causing more difficulties, especially for students of color, as when, for example, teachers run simulations where students are told to kneel in the hold of a make-believe slave ship with their hands taped behind their backs, or when classes engage in simulations that assign positive roles to blue-eyed students and negative ones to brown-eyed kids.[21]

CONFRONTATION IS KEY

The fact that teaching tolerance requires reaching into students' deepest sensitivities, however, is not a reason to dodge the topic. Unfortunately, too many teachers avoid teaching about race and prejudice and the need for tolerance precisely because they feel like they'll do the wrong thing or bring up a Pandora's box of issues they won't be able to handle. Mica Pollock, director of the Center for Research on Educational Equity, Assessment, and Teaching Excellence, uses the term *colormute* to describe the censoring of race words that one is anxious about.[22] This practice is regrettable, because to counter racism and other forms of prejudice, it is important to meet it head on, as for example, when someone in the classroom or out in the hallways uses a racial slur or expresses an intolerant point of view. This is precisely the time to teach about discrimination, stereotypes, and bias—in context, as a "teachable moment." Experts in the field of tolerance education agree that the wrong thing to do in this instance is to remain silent, which serves as a form of tacit agreement that the slur or intolerant point of view is acceptable.

Discussions about racism and other forms of prejudice should be conducted in a democratic climate of free and respectful deliberation. In one study of the use of deliberation of controversial political issues in several midwestern high schools, researchers Paula McVoy, now an assistant professor at North Carolina State University, and Diana Hess, currently dean of the University of Wisconsin, Madison, School of Education, asked teachers why they were using deliberation in their classrooms. They most often said that it was to prepare students for democratic life. One teacher commented, "I think students should be able to carry out an intelligent conversation using civil discourse to . . . express themselves in an appropriate manner and have honest, genuine discussions with one another about these issues. I think what they see a lot of times, in the media today, it is not really modeling civil discourse."[23] To help cut down on the heated nature of controversial class discussions, Steve Caudill, at Bremen High School in Bremen, Indiana, for example, insists that students back up statements they make with evidence. He also requires that when students speak, they restate what the previous speaker has said to show that they were listening.[24]

CELEBRATING DIVERSITY IS VITAL

Another crucial approach for combating racism, heterosexism (prejudice toward people in the LGBTQ community), sexism, ethnicism, and other forms of bias, is to create an environment where diversity is celebrated. One study, for example, suggested that diversity education could reduce both implicit and explicit antiblack biases.[25] Elementary school principal Don Vu, at Barrett Ranch Elementary School in Antelope, California, writes, "Our school has partnered with neighboring schools to host a World Fair event every spring. Our vision is to highlight and celebrate all the diverse cultures that are in our schools. Families volunteer to run a booth in which they share cultural artifacts and food samples. From Russia to Mexico, we have nearly 30 countries represented every year. Every student 'traveler' is given a booklet for the event, a passport to be stamped as they visit the different countries at the World Fair. Throughout the evening, the main stage may feature performances from a student baile folklórico dance group or a Ukrainian bandura quartet."[26] Second-grade teacher Aeriale Johnson, at Washington Elementary School in San Jose, California, has each student in her class mix up paint to match their skin color. She then asks them, "In what ways does the color of our skin influence who we are and what our place is in the world?" She wrote that when she was growing up, teachers pretended that they didn't see color but that she felt it was important to raise this issue. She wrote, "My culture, my language, my religion, and even the texture of my hair are all inextricably linked to the color of my skin. To erase it is to erase me."[27]

SEEING THE WORLD THROUGH ANOTHER'S EYES

An important feature of learning tolerance is developing the capacity to take on the perspective of another individual whose race, ethnic group, or other classification differs from one's own. Education expert Molly Barker teaches tolerance to primary school students by taking pairs of cast-off shoes and labeling them "poor," "rich," "boy," "girl," "homeless," "physically disabled," "old," "young," "sick," "from a different country," "different religion," "different ethnicity," and "different political beliefs." She then asks the kids to literally "walk in another person's shoes."[28] Antoinette Dempsey-Waters, a black social-studies educator at Wakefield High School in Arlington, Virginia, said she uses autobiographies to deliver a vivid image of enslavement that assists all students in her highly diverse school to "walk away with the knowledge of the evil of slavery" as they come to "understand and respect . . . the fight for freedom waged by enslaved people."[29] Another novel approach on the horizon that could be adopted in schools of the future is the use of virtual reality to embed an individual in the virtual body of someone of another race or ethnic group. In particular, embodying white people in black virtual bodies has been associated in research with an immediate decrease in their implicit racial bias against black people.[30]

Educators have also sought to facilitate perspective taking by encouraging student friendships in school with individuals who are different from themselves. Cross-group friendships have been shown to reduce intergroup anxiety and promote empathy, and studies have found that contact is particularly effective at helping to reduce prejudice among children.[31] Students at Springfield Middle School in Lucama, North Carolina, plan "mix it up" days when lunch tables have different colors and students sit with a different group of students than they normally would. The groups are assembled with people of varying races and backgrounds. One student commented, "I think it is a good experiment because it is teaching us to get along with different races and different kind of people."[32] Part and parcel of this approach is forging connections between schools and the multicultural communities of which they find themselves a part.[33]

PROMOTING SOCIAL JUSTICE

Finally, a significant ingredient in fostering tolerance in the classroom is an emphasis on social justice. Prejudices have important consequences for life in the way that institutions are run, assets are distributed, laws are regulated, social groups are formed, and moral sensibilities are articulated. By putting an emphasis on social justice, educators can help students right wrongs and create positive changes in the world. Three students at Ladue Horton Watkins High School in St. Louis, Missouri, for example, covered the Michael Brown murder (where a black eighteen-year-old was fatally shot by a white policeman) alongside professional journalists, with support from their school, and produced a successful video news story.[34] At Saul Mirowitz Jewish Day School, also in St. Louis, students go on multiday class trips to explore different topics related to social justice. Head of School Cheryl Maayan writes, "On the Civil Rights trip, students are agape as their bus passes Confederate flags on the highway heading south. They stare shocked at the KKK uniforms in the Civil Rights museums in Montgomery. They sing 'We Shall Overcome,' as we march across the Edmund Pettus Bridge in Selma. For our students, racial discrimination feels like ancient history—until they notice that the plaque next to the KKK uniform staring out at them is from ten years ago. In Memphis, they walk in the shoes of Martin Luther King Jr., just before he was shot. The students are challenged to think about what it would take for them to give up their safety for a cause, like those who joined the Civil Rights movement."[35]

TOLERANCE WORKS FROM THE INSIDE OUT

Finally, a word needs to be said about the ways in which tolerance activities are structured in schools. There seems to be a dichotomy between approaches that are external and "top-down" (e.g., pledges, T-shirts, poster campaigns), and those that are internal and "bottom-up" (e.g., small-group conversations about race, journaling about prejudice, sensitive whole-class discussions). The research seems to suggest that the more effective interventions involve students achieving a tolerant attitude through their own internal reflection—in other words, through having personal insights and revelations about the injustices of racial prejudice or antigay bias or sexism, for example—rather than having it externally pounded into them that these attitudes are wrong and should be discarded. One study put it this way: "Motivating people to reduce prejudice by emphasizing external control *produced more explicit and implicit prejudice than did not intervening at all* [emphasis mine]. Conversely, participants in whom autonomous motivation to regulate prejudice was induced displayed less explicit and implicit prejudice compared with no-treatment control participants."[36] Teaching tolerance, then, is a delicate process of dismantling the impact of years of conditioning from parents, schools, the media, and other institutions. Rather than letting this curtail our actions, however, we should redouble our efforts, given the acute level of seen and unseen intolerance that permeates our culture.

CHAPTER THIRTEEN

Beauty: Sensitizing Kids to an Aesthetic Appreciation of the World

---

To sense that behind anything that can be experienced there is something that our minds cannot grasp, whose beauty and sublimity reaches us only indirectly, this is religiousness. In this sense, and in this sense only, I am a devoutly religious man.

—Albert Einstein[1]

If Einstein ran the schools, he most assuredly would include approaches that guide students in an appreciation of beauty in its manifold aspects. He saw beauty as an integral part of his own work. In 1915, after he had formulated his general theory of relativity, he mailed out four of his lectures on this groundbreaking idea to friends of his, and to one he commented, "Be sure you take a good look at them . . . the theory is of incomparable beauty."[2] Elsewhere, Einstein wrote, "It is essential that the student acquire an understanding of and a lively feeling for values. He must acquire a vivid sense of the beautiful and of the morally good. Otherwise he—with his specialized knowledge—more closely resembles a well-trained dog than a harmoniously developed person."[3] Most people associate beauty with physical attractiveness or art appreciation or the beauty of nature, and most assuredly these are important avenues of entry into these aesthetic realms. But it's important to recognize that Einstein regarded aesthetic appreciation as something that went beyond these forms of beauty and constituted an integral part of the life of the mind. In this sense, he agreed with the philosopher and educator John Dewey, who wrote, "Aesthetic [experience] cannot be sharply marked off from intellectual experience since the latter must bear an aesthetic stamp to be itself complete."[4]

BEAUTY IN MIND, BRAIN, AND CULTURE

There's evidence from neuroscience that the experience of beauty is associated with activity in the brain, particularly in one specific area called the medial orbitofrontal cortex (mOFC) situated behind the forehead just above the orbits of the eyes. In one study, subjects rated different paintings and pieces of music on a scale from 1 to 9, with 9 representing the most beautiful. Scientists then scanned the subjects' brains while they were viewing the same visual work or listening to the same musical excerpts while inside the scanner. The results indicated that only one cortical area, located in the mOFC, was active during the experience of musical and visual beauty, with the activity produced by the experience of beauty derived from either source overlapping the other almost completely. The strength of activation in this part of the mOFC was proportional to the strength of the declared intensity of the experience of beauty.[5] A later study scanned the brains of fifteen mathematicians after they had rated mathematical formulae as beautiful, indifferent, or ugly and found the same thing: activation of the mOFC.[6] Interestingly, this area of the brain has also been linked with moral judgments, suggesting that an individual's moral attitudes might be considered "beautiful," "ugly," or "indifferent."[7]

Beauty is also embedded, to a greater or lesser degree, within human culture. Certain cultures value aesthetic principles more than others. Japan, for instance, puts great importance upon beauty, especially when found in nature. The Japanese like to time their family celebrations with special seasonal events such as the blossoming of cherry trees or the autumnal full moon. They assign a high priority to places and times in nature where the possibilities of aesthetic perception are greatest and enshrine those places and moments in their poetry and novels. In the eleventh-century novel *The Tale of Genji*, for example, each of its fifty-four chapters begins with an invocation to something beautiful in nature. And in the foreword to the seventeenth-century poet Matsuo Bashō's *The Narrow Road to the Interior*, the authors write,

> In Japan, where the first large-scale collection of verse dates from the eighth century, a great many places were routinely described or mentioned in poetry from the outset, and many of these came to be known as uta-makura, "poetic pillows." Uta-makura then acquired the same significance as kidai or kigo, "seasonal subjects." . . . For Bashō the purpose of visiting such places

was, as he said to Kikaku in a letter . . . to "feel the truth of old poems." His passion in this regard was intense. Once, in 1688, he walked 160 mountainous miles in five days so that he might see the full moon at one particular "poetic pillow"—in this instance Mount Obasute.[8]

CONFRONTING DYSBEAUTIA IN OUR SCHOOLS

In the United States, we do not have anything near this kind of depth of appreciation for beauty. For us, beauty means "beauty pageants," "beauty creams," and "beauty salons." As far as cultivating an aesthetic for nature, the bulldozer, the backhoe, and the logging truck are more appropriate symbols than the begonia, the black birch, and the long-tailed duck. Ours is a culture of practicality and utilitarian values. As the German poet and philosopher Friedrich Schiller wrote, "Utility is the great idol of the time, to which all powers do homage and all subjects are subservient."[9] We might even say that American culture suffers from a strong case of *dysbeautia*. Unfortunately, our schools, which should be places where the love of beauty is kindled, seem to give scant attention to aesthetic sensibilities. Our classrooms are designed with straight rows, confining cubicles, industrial-grade furniture, and bland wall decorations. University of Calgary professor Patricia Tarr commented upon the lack beauty in our early childhood classrooms:

> The commercial posters and materials usually include simplified, black outlined figures reminiscent of coloring books. . . . The seasonal materials bear a "greeting card" aesthetic reminiscent of decorations purchased at the local mall or products created from popular crafts kits such as those featuring bunnies and teddy bears. . . . The flatly colored, outlined stereotyped images of the posters and bulletin board borders talk down to children and assume that they are not capable of responding to the rich, diverse images and artifacts . . . which the world's cultures have created.[10]

A school's quest to achieve some type of sublime aesthetic experience for its students comes nearest to the goal when it engages children and teens in art activities. Yet this, too, is often tempered by utilitarian values. Students are engaging less and less in formal art education due to the climate of accountability and standardized testing in the United States. A 2011 report from the President's Committee on the Arts and Humanities states, "Due to budget constraints and emphasis on the subjects of high stakes testing, arts instruction in schools is on a downward trend."[11] The same thing is true of creative writing, and poetry in particular. Writer, teacher, and musician Andrew Simmons writes, "In an education landscape that dramatically deemphasizes creative expression in favor of expository writing and prioritizes the analysis of non-literary texts, high school literature teachers have to negotiate between their preferences and the way the wind is blowing. That sometimes means sacrifice, and poetry is often the first head to roll."[12]

ART FOR ACADEMICS' SAKE

Partly to justify the disappearance of fine-arts classes in U.S. schools, there's been an increased emphasis on integrating the arts into other subjects.[13] While the linkage of art to these other disciplines is certainly better than nothing, these programs all too often lack the aesthetic quality that a deeper exploration of music, dance, visual art, and drama demands. Students make up raps to learn math formulae, measure the angles in a painting by Kandinsky, or create skits out of historical events. The problem with these kinds of activities is that the arts are being made the handmaiden of academic standards rather than being considered worthy of exploration in their own right. More importantly for this chapter, the activities usually don't include as a learning goal the deepening of a child's aesthetic sensibility.[14] As Ellen Winner, professor of education at Boston College, and Lois Hetland, professor of art at the Massachusetts Institute of Art and Design, implore,

> Let's stop requiring more of the arts than of other subjects. The arts are the only school subjects that have been challenged to demonstrate transfer [to academics] as a justification for their usefulness. If we required physical education to demonstrate transfer to science, the results might be no better, and probably would be worse. So, it is notable that the arts can demonstrate any transfer at all. Perhaps with more attention to how the arts foster transfer, we can understand how to exploit that capacity further. But even when the relationships are understood, we still maintain that the justification for arts programs must be based on their inherent merit.[15]

THE ART CLASS SPECTRUM

Even when art instruction is specifically taught for its own sake, it often fails to address the important issue of deepening students' aesthetic appreciation of the world. In my rough-and-ready conceptualization of visual art instruction, for example, there seem to be three levels of art instruction. The most rudimentary form of art is represented by the "arts and crafts" teacher. At the low end of the arts and crafts spectrum, the teacher engages children in "tasks" and "projects" such as coloring in pumpkins and witches for Halloween (students are reminded to use the color orange for pumpkins and black for witches), cutting out shapes for "school pride" posters to display in the halls, making "cat's eyes" with yarn, or fashioning soap dishes out of clay. Further up the spectrum of the arts-and-crafts art approach is the teacher who involves students in weaving, knitting, macramé, pottery, and formulaic types of drawing and painting (e.g., draw-by-number or painting approaches that are based on the five universal shapes, as is the case with Monart).[16] It should be noted that at the highest end of this continuum, students may be introduced to, and learn at a deep level, aesthetic principles, as they create weavings, clay structures, or other artisanal productions.

One step up from the arts-and-crafts art teacher is the "content" art teacher. This is the teacher who regards art as a "subject," like math or science, which has its own distinct knowledge base and its own unique set of competencies or skills that can be mastered to one degree or another in the course of a term, semester, or academic year. Here, students are exposed to luminary artists, such as Van Gogh, Picasso, and Matisse. At the lower end of this spectrum they may do book reports on them, and at the upper level they may do projects that involve creating paintings that mimic the unique styles of these masters (note the inherent paradox in the juxtaposition of *mimic* and *unique*). Students are also taught specific "rote aesthetic principles" that they are expected to adhere to in their drawings and paintings, including the use of proper color schemes, perspectival techniques, and appropriate juxtaposition of design elements on a canvas. An example of this level of art instruction is the Getty Center for Education in the Arts curriculum. For grades 5 and 6, for example, the curriculum stipulates that students, when looking at a work of art, should be able to "identify light sources and discuss depiction of light and shadow, identify positive and negative space, and discuss concepts of hue, values, and intensity in color."[17]

The third, and highest level of visual art education is essentially the cultivation of aesthetic sensibilities through art. Aspects of the two lower levels of art education may be present at this stage, but they are subsumed under the broader and more significant goal of helping to unleash the inner artist and art lover within each student. The emphasis here is on students creating and viewing artworks that are individual, idiosyncratic, unique, and free of stereotypical imagery and formulaic methods of composition, unless these are incorporated in the service of students' creative imagination. Another feature of this level of art instruction is that the greater emphasis here is upon process rather than product. The act of creating something new is regarded as far more significant than the fashioning of something deemed worthy of admiration or esteem by others. While at the arts and crafts level, the primary determinant of success is the creation of something functional, and at the "content art" level the key factor is "mastery" based on the use of rubrics and benchmarks, the overriding element at this highest level of art education is "self-discovery" or "self-realization." Grades and tests are often used in the first two levels of the art education described here. On the 2016 National Assessment of American Progress, for example, students scored an average 147 in music and 149 in visual arts on a scale of 300, which strikes me as evidence of the utter vacuity of these efforts. Such evaluative tools have absolutely no place in an art program based on cultivating a love of beauty.[18]

CREATING BEAUTIFUL CLASSROOMS

The deepening of students' aesthetic sensibilities can be approached in a number of ways. One can, for example, surround students with a beautiful classroom environment. The Reggio Emilia schools regard the environment as a student's "third teacher" and give special attention to how objects are arrayed, stored, and displayed. Teachers may place mirrors around objects to expand students' perspective, and create "provocations" by putting paper and pencil in the blocks center or by wafting aromatic scents to heighten students' olfactory sense when they first enter the classroom. On the shelves, there are transparent jars of shells, buttons, beads, wires, tiny pine cones, dried rose metals, sequins in the shape of flowers, and spiral shavings from colored pencils, all of which beckon to the children. The classrooms are even called "ateliers" (artists' studios) to emphasize the idea of education as the process of training artists, in the broadest sense of this word.

Similarly, in Waldorf classrooms, great attention is placed on creating a beautiful environment and sensitizing children to the beauty around them. The core values of Waldorf education are truth, beauty, and goodness, and a Waldorf school is designed to emphasize its aesthetic qualities. The walls of a Waldorf classroom are painted using a technique called lazure, where a very thin paint medium consisting of binder, pigment, and water is prepared and applied to a white wall in several layers with large brushes using rhythmical movements, generating warm tones in the earlier grades and cooler tones in the upper grades. Waldorf school architecture, likewise, is rendered artistically, through naturalistic curves, patterns, and slopes, which may convey the impression of a forest stream or a stony cave, and both the classroom itself and the playthings and learning materials used are made with natural unpainted woods to reflect their inner beauty. As the originator of Waldorf education, Rudolf Steiner, writes, "An intense feeling for beauty—as it was then conceived—existed in earlier ages. Nothing of the same kind is present in modern civilization. Man cannot be truly man if he has no sense of beauty."[19]

LOOKING FOR ART OUTSIDE AND IN

Another way to deepen students' appreciation for beauty is by pointing to beautiful things in nature. One fifth-grade teacher, for example, demonstrated the power of aesthetic education by teaching a lesson on the atmosphere, where students went outside, lay on their backs, and looked up at the clouds. He then asked them: 'Can you see those treetops over there? Can you see those birds flying above the trees? Can you see those low puffy clouds? Can you see above those clouds to the thin, wispy ones beyond? There's depth to the sky; some things in the sky are higher than others. That's because the sky is actually like an ocean of air." In this case, a lesson on the atmosphere was directly linked to an appreciation of beauty.[20] Similarly, another teacher began a fifth-grade lesson on molecular motion by stating, "Last night I noticed that the condensation was freezing on my garage windows. It was making the most interesting and spectacular little patterns of ice crystals. I couldn't help but imagine how the molecules were moving more and more slowly as the temperature dropped, until finally, they formed these amazing little crystals."[21]

Students can also train their aesthetic sensibilities by visiting art museums. Carl Connelly, an art educator and thirty-year veteran of teaching in the Chicago public schools led fifth and sixth graders through the Art Institute of Chicago. Students brought sketchbooks to take notes or to make drawings of particularly interesting works. As they viewed the different pieces, Carl would provide a little background information, answer questions, and then at times ask questions of his own. In front of an abstract by twentieth-century American Clyfford Still, Carl asked students to describe what they saw in the painting. Some of their responses were "blood coming down," "a cave in the dark," "an Oreo cookie," and the "inside part of an eyeball." Carl then described what he saw: "I see a cliff with rocks and then I see the sun coming up. Do you see that part with the red on it?"[22] When they returned to their classrooms, students were asked to reflect on their art visit through writing and sketching and were asked to identify an artwork that held their attention.

This type of approach to encountering a work of art views the aesthetic experience as a fusion of students' own questions, background, and experience with the artist's own quest to make his expressions in paint meaningful to the viewer. In this sense, it echoes the thoughts of Columbia University art educator and educational philosopher Maxine Greene, with respect to an individual's confrontation with an object of beauty: "You have to be fully present to it—to focus your attention on it and, again, to allow it to exist apart from your everydayness and your practical concerns. I do not mean that you, as a living person with your own biography, your own history, have to absent yourself. No, you have to be there in your personhood, encountering the work much in the way you encounter other persons."[23]

ARTISTS IN THE MAKING

Finally, there is the act of art making itself and its link to students' aesthetic development. Students can be initiated into the mysteries of art creation through artist-in-residence programs, where bona fide artists illustrate the process that a creative work of art, literature, music, dance, or theater goes through from start to completion. At C. A. Donehoo Elementary School in Gadsden, Alabama, students crowded into the gym to watch potter Park Hunt spin clay into pots and vases. Donehoo principal Chance Goodwin commented, "I wanted the whole school to be able to see this . . . a lot of these kids, they didn't know what pottery was. They felt like these things are made at Walmart, literally."[24] Another artist-in-residence program involved composer and musician Andrew Lipke, who took a group of thirty middle school students in Philadelphia, Pennsylvania, through the entire process of creating a music album from original conception to final product. "We wanted it to be something that could stand on its own," said Lipke, "that was enjoyable to listen to as music, that has artistic integrity and has an aesthetic appeal. That was very important to us. . . . But in the same moment, we wanted the process, the material, to be driven by the kids and be a reflection of their voice."[25]

Ultimately, what aesthetic education offers to students is the opportunity to be regarded as creative artists rather than passive consumers of knowledge or generators of stereotypical images. As one fourth-grade art teacher points out with regard to his students' art making, "This is a challenging activity because a lot of kids just want to draw a heart and put love, love, love in the background. I talk to them about how it doesn't have to be so literal. I want them to struggle through it and it is a little bit of a struggle. I want them to come to some kind of agreement in their mind of how to convey how they feel, visually."[26] If we believe the words of educators like John Dewey, Herbert Read, and Elliot Eisner, the function of education itself may be the creation of artists who, regardless of the field they choose, seek to inject into their work a measure of the sublime, a reflection of cosmic beauty and grace.[27] In order for this to happen, though, teachers must take a hard look at themselves. As psychologist and art educator Howard Gardner points out, "Unless teachers can and will expose their own aesthetic values, no change will take place."[28] The rewards of doing so will benefit not only themselves but the students they instruct, and the rewards can be immense. Architect Frank Lloyd Wright put it this way, "The longer I live the more beautiful life becomes. If you foolishly ignore beauty, you will soon find yourself without it. Your life will be impoverished. But if you invest in beauty, it will remain with you all the days of your life."[29]

CHAPTER FOURTEEN

The Einstein Classroom: Education for Our Children's Future

The wit was not wrong who defined education in this way: "Education is that which remains, if one has forgotten everything he learned in school."
—Albert Einstein[1]

Most people think of a genius as that one in a million individual who can paint, compose, or think in an extraordinary way—like an Einstein. Yet the word *genius* itself means "to give birth" or "to create" and is also etymologically related to the adjective *genial*, or *joyful*. It is in this sense that every child ought to be considered a genius: every child who comes into the world brings with him or her a joy of learning. In an Einstein-inspired classroom, each and every child would be treated like a genius with untold potential. This is radically different from today's classrooms, where children are sorted into ability categories like "low achieving" "reluctant reader," "average," "learning disabled," and "gifted and talented." Some educators might argue that such and such a child is not only *not* a genius but is a holy terror in the classroom or a complete dunce. But we've got to keep in mind Goethe's saying: "If we treat [people] not as they are but as they should be, we help them to become what they can become."[2]

We saw in chapter 9 that there are countless instances of individuals who were thought to be dull or stupid as children but made invaluable contributions to the world as adults. Einstein's teachers thought he was backward and insolent.[3] A teacher said of the French novelist Honoré de Balzac, "This fat little fellow goes around in a state of intellectual coma."[4] Beethoven's teacher, Johann Georg Albrechtsberger, said of his student, "He has learned nothing. He never will learn anything."[5] John Gurdon's high school biology teacher said, "I believe Gurdon has ideas about becoming a scientist; on his present showing this is quite ridiculous. If he can't learn simple biological facts, he would have no chance of doing the work of a specialist, and it would be a sheer waste of time, both on his part and of those who would have to teach him."[6] What happened to John? He grew up, became a scientist, and received the 2012 Nobel Prize in Physiology or Medicine. The fact is that since we simply *can't know* who the great individuals in our classrooms are, we have to treat *every student* like a genius.

A PASSION FOR TEACHING

Likewise, all teachers in an Einstein-inspired classroom would be entrusted to draw upon the best they have within themselves and teach with fire in their belly. Too often in the schools today, teachers teach without passion. In a Gallup survey, just over half of K–12 educators (56 percent) said they were "not engaged" in their work, meaning they were not connected emotionally with their work and were unlikely to devote much extra time to their teaching duties. Another 13 percent were "actively disengaged," meaning they were not satisfied with their workplace and were likely to spread negativity among their coworkers. The survey's authors concluded, "So if nearly 70% of teachers are just going through the motions at work—or worse, undermining student learning by spreading negativity—that's a big problem facing the nation's schools."[7] As primatologist Jane Goodall writes, "When I think back to when I was at school, there were so many bad teachers, they were boring and how sad to have a fascinating subject and talk about it in such a way that the people listening to you feel like going to sleep or doing anything but listening to you."[8] Part of the problem, as we've noted, is that teachers are being evaluated by standardized test scores and are forced to teach to those standards, thus having little room to inject their own vitality and creativity into their teaching.

Teachers in an Einstein-inspired classroom would engage students in activities designed to provoke curiosity, inspire wonder, stimulate playfulness, and activate creativity. They would give their students plenty of "learning moments" to be remembered by, years after the students' school experience was over. How many of us remember the learning activities we engaged in at school thirty to fifty years ago? Would any of us say, "Yes, I remember you. You were the teacher who took me from the twenty-sixth percentile to the eighty-first percentile on the Stanford Achievement Test in third grade"? These aren't the teachers that we remember. We remember the teachers who told us stories, who had us doing plays, who sang to us, who took us outside to experience the wonders of nature, who had us questioning life's imponderables.

I was just reading an essay on education by the early twentieth-century American journalist H. L. Mencken, and I really liked what he had to say about what makes for a good teacher (please make allowances for his early twentieth-century gender bias):

> It consists, first, of a natural talent for dealing with children, for getting into their minds, for putting things in a way that they can comprehend. And it consists, secondly, of a deep belief in the interest and importance of the thing taught, a concern about it amounting to a kind of passion. A man who knows a subject thoroughly, a man so soaked in it that he eats it, sleeps it, and dreams it—this man can almost always teach it, with success, no matter how little he knows of technical pedagogy. This is because there is enthusiasm in him, and because enthusiasm is as contagious as fear or the barber's itch. An enthusiast is willing to go to any trouble to impart the glad news bubbling within. He thinks that it is important and valuable for [students] to know; given the slightest glow of interest in a pupil to start with, he will fan that glow to a flame.[9]

These are the criteria that should be utilized when evaluating whether teachers are any good. What this means is that the people who are assessing the teachers should themselves be passionate individuals who have enlivened the worlds of students. It takes one to know one. And the way you do this is by observing the teacher in the course of teaching her students. You can't get at teacher excellence by gathering objective data. This is the big error that is being made by educational bureaucrats—the idea that teachers should be accountable for the test scores of their students. Instead, we should be looking at how teachers inspire their students to make breakthroughs in their own learning—having aha experiences during science experiments, writing powerfully affecting stories in writing class, asking interesting and unlikely questions in the literature classroom, and having wonderful ideas during history lessons.

These sorts of events occur spontaneously throughout a school day; you cannot sit a child down in a desk with a stopwatch and expect these miracles to happen. Standardized tests are laughably inadequate in probing the inner depths of a child's brain (see Appendix A). We shouldn't even be using them, let alone evaluating teachers by their data. Instead, we should be looking for that inner passion and love of children that cannot be encapsulated within the domain of some cold, dead, test scores. Let's look for inspiration, empathy, vitality, and compassion in our teachers!

THE DINOSAUR IN THE ROOM SEPARATING GENIUS KIDS FROM REAL LEARNING

This brings us full circle to the question I asked at the beginning of this book: How is it possible for educators to ever screw up their mission to introduce these genius kids to the amazing world around them? Now we are closer to an answer. The simplest answer is that there is a gigantic barrier the size of a Tyrannosaurus Rex standing between the incredible children in this country and the vibrant amazing world around them, and this massive creature is crippling their chances for joyful learning. Let me enumerate some of the components of this sprawling theropod. There are the laws that state and federal legislatures pass that specify what students are to learn, how they are to learn it, and how fast they are to learn it.[10] There are the textbook and test manufacturers who make billions of dollars every year by commodifying knowledge—by manufacturing, to use Friedrich Nietzsche's neat little phrase "indigestible knowledge-stones" for consumption by millions of unwary students.[11] There are the test preparation companies, testing coaches, and even bribes that well-to-do parents are able to pay to give their kids a leg up in the competition.[12] There are the thousands of educational researchers, or "bean counters," in American universities, who are carrying on American educational psychologist Edward Thorndike's 1910 science-mad mission to "tell every fact about everyone's intellect and character and behavior . . . tell the cause of every change in human nature . . . tell the result of every educational force—every act of every person that changed any other or the person himself" (and to do it all with statistics).[13]

What else gets in the way? There are the websites that provide school ratings, such as GreatSchools.org, which reduce a school's performance to a single number on a scale of one to ten. Since real estate values are tied to those ratings, people's territoriality, or lizard brains, are activated in the process.[14] There are the educational bureaucrats at the local, state, and federal level who live in a world of acronyms (ESSA, Title 1, NCLB, SAT, IEP, BIP, IDEA, LRE, etc.) that blur the outlines of real human children and their unique experiences in classroom.[15] There are the local school boards and statewide textbook adoption committees who let their political and sometimes religious beliefs dictate public school policy.[16] There are the mass media dispensers, who are first out of the block to publish the latest test scores to alarm parents. There are the increasing number of for-profit schools that turn away students who might lower their schoolwide test results and that create outcomes that will maximize potential profits for their shareholders.[17] There are the corporations that use ingenious marketing methods to pack the schools with depersonalized computer learning programs, and who import an ethos of "twenty-first-century skills" that are simply corporate values bent on turning today's students into tomorrow's cube farmers and consumers of their branded products.

TURNING IDEALS INTO PRACTICAL IDEAS

The list is enough to ruin your day! How could it ever be possible, you might ask, to marshal enough force to counteract the influence of these and other barriers between the incredible child and the amazing world? The first thing we need to do is speak truth to power. We need to change the conversation about education in our country from "Why are we losing out in the international marketplace of ideas?" to "Why are we using those worthless standardized tests in the first place?" We need to neatly excise from our vocabulary, words like *standards, accountability, benchmarks, rubrics, rigor,* and *testing* and replace them with words like *joy, creativity, curiosity, playfulness,* and *wonder.* We need to join up with other parents around the country who are deciding to opt out of standardized testing for their kids, and support teachers' unions that are striking for better teaching conditions, including a reduction in high-stakes testing and the elimination of "value-added" assessment of teachers.[18]

We also need to learn the magic and craft of those educators who make the many wonderful things described in this book happen with their students. What did they do? Find a receptive principal? Create a support group? Take a risk and dedicate fifteen minutes every day to real learning? Find a rich friend in the community who could help fund an initiative in the school? There are creative mechanisms involved in making substantive change in schools, and we need to know the rules for how these things work.[19] We need to know about the organizations and resources (many of them listed in Appendix C, the resource guide for this book) that support learning through imagination, wonder, playfulness, creativity, and each of the other components of natural learning described here. Of course, we could always wait around for a new administration, school board, or federal law to support us in making it easier for teachers to directly engage students in the amazing world. But I wouldn't hold my breath. Instead, I'd be directing my gaze to the beacons in this country who are shining brightly and passionately inspiring kids to develop their full potential. And I'd make sure that all parties to the education of kids know about and understand the significance of these incredible teachers and genius kids: that they are the foundation of our culture, and that curiosity and creativity are the new standards upon which the future of our nation rests.

STAND UP FOR WHAT YOU BELIEVE IN

We've got to do some prioritization to help the status quo-ers understand what is actually at stake. We need to ask them, Is it better to have good test-takers or curious kids? Is it more important to raise test scores or to eliminate bullying and hate in our schools? Is it a better use of our resources and energies to save the planet from environmental destruction or to have compliant kids who meet all their grade-level standards in math and English language arts? Is it better to have a student who can make subject and predicate agree in a sentence or to have a child who can feel a sense of wonder toward the mysteries of the universe? Some people would like to get out of this forced-choice format and say that both are important. But that's really not the way this game is played. Time and money resources are allocated based on priorities. If there's not enough in the school budget, do we remove art class or science class? If there're forty-two minutes in a high school class session, how much of that time should be spent preparing kids to take the next high-stakes test, and how much should be devoted to feeding students' innate love of learning? We should make each and every stakeholder in education answer these questions, take a stand, and show where their own priorities lie. Just as we need to confront individuals who say or do racist things, we need to confront people who want to turn a student's life into "data" or who want to make students' future depend upon their grades and test scores, not their character and virtues.

If we all just take a stand for what we believe in, then at least we will know where we are with respect to the chances that our students might have to dynamically encounter the real world during the roughly twelve thousand hours they spend in school. In the decades during which I worked with teachers, I would often ask them why they got into teaching in the first place. Was it to raise test scores or to help unfold a student's potential? I never saw a raised hand for test scores. That means that every one of them wanted to strive for the virtues and values that make up the substance of this book. It's easy to get derailed by the conformists and say something like, "Well, I need to follow the regulations," or "I'm afraid I'd get fired." The existentialists have a term for this kind of diversion; they call it "bad conscience." Instead of aligning our actions to our most deeply held beliefs about education, children, and learning, we end up giving ourselves away and explaining our conforming actions through a series of excuses. What is required here is a certain amount of risk, to step away from the poor decisions and ill-conceived actions of the last thirty-five years of U.S. education, and initiate a *true* reform of our nation's schools. That reform would be based upon those values and skills that are fundamental to the establishment of a sound society: creativity, curiosity, tolerance, compassion, care for nature, playfulness, individuality, beauty, diversity, wonder, imagination, and love of learning.

There's never been a better time in U.S. history for such a transformation to take place. It rests in your hands whether you do something tangible about it or not. I trust that you will be moved to take action. If Einstein ran the schools, I'm sure he'd do the right thing.

APPENDIX A

Weapons of Mass Instruction: Fifteen Reasons Standardized Tests Are Worthless

None of the great individuals discussed in this book valued standardized testing or standardization in general as a legitimate practice in education. On the contrary, they all emphasized developing the unique character of each individual. Despite this fact, the use of standardized testing goes on mostly unchallenged as a so-called legitimate approach to determining student understanding. The following fifteen arguments provide a basis for supporting a campaign to discontinue their use in American schools.

1. Because students know that test scores may affect their future lives, they do whatever they can to pass them, including cheating and taking performance drugs (e.g., psychostimulants like Adderall "borrowed" from their friends).[1]

2. Because teachers know that test scores may affect their salaries and job security, they also cheat (see the best seller *Freakonomics* for some interesting statistics on this issue).[2]

3. Standardized tests don't provide any feedback on how to perform better. The results aren't even given back to the teachers and students

until months later, and there are no instructions provided by test companies on how to improve these test scores.

4. Standardized tests don't value creativity. A student who writes a more creative answer in the margins of such a test doesn't realize that a human being won't even see this creative response, that machines grade these tests, and that a creative response that doesn't follow the format is a wrong response.[3]

5. Standardized tests don't value diversity. There is a wide range of differences among the people who take standardized tests: they have different cultural backgrounds, different levels of proficiency in the English language, different learning and thinking styles, different family backgrounds, and different past experiences. And yet the standardized test treats them as if they were all identical—and identical to the group that took the test several years ago to which the test has been "normed" (i.e., this original group is the "norm group" against which any future test takers must be compared).

6. Standardized tests favor those who have socioeconomic advantages. Test companies not only manufacture the tests but also manufacture the courses and programs that can be taken to "prepare for the test" (constituting a multibillion dollar a year industry). If you have the money, you can even get special tutors that will help you do well on a test. If you don't have the money and your school is in a low socioeconomic area that gets less funding than rich suburban schools, then you're not getting the same preparation for the test that those at higher socioeconomic levels do, and that's unfair.[4]

7. Because so much emphasis is placed on standardized test results these days, teachers are spending more and more time "teaching to the test." If there is something that is interesting, compelling, useful, or otherwise favorable to the development of a student's understanding of the world, but it is not going to be on the standardized test, then there really isn't any incentive to cover this material. Instead, most of classroom time consists of either taking the tests or preparing for the tests, and this shuts out the possibility of learning anything new or important.[5]

8. Standardized tests occur in an artificial learning environment: they're timed, you can't talk to a fellow student, you can't ask questions, you can't use references or learning devices, you can't get up and move around. How often does the real world look like this? And yet, even the most hardheaded conservative will say that education must prepare students for "the real world." Clearly standardized testing doesn't do this.

9. Standardized tests create stress. Some kids do well with a certain level of stress. Other students fold. So, again, there isn't a level playing field. Brain research suggests that too much stress is psychologically and

physically harmful. And when stress becomes overwhelming, the brain shifts into a "fight or flight" response, where it is impossible to engage in the higher-order thinking processes that are necessary to respond correctly to the standardized test questions.[6]

10. Standardized tests reduce the richness of human experience and human learning to a number or set of numbers. This is dehumanizing. A student may have a deep knowledge of a particular subject but receive no acknowledgment for it because his or her test score may have been low. If the student were able to draw a picture, lead a group discussion, or create a hands-on project, he or she might show that knowledge. But not in a standardized testing room. Tough luck.[7]

11. Standardized tests weren't developed by geniuses. They were developed by mediocre minds. One of the pioneers of standardized testing in this country, Lewis Terman, was a racist (see *The Mismeasure of Man*, by Stephen Jay Gould). Another pioneer, Edward Thorndike, was a specialist in rats and mazes—just the kind of mind you want your students to be led by, right? Albert Einstein never created a standardized test (although he failed a number of them), and neither did any of the great thinkers of our age or any age. Standardized tests are usually developed by pedantic researchers with PhDs in psychometrics or educational psychology. If that's the kind of mind you want your child to have, then go for it![8]

12. Standardized tests provide parents and teachers with a false sense of security. If a student scores well on a test, then it is assumed that the student knows the material. However, this may not be true at all. The student may have simply memorized the facts or formulas or tricks necessary to do well on the test (some students are naturally gifted in taking standardized tests; others are not). A group of Harvard graduates were asked why it is colder in the winter and warmer in the summer. Most of them got the question wrong. They were good test takers but didn't understand fundamental principles that required a deeper comprehension.[9]

13. Standardized tests exist for administrative, political, and financial purposes, not for educational ones. Test companies make billions. Politicians get elected by promising better test results. Administrators get funding and avoid harsh penalties by boosting test scores. Everyone benefits except the children. For them, standardized testing is worthless and worse.

14. Standardized testing creates "winners" and "losers." The losers are those who get labeled as "my low students," "my learning-disabled kids," "my reluctant learners." Even the winners are trapped by being caught up on a treadmill of achievement that they must stay on at all costs through at least sixteen years of schooling, and more often

twenty years. The losers suffer loss of self-esteem, and the damage of "low expectations."[10] The winners suffer loss of soul, since most of them are functioning as performing seals for fast-track parents and may reach midlife on a pinnacle of power and achievement yet lack any connection to their deeper selves, to ethical principles, to aesthetic feelings, to spiritual aspirations, to compassion, creativity, and/or commitment to life.

15. Finally, my most important reason that standardized tests are worthless: During the time that a child is taking a test, she or he could be doing something far more valuable: actually learning something new and interesting!

APPENDIX B

Leonardo da Vinci's IEP Meeting: The Problem with Special Education

Imagine that Leonardo da Vinci has been whisked away from fifteenth-century Italy as a nine-year-old child and is now a student at a typical public elementary school in the United States. Given Leo's specialness and the penchant in special education programs for emphasizing disorder, disability, and dysfunction, here is how his Individual Education Plan (IEP) meeting might unfold:

> *Principal*: "Okay, I think we're ready to start. Who wants to get the ball rolling?"
>
> *School Psychologist*: "Well, I ran him through some tests, but his attention was all over the place. He kept looking at a part of the wall in my office where the plaster had fallen off, and said he saw a battleship fighting a dragon. I'm wondering whether he needs a workup by a psychiatrist to rule out possible psychotic features."
>
> *Learning Disability Specialist*: "I'm concerned that he occasionally writes backward. As you probably know, this is a soft sign for neurological dysfunction."
>
> *Classroom Teacher*: "Yes, I've seen those reversals in my classroom. He never seems to get any work done. He'll start one thing and then lose interest. He's always doodling in the margins of the worksheets I give

him. And when he's not doing that, he's looking out the window daydreaming."

Learning Disability Specialist: "I've also noticed that in my remediation sessions with him. He appears to be a good candidate for psychostimulant medication."

Classroom Teacher: "Yes! That would help me *so much*! Last week, we found him in the boiler room with a screwdriver. He said he had a great idea about how to improve the heating duct system in the school. We had to put him on detention."

Learning Disability Specialist: "He's falling way behind in reading and most of his other academic subjects, although his math and science aren't too bad. I recommend that we take him out of his art class for more one-on-one remediation to focus on his spelling, handwriting, and phonemic awareness skills."

Principal: "That sounds like a great idea. And can you set up some workable instructional objectives. I'm concerned that he's not going to be able to perform at grade level on his Common Core Standards. And then what's going to happen to him? I mean, he can't exactly make a living by doodling, now, can he?"

Educators: Don't let this happen to the little Leonardos in your class! Do everything you can to discover their strengths, talents, gifts, and abilities!

APPENDIX C

A Resource Guide for Revitalizing U.S. Education

The resources listed below are intended to provide some of the "muscle" needed to take on the corporate-driven politically motivated process of miseducation that the country has suffered from over these past thirty-five years. The list includes everything from training programs in compassionate education for teachers, to opt-out campaigns for parents, to children's literature. As this is a partial list, I encourage readers to look for other opportunities to speak truth to power and take the risks necessary to bring American education out of the Dark Ages.

IMAGINATION

Berne, Jennifer. *On a Beam of Light: A Story of Albert Einstein*. San Francisco: Chronicle Books, 2016 (ages 6–9 years).

DK. *Unlock Your Imagination: More than 250 Boredom Busters*. New York: DK, 2018 (ages 6–9 years).

Imaginative Education Research Group (IERG). http://ierg.ca. Learning materials for educators showing how learners' imaginations can be routinely engaged in any classroom.

Johnson, Crockett. *Harold and the Purple Crayon*. New York: HarperCollins, 2015 (ages 4–8 years).

Portis, Antoinette. *Not a Box*. New York: HarperCollins, 2006 (ages 2–4 years).

LOVE OF LEARNING

edX. https://www.edx.org. Online learning destination and MOOC provider, offering high-quality courses from the world's best universities and institutions for learners everywhere.

Fadiman, Clifton, and John S. Major. *The New Lifetime Reading Plan: The Classical Guide to World Literature, Revised and Expanded.* New York: Collins Reference, 1999.

Genius Hour. http://geniushour.com. An initiative where teachers set aside a set amount of time each day for students to engage in a project that they have a passion about.

The Great Courses. https://www.thegreatcourses.com. For older students, this organization sells DVDs, CDs, and video streaming of courses in a wide range of fields taught by highly rated professors from well-regarded colleges and universities; subjects include fine arts, economics, literature, philosophy, religion, music, mathematics, and science.

The Khan Academy. https://www.khanacademy.org. Consists of thousands of short videos that teach specific content or skills in a wide range of fields.

CREATIVITY

Capacchione, Lucia. *The Creative Journal for Teens: Making Friends with Yourself.* Newburyport, MA: Red Wheel/Weiser, 2008 (ages 12–17 years).

Conner, Bobbi. *The Giant Book of Creativity for Kids: 500 Activities to Encourage Creativity in Kids Ages 2 to 12—Play, Pretend, Draw, Dance, Sing, Write, Build, Tinker.* Boulder, CO: Roost Books, 2015.

National Art Education Association. https://www.arteducators.org. The leading professional membership organization exclusively for visual arts educators. Members include elementary, middle, and high school visual arts educators, college and university professors, university students preparing to become art educators, researchers and scholars, teaching artists, administrators and supervisors, and art museum educators—as well as more than fifty-four thousand students who are members of the National Art Honor Society.

National Novel Writing Month. https://www.nanowrimo.org. Invites students and others to write a complete novel in the month of November (recommended number of total words depends upon grade level). Provides support and resources to help with this project.

Teachers and Writers Collaborative. https://www.twc.org. Seeks to educate the imagination by offering innovative creative writing programs for students and teachers and by providing a variety of publications and resources to support learning through the literary arts.

PLAYFULNESS

Alliance for Childhood. http://www.allianceforchildhood.org. Builds, strengthens, and empowers advocacy networks to encourage free play that supports the developmental needs of children.

American Association for the Child's Right to Play. http://www.ipausa.org. Provides advocacy and an international forum for the promotion of play.

Conner, Bobbi. *Unplugged Play: No Batteries. No Plugs. Pure Fun.* New York: Workman, 2007.

The National Institute for Play. http://www.nifplay.org. Seeks to unlock human potential through play in all stages of life, using science to discover all that play has to teach us about transforming our world.

Olfman, Sharna, ed. *All Work and No Play: How Educational Reforms Are Harming Our Preschoolers.* Santa Barbara, CA: Praeger, 2003.

CURIOSITY

Association of Children's Museums. https://www.childrensmuseums.org. Supports the values of children's museums and has a search function on its website to find children's museums in your area.

Grice, Gordon. *Cabinet of Curiosities: Collecting and Understanding the Wonders of the Natural World.* New York: Workman, 2015.

McFall, Matthew. *The Little Book of Awe and Wonder: A Cabinet of Curiosities.* Carmarthen, UK: Independent Thinking Press, 2013.

Tough, Paul. *How Children Succeed: Grit, Curiosity, and the Hidden Power of Character.* Wilmington, MA: Mariner Books, 2012.

WONDER

Foer, Joshua, Dylan Thuras, and Ella Morton. *Atlas Obscura: An Explorer's Guide to the World's Hidden Wonders.* New York: Workman, 2016.

From Conception to Birth. https://www.youtube.com/watch?v=7ItmwtLCDVY. A four-minute video showing through realistic animation the unfolding of the human being over nine months.

Guinness World Records. London: Guinness World Records, 2019.

Our Story in One Minute. https://www.youtube.com/watch?v=ZSt9tm3RoUU. A video tracing the cosmic and biological origins of our species.

Powers of Ten. https://www.youtube.com/watch?v=0fKBhvDjuy0. A mind-boggling video that in nine minutes takes the viewer to the outermost extremities of space and the innermost components of a leaf's cell.

INDIVIDUALITY

Andreae, Giles. *Giraffes Can't Dance.* New York: Cartwheel Books, 2012 (ages 4 and up).

Bar-el, Dan. *Not Your Typical Dragon.* New York: Viking, 2012 (ages 3–5 years).

Blabey, Aaron. *Thelma the Unicorn.* New York: Scholastic, 2017 (ages 3–5 years).

Dismondy, Maria. *Spaghetti in a Hot Dog Bun: Having the Courage to Be Who You Are.* Wixom, MI: Cardinal Rule Press, 2008 (ages 4–11 years).

Hall, Michael. *Red: A Crayon's Story.* New York: Greenwillow Books, 2015 (ages 4–8 years).

Helakoski, Leslie. *Woolbur.* New York: HarperCollins, 2008 (ages 4–8 years).

Hoffman, Mary. *Amazing Grace.* New York: Dial Books, 1991 (ages 4–8 years).

Kraus, Robert. *Leo the Late Bloomer.* New York: HarperCollins, 1999 (ages 4–8 years).

Lovell, Patty. *Stand Tall, Molly Lou Melon.* New York: G. P. Putnam's Sons, 2001 (ages 4–8 years).

Parr, Todd. *Be Who You Are.* Boston, MA: Little, Brown Books for Young Readers, 2016 (ages 4–8 years).

Rose, Todd. *The End of Average: Unlocking Our Potential by Embracing What Makes Us Different.* New York: HarperOne, 2017.

NEURODIVERSITY

Armstrong, Thomas. *Neurodiversity in the Classroom: Strategies for Helping Students with Special Needs Succeed in School and Life.* Alexandria, VA: ASCD, 2012.

Armstrong, Thomas. *The Power of Neurodiversity: Unleashing the Advantages of Your Differently Wired Brain.* Cambridge, MA: Da Capo Lifelong, 2011.

Eide, Brock L., and Fernette F. Eide. *The Dyslexic Advantage: Unlocking the Hidden Potential of the Dyslexic Brain.* New York: Plume, 2011.

Honos-Webb, Lara. *The Gift of ADHD: How to Transform Your Child's Problems into Strengths.* Oakland, CA: New Harbinger, 2010.

Kluth, Paula. *Just Give Him the Whale! 20 Ways to Use Fascinations, Areas of Expertise, and Strengths to Support Students with Autism.* Baltimore, MD: Brookes Publishing, 2008.

COMPASSION

Bluth, Karen. *The Self-Compassion Workbook for Teens: Mindfulness and Compassion Skills to Overcome Self-Criticism and Embrace Who You Are.* Oakland, CA: Instant Help/New Harbinger Publications, 2017.

Center for Healthy Minds, University of Wisconsin, Madison. https://center healthyminds.org. Sponsors of the Kindness Curriculum for preschools. For a free copy, go to https://centerhealthyminds.org/join-the-movement /sign-up-to-receive-the-kindness-curriculum.

Compassionate Schools Project (University of Virginia's Curry School of Education). https://www.compassionschools.org. A seven-year research program in fifty schools, with more than twenty thousand students, the project interweaves support in academic achievement, mental fitness, health, and compassionate character.

Random Acts of Kindness Foundation. https://www.randomactsofkindness.org /for-educators. Offers free K–8 lesson plans to lead a kindness project or form a kindness club at school.

Silverstein, Shel. *The Giving Tree.* New York: Harper & Row, 1963 (ages 1–8).

CARE FOR NATURE

Beetles: Science and Teaching for Field Instructors. http://beetlesproject.org. Environmental education resources that serve both students and teachers, offered by UC, Berkeley's Public Science Learning Center.

Children & Nature Network. https://www.childrenandnature.org. A global movement to increase equitable access to nature so that children—and natural places—can thrive. Includes directories to local, state, national, and international nature projects.

Eco-Schools USA (National Wildlife Federation). https://www.nwf.org/Eco-Schools-USA National program for K–12 involving the effective green management of school grounds, environmental curriculum, climate change skills, and more.

The Geo-Inquiry Process (National Geographic). https://www.nationalgeographic.org/education/programs/geo-inquiry. Using a geographic perspective, offers students a unique lens with which to analyze space, place, and the interconnections between the human and natural worlds.

Green Schoolyards America. http://www.greenschoolyards.org. With student involvement, transforms school grounds into green spaces with trees, grass, edible plants, and local biodiversity, so that students can experience nature for immediate access.

Roots and Shoots (The Jane Goodall Institute). https://www.rootsandshoots.org. Students create projects and groups to engage in actions designed to make the world a better place for people, other animals, and the environment.

TOLERANCE

Facing History and Ourselves. https://www.facinghistory.org. Engages students of diverse backgrounds in an examination of racism, prejudice, and anti-Semitism in order to promote the development of a more humane and informed citizenry.

No Place for Hate (Anti-Defamation League). https://www.adl.org/who-we-are/our-organization/signature-programs/no-place-for-hate. A self-directed campaign by individual schools that helps all stakeholders take the lead in improving and maintaining school climate so all students can thrive.

Project Implicit (Harvard University). https://implicit.harvard.edu/implicit/takeatest.html. For older students, this website offers the opportunity to take variations of the Implicit Association Tests online, which can reveal one's subconscious attitudes toward people of different ages, genders, ethnicities, races, religions, skin tones, and sexual preferences (parent or teacher discretion advised).

Teaching Tolerance (Southern Poverty Law Center). https://www.tolerance.org. Provides resources (including a biannual magazine sent out free to more than 450,000 educators), ideas, curriculum, and projects for combating racism, sexism, and other forms of discrimination on school grounds and in local communities.

BEAUTY

Diaz, Gene, and Martha Barry McKenna, eds. *Teaching for Aesthetic Experience: The Art of Learning.* New York: Peter Lang Publishers, 2004.

DK Children. *Universe: Marvel at the Beauty of the Universe from Our Solar System to Galaxies in the Farthest Reaches of Space.* New York: DK Children, 2015.

Gardner, Howard. *Truth, Beauty, and Goodness Reframed: Educating for the Virtues in the Age of Truthiness and Twitter.* New York: Basic Books, 2012.

Richardson, Joy. *Inside the Museum: A Children's Guide to the Metropolitan Museum of Art.* New York: Harry N. Abrams, 1993.

Sinclair, Nathalie. *Mathematics and Beauty: Aesthetic Approaches to Teaching Children.* New York: Teachers College Press, 2006.

Wyeth, Sharon Dennis. *Something Beautiful.* Decorah, IA: Dragonfly Books, 2002 (ages 3–7 years).

OTHER CHILD-CENTERED RESOURCES

Association Montessori International—USA. https://amiusa.org. Includes articles and links related to Montessori for parents and families, future teachers, and school staff, plus a school locator for the United States.

Association of Waldorf Schools of North America. https://www.waldorfeducation.org. Provides information, a blog, links, and a search feature for Waldorf schools in North America.

Campaign for a Commercial-Free Childhood. https://commercialfreechildhood.org. Educates the public about commercialism's impact on kids' well-being and advocates for the end of child-targeted marketing.

Children's Defense Fund. https://www.childrensdefense.org. Advocates for the needs of children regarding education, health, welfare, equity, social justice, gun violence prevention, and early childhood development.

Defending the Early Years. https://www.deyproject.org. Defending children's right to play, grow, and learn in an era of so-called standards and accountability.

Diane Ravitch's Blog. https://dianeravitch.net. Includes frequent timely opinions and news items that support our public schools and criticizes the privatization of schools in the United States and the depersonalization of learning due to corporate involvement in education.

Edwards, Carolyn, Lella Gandini, and George Foreman. *The Hundred Languages of Children: The Reggio Emilia Experience in Transformation, 3rd Edition.* Santa Barbara, CA: Praeger, 2011.

FairTest—The National Center for Fair and Open Testing. http://www.fairtest.org/get-involved/opting-out. Works to end the misuses and flaws of standardized testing and to ensure that evaluation of students, teachers, and schools is fair, open, valid, and educationally beneficial; provides information about how to get involved with the opt-out movement (opting out of standardized testing).

Meier, Deborah, and Matthew Knoester. Beyond Testing: Seven Assessments of Students and Schools More Effective Than Standardized Tests. New York: Teachers College Press, 2017.

Network for Public Education. https://networkforpubliceducation.org. Provides information, research, and networking on vital issues that concern the future of public education at a time when it is under attack.

North American Reggio Emilia Alliance (NAREA). https://www.reggioalliance .org/narea. Connects early childhood educators and advocates together in discovering, interpreting, and promoting Reggio Emilia–inspired education, including the inherent abilities and basic rights of children and adults, particularly with regard to their competence and right to actively construct relations, knowledge, feelings, and identity.

Parent Coalition for Student Privacy. https://www.studentprivacymatters.org. A national alliance of parents and advocates defending the rights of parents and students to protect their school data.

Race to Nowhere. An independently produced documentary film written by Maimone Attia and directed by Vicki Abeles and Jessica Congdon, which is critical of overtesting, overscheduling, and the relentless pressure on children to achieve in school. To schedule a viewing at your school or in your community, go to http://www.racetonowhere.com.

Ravitch, Diane. Reign of Error: The Hoax of the Privatization Movement and the Danger to America's Public Schools. New York: Vintage, 2014.

Rethinking Schools. https://www.rethinkingschools.org. Magazine, bookstore, blog, and advocacy group supporting social justice, multiculturalism, tolerance of differences, social activism, and issues of equity in our nation's schools.

We the Educators. https://wetheeducators.com. An international initiative of teachers crusading against the depersonalization, datafication, and standardization of education.

Notes

CHAPTER ONE. THE PURPOSE OF EDUCATION: INTRODUCING INCREDIBLE KIDS TO AN AMAZING WORLD

1. Albert Einstein is quoted in "Assails Education Today; Einstein Says 'It Is Miracle' Inquiry Is Not 'Strangled,'" *New York Times*, March 13, 1949, 34.

2. J. Robert Oppenheimer is quoted in International Center for the Typographical Arts, *Vision 65: New Challenges for Human Communications* (Carbondale, IL: Southern Illinois University, 1965), 221.

3. Marian Diamond is quoted in Marian Diamond and Janet Hopson, *Magic Trees of the Mind: How to Nurture Your Child's Intelligence, Creativity, and Healthy Emotions from Birth through Adolescence* (New York: Plume, 1999), 54.

4. Stephen Jay Gould's writings on the importance of neoteny in human evolution include his books *Ontogeny and Phylogeny* (Cambridge, MA: Belknap Press, 1985) and *The Mismeasure of Man* (New York: W. W. Norton, 1996). In addition, see his "A Biological Homage to Mickey Mouse," in *The Panda's Thumb* (New York: W. W. Norton, 1992). Also note the indirect reference to neoteny in this quote from Albert Einstein writing to a colleague: "People like you and I, though mortal of course like everyone else, do not grow old no matter how long we live. What I mean is we never cease to stand like curious children before the great Mystery into which we were born." Quoted in a letter to Otto Juliusburger, September 29, 1942, in *The Ultimate Quotable Einstein*, ed. Alice Caprice (Princeton, NJ: Princeton University Press, 2013), 55–56.

5. To learn more about children creating their own unique language, see Derek Bickerton, "Creole Languages," *Scientific American* 249 (July 1983): 116–22.

6. Hans Christian Andersen, quoted in Pat Shaw Iversen, "Afterword," *Andersen's Fairy Tales* (New York: Signet, 1987), 378.

7. Michael Parker is quoted in Claudia Wallis, "Does Kindergarten Need Cops?" *Time*, December 7, 2003, http://content.time.com/time/mag azine/article/0,9171,556865,00.html. Note that this identification of more aggressive kindergartners and first graders took place just one year after the implementation of the federal No Child Left Behind Act.

8. Statistics cited about suicidal thoughts among preschoolers are from Diana J. Whalen et al., "Correlates and Consequences of Suicidal Cognitions and Behaviors in Children Ages 3 to 7 Years," *Journal of the American Academy of Child & Adolescent Psychiatry* 54, no. 11 (November 2015): 926–37.

9. The increase in elementary school children presenting with ulcers and migraines is cited in Alexa Abeles, "Is the Drive for Success Making Our Children Sick?" *New York Times*, January 2, 2016, https://www.nytimes .com/2016/01/03/opinion/sunday/is-the-drive-for-success-making-our -children-sick.html.

10. Figures on the increase in ADHD diagnoses from 2003 to 2016 are taken from the Centers for Disease Control and Prevention, "Data and Statistics about ADHD," accessed March 29, 2019, https://www.cdc.gov /ncbddd/adhd/data.html.

11. The decline in measures of creativity in schoolchildren comes from Kyung Hee Kim, "The Creativity Crisis: The Decrease in Creative Thinking Scores on the Torrance Tests of Creative Thinking," *Creativity Research Journal* 23, no. 3 (October 2011): 285–95.

12. The statistic on threats and attacks on teachers is from Frances L. Huang, Colleen Lloyd Eddy, and Emily Camp, "The Role of the Perceptions of School Climate and Teacher Victimization by Students," *Journal of Interpersonal Violence*, July 27, 2017, https://doi.org/10.1177/08862605177 21898.

13. The figure on adolescents' school-related stress is from the American Psychological Association, "American Psychological Association Survey Shows Teen Stress Rivals That of Adults," February 11, 2014, http:// www.apa.org/news/press/releases/2014/02/teen-stress.aspx.

14. Information about "robo-students" is from J. O. Conner and D. C. Pope, "Not Just Robo-Students: Why Full Engagement Matters and How Schools Can Promote It," *Journal of Youth and Adolescence* 42, no. 9 (September 2013): 1426–27.

15. The figure on college students' thoughts of suicide is from Alina Tugend, "Colleges Get Proactive in Addressing Depression on Campus," *New York Times*, June 7, 2017, https://www.nytimes.com/2017/06/07/edu cation/colleges-get-proactive-in-addressing-depression-on-campus.html.

16. The falling number of teachers in teacher preparation programs is from Eric Westervelt, "Frustration, Burnout, Attrition: It's Time to Address

the National Teacher Shortage," nprED, September 15, 2016, https://www
.npr.org/sections/ed/2016/09/15/493808213/frustration-burnout-attrition
-its-time-to-address-the-national-teacher-shortage.

17. For a look at the neurodevelopmental needs of middle school and high
school students, and how the schools are failing to meet them, see Thomas
Armstrong, *The Power of the Adolescent Brain* (Alexandria, VA: ASCD, 2016).

18. The third-grade standard was taken from the Common Core State
Standards for English Language Arts & Literacy in History/Social Studies,
Science, and Technical Subjects, June 2, 2010, http://www.corestandards
.org/wp-content/uploads/ELA_Standards1.pdf.

19. The federal report was quoted in "A Nation at Risk," U.S. Department of Education Archives, April 1983, https://www2.ed.gov/pubs/NatA
tRisk/risk.html. One could go back even farther historically to the moment
when Russia put the satellite Sputnik in orbit on October 4, 1957, and
Edward Teller, the father of the hydrogen bomb, wrote a cover piece for
Time six weeks later (November 18, 1957), decrying the poor state of
American mathematics and science education compared with Russian
education. One consequence of Sputnik and Teller's appeal was the passage of the National Defense Education Act on September 2, 1958, which
allocated hundreds of millions of dollars to revamping America's science
and math programs (and gave us, incidentally, "the new math," BSCS biology, CHEM study, and a number of other courses I had to take in junior
high and high school from 1963–1967). For a more recent linkage of school
reform with national security, see "U.S. Education Reform and National
Security," *Council on Foreign Relations*, March 2012, https://www.cfr.org
/report/us-education-reform-and-national-security.

20. Portions of the following chronology of American efforts toward a
standards-based, high-stakes testing environment are adapted from "Are We
There Yet? Business, Politics, and the Long (Unfinished) Road to National
Standards," *Frontline*, accessed March 29, 2019, http://www.pbs.org/wgbh
/pages/frontline/shows/schools/standards/bp.html.

21. For a look at how business became interested in education in the
1980s, see Pamela G. Hollie, "Why Business Is Barging into the Classroom,"
New York Times, July 12, 1987, http://www.nytimes.com/1987/07/12/busi
ness/why-business-is-barging-into-the-classroom.html.

22. Gerstner is quoted in "Are We There Yet?"

23. Stan Karp is quoted from his article, "ESSA: NCLB Repackaged,"
Rethinking Schools 30, no. 3 (Spring, 2016), https://www.rethinkingschools
.org/articles/essa-nclb-repackaged.

24. For the role of Bill Gates in creating the Common Core State Standards, see Lyndsey Layton, "How Bill Gates Pulled Off the Swift Common
Core Revolution," *Washington Post*, June 7, 2014, https://www.washington
post.com/politics/how-bill-gates-pulled-off-the-swift-common-core-revo
lution/2014/06/07/a830e32e-ec34-11e3-9f5c-9075d5508f0a_story.html.

25. President Trump's 2019 budget requests for education are described in Andrew Ujifusa, "Trump K–12 Priorities Outlined in Budget," *Education Week*, March 20, 2019, https://www.edweek.org/ew/articles/2019/03/20/trump-k-12-priorities-outlined-in-budget.html.

26. Diane Ravitch is quoted from her article, "Are Donald Trump and Betsy DeVos the Civil Rights Leaders of Our Time?" *Huffington Post*, March 1, 2017, http://www.huffingtonpost.com/entry/are-donald-trump-and-betsy-devos-the-civil-rights-leaders-of-our-time_us_58b6fb34e4b023018c6c1d34.

27. For America's poor performance on the PISA test, see Jill Barshay, "U.S. Now Ranks near the Bottom among 35 Industrialized Nations in Math," *Hechinger Report*, December 6, 2016, http://hechingerreport.org/u-s-now-ranks-near-bottom-among-35-industrialized-nations-math.

28. The Brookings Institution's report of no significant change in PISA test results among U.S. students is from Louis Serino, "What International Test Scores Reveal about American Education," Brookings Institution, April 7, 2017, https://www.brookings.edu/blog/brown-center-chalkboard/2017/04/07/what-international-test-scores-reveal-about-american-education. Note: PISA scores in any given year are reported at the end of the following year.

29. Statistics on Americans who reported not having read a book in a given twelve-month period come from Andrew Perrin, "Who Doesn't Read Books in America?" Pew Research Center, November 23, 2016, http://www.pewresearch.org/fact-tank/2016/11/23/who-doesnt-read-books-in-america.

30. Statistics on Americans' answers to science literacy questions come from Tania Lombrozo, "Scientific Literacy: It's Not (Just) about the Facts," *Cosmos & Culture*, September 14, 2015, http://www.npr.org/sections/13.7/2015/09/14/440213603/scientific-literacy-it-s-not-just-about-the-facts.

31. Figures about the decline in arts attendance nationwide come from the "National Endowment for the Arts, a Decade of Arts Engagement: Findings from the Survey of Public Participation in the Arts, 2002–2012," *NEA Research Report #58*, January 2015, https://www.arts.gov/sites/default/files/2012-sppa-feb2015.pdf.

32. Albert Einstein is quoted in Walter Isaacson, *Einstein: His Life and Universe* (New York: Simon & Schuster, 2008), 49.

CHAPTER TWO. IMAGINATION: UNLEASHING OUR CHILDREN'S ABILITY TO MENTALLY SOAR

1. Albert Einstein is quoted in "What Life Means to Einstein: An Interview by George Sylvester Viereck," *Saturday Evening Post*, October 26, 1929, 117, http://www.saturdayeveningpost.com/wp-content/uploads/satevepost/what_life_means_to_einstein.pdf.

2. Albert Einstein is quoted in Gerald Holton, "On Trying to Understand Scientific Genius," *American Scholar* 41, no. 1 (Winter 1971–72): 95–110.

3. Einstein made virtually all of his pioneering discoveries in science in early adulthood and then spent the rest of his life trying to harmonize the consistency of his relativity theories with the probabilistic features of quantum theory. Interestingly, Richard Feynman suggested that Einstein may have failed to discover a unified field theory "because he stopped thinking in concrete physical images and became a manipulator of equations." Feynman is quoted in Freeman Dyson, *Disturbing the Universe* (New York: Basic Books, 1981), 62.

4. Albert Einstein is quoted in Jacques Hadamard, *The Psychology of Invention in the Mathematical Field* (Princeton, NJ: Princeton University Press, 1945), 142–43.

5. These and other accounts of scientific imagination can be found in Roger Shepard, "The Imagination of the Scientist," in *Imagination and Education*, eds. Kieran Egan and Dan Hadaner (New York: Teachers College Press, 1988), 153–85.

6. Richard Feynman is quoted in Dyson, *Disturbing the Universe*, 55.

7. Stephen Hawking is quoted in Shepard, "The Imagination of the Scientist," 178.

8. Csikszentmihalyi is quoted in Mihaly Csikszentmihalyi, *Applications of Flow in Human Development and Education: The Collected Works of Mihaly Csikszentmihalyi* (New York: Springer 2014), 131.

9. For a list of states that have adopted the Common Core and those who are using their own standards, see "Map: Tracking the Common Core State Standards," *Education Week*, September 18, 2017, https://www.edweek.org/ew/section/multimedia/map-states-academic-standards-common-core-or.html.

10. Peter Wood is quoted in Sol Stern and Peter Wood, *Common Core: Yea & Nay* (New York: Encounter Books, 2014), 9–10.

11. These Common Core State Standards were downloaded from the website Common Core State Standards Initiative, accessed March 29, 2019, http://www.corestandards.org/ELA-Literacy.

12. Ron Maggiano is quoted in Valerie Strauss, "11 Problems Created by the Standardized Testing Obsession," *Washington Post*, April 22, 2014, https://www.washingtonpost.com/news/answer-sheet/wp/2014/04/22/11-problems-created-by-the-standardized-testing-obsession.

13. The lesson on "The Capture of Father Time" and sample questions are given in Smarter Balanced Assessment Consortium, *ELA Practice Test Scoring Guide, Grade 7*, January 3, 2017, https://portal.smarterbalanced.org/library/en/grade-7-ela-practice-test-scoring-guide.pdf.

14. This method of "close reading" is essentially borrowed from a branch of university-level literary criticism called the New Criticism, which was

given its name in 1941 by poet John Crowe Ransom in his book *The New Criticism* (New York: Praeger, 1979). It was especially popular in the mid-1950s in colleges and universities in the United States and Europe (and was particularly associated, unsurprisingly, with Yale University, where David Coleman was educated). For information about the New Criticism, see Mark Jancovich, *The Cultural Politics of the New Criticism* (Cambridge: Cambridge University Press, 1993).

15. David Coleman is quoted in "Bringing the Common Core to Life," transcript of a speech at Chancellors Hall, State Education Building, Albany, New York, April 28, 2011, http://usny.nysed.gov/rttt/docs/bringingthecom moncoretolife/fulltranscript.pdf.

16. The Common Core State Standard in seventh-grade mathematics was retrieved from the Common Core website, accessed March 29, 2019, http://www.corestandards.org/wp-content/uploads/Math_Standards1.pdf.

17. Einstein's uncle is quoted in Ronald Clark, *Einstein: The Life and Times* (New York: Avon Books, 1984), 27–28. In my own teaching, before introducing x, I'd ask my students to think about the unknowns in their own lives as a way of activating their imaginations. My own excitement about mathematics was fueled as a child when I watched the 1959 Disney Academy Award–nominated television production called "Donald Duck in Mathmagic Land." This video can be viewed on YouTube at: https://www .youtube.com/watch?v=U_ZHsk0-eF0.

18. For a look at the imaginative dimensions of mathematics, see Edward Kasner and James Newman, *Mathematics and the Imagination* (New York: Dover, 2001).

19. The example of kids comparing a playground slide to Rapunzel's hair is given in Brian Smith, "Imagination: The Forgotten 21st Century Skill?" *Scholastic*, December 31, 2014, https://www.scholastic.com/teachers/blog -posts/brian-smith/imagination-forgotten-21st-century-skill.

20. Leo's imaginative experience is cited in Mark Girod, Cheryl Rau, and Adele Schepige, "Appreciating the Beauty of Science Ideas: Teaching for Aesthetic Understanding," *Science Education* 87, no. 4 (July 2003), http://www.wou.edu/~girodm/670/beauty_of_ideas.pdf.

21. The imaginative lesson about Dutch resistant fighters is given in S. W. Cawthon, K. Dawson, and K. S. Ihorn, "Activating Student Engagement through Drama-Based Instruction," *Journal for Learning through the Arts* 7, no. 1 (2011): 6.

22. The Queen of the Giants math lesson is given in Lindsay Zebrowski, "Queen of the Giants: A Narrative for Guiding Measurement Explorations through Blogging in Early Primary," *imaginED*, December 9, 2016, http:// www.educationthatinspires.ca/2016/12/09/queen-of-the-giants-a-narrative -for-guiding-measurement-explorations-through-blogging-in-early-primary.

23. The lesson about why bananas are green is given in Brandon and Kristin Hendrickson, "How Imaginative Education (IE) Tricked Us Into

Teaching Atomic Physics . . . to Squirrely 7-Year-Olds," *imaginED*, January 16, 2017, http://www.educationthatinspires.ca/2017/01/16/how-imaginative -education-ie-tricked-us-into-teaching-atomic-physicsto-squirrely-7-year -olds. For more information about IE, see Kieran Egan, *An Imaginative Approach to Teaching* (San Francisco: Jossey-Bass, 2005).

24. The poll on voters' opinions about imagination in learning is reported on in "New Poll Reveals Stifling Imagination in Schools Underlies Innovation and Skills Deficit," National Association of Music Merchants (NAMM), January 24, 2008, https://www.namm.org/news/press-releases /new-poll-reveals-stifling-imagination-schools-unde.

25. The research on imagination with 1,700 children is cited in Raya A. Jones et al., "The Dialectical Mind: On Educating the Creative Imagination in Elementary School," in *Education and Imagination: Post-Jungian Perspectives*, ed. Austin Clarkson (Hove, East Sussex, UK: Routledge, 2008), 127.

26. "Waldorf education" provides a good example of an approach that is sensitive to features of modern life that serve to shut down the imagination. Television watching (which provides ready-made images) is frowned upon, and dolls in a Waldorf kindergarten are given a minimal set of facial features so that children can use their imagination to fill in the rest. See Todd Oppenheimer, "The Primacy of Imagination," *Atlantic Online*, September 1999, https://www.theatlantic.com/past/docs/issues/99sep/9909 waldorf2.htm.

CHAPTER THREE. LOVE OF LEARNING: AFFIRMING THE MOST IMPORTANT GOAL OF EDUCATION

1. Albert Einstein is quoted in Isaacson, *Einstein*, 548.

2. Exemplary lectures on a wide range of subjects are available from The Great Courses, 4840 Westfields Blvd, Suite 500, Chantilly, VA 20151. 1-800-832-2412, accessed March 29, 2019, http://www.thegreatcourses.com.

3. For information about The Criterion Channel, visit their website at: https://www.criterionchannel.com.

4. For the quote on selling "love of learning" to students, see Dan Pink: "How Teachers Can Sell Love of Learning to Students," *MindShift*, January 18, 2013, https://ww2.kqed.org/mindshift/2013/01/18/dan-pink-how-teachers -can-sell-love-of-learning-to-students.

5. The suggestion for learning five new words is quoted from the website of the VIA Institute on Character, accessed March 29, 2019, http:// www.viacharacter.org/www/Character-Strengths/Love-of-Learning.

6. Carol Dweck is quoted in "How to Help Your Child Develop a Love of Learning," *Kids in the House*, accessed March 29, 2019, https://www .kidsinthehouse.com/teenager/education/academic-pressure/how-help -your-child-develop-love-learning.

7. For the Jewish tradition of sweetening a child's alphabet board, see Vered Guttman, "The Sweet Taste of the Torah, Baked with a Little Butter and Jam," *Haaretz*, October 9, 2012, https://www.haaretz.com/.premium-the-sweet-taste-of-torah-with-jam-1.5178244.

8. The Hadith or saying of the Prophet Muhammad is from The Book of Knowledge, Hadith 13, Sunnah.com, accessed March 29, 2019, https://sunnah.com/riyadussaliheen/13.

9. Confucius is quoted in *The Analects of Confucius*, trans. Simon Leys (New York: W. W. Norton, 1997), 86–87.

10. Plato is quoted in *The Republic*, trans. Allan Bloom (New York: Basic Books, 1991), 53.

11. Alfred North Whitehead is quoted from his book *The Aims of Education and Other Essays* (New York: Free Press, 1967), 17–18.

12. For a look at how learning serves to expand adaptability to changed life circumstances, see M. Sutter and T. J. Kawecki, "Influence of Learning on Range Expansion and Adaptation to Novel Habitats," *Journal of Evolutionary Biology* 22, no. 11 (November 2009): 2201–14. It seems telling to me that discourse on the evolutionary basis of learning is almost completely absent within the educational community.

13. Jean Piaget is quoted from his book *The Origins of Intelligence in Children* (New York: International University Press, 1952), 185.

14. Daniel Stern's observations of six-week old Joey are from his book *Diary of a Baby: What Your Child Sees, Feels, and Experiences* (New York: Basic Books, 1990), 18.

15. Piaget's story about his mathematical friend's childhood experience was quoted in Herbert Ginsburg and Sylvia Opper, *Piaget's Theory of Intellectual Development: An Introduction* (Englewood Cliffs, NJ: Prentice-Hall, 1969), 216.

16. The adult's reminiscences about walking home are given in Edward Robinson, *The Original Vision: A Study of the Religious Experience of Childhood* (New York: Seabury Press, 1983), 112.

17. The adult's reminiscences about learning words in school ending in "-ness" are given in Robinson, *Original Vision*, 27–28.

18. For information about two brothers who have looked at "peak moments" in life and begun to speculate on how this approach might be applied to an educational setting, see Chip Heath and Dan Heath, "The Secret to Student Engagement," *Education Week*, January 10, 2018, https://www.edweek.org/ew/articles/2018/01/10/the-secret-to-student-engagement.html. Also note their book *The Power of Moments: Why Certain Experiences Have Extraordinary Impact* (New York: Simon and Schuster, 2017). For a look at a group of individuals called "extreme learners" who are said to possess an intense, almost obsessive, love of learning, see Milton Chen, "The 5 Habits of Extreme Learners," *Education Week*, December

11, 2017, https://www.edweek.org/ew/articles/2017/12/13/the-5-habits-of -extreme-learners.html.

19. A seminal paper on the idea of crystallizing experiences is Joseph Walters and Howard Gardner, "The Crystallizing Experience: Discovering an Intellectual Gift," ERIC Institute of Education Sciences, March 30, 1984, https://files.eric.ed.gov/fulltext/ED254544.pdf.

20. Helen Keller is quoted from her autobiography *The Story of My Life* (New York: Dover Publications, 1996), 12.

21. Anna Pavlova is quoted in Ronald Stanley Illingworth and Cynthia M. Illingworth, *Lessons from Childhood: Some Aspects of the Early Life of Unusual Men and Women* (Baltimore, MD: Williams and Wilkins Co., 1966), 261.

22. Ingmar Bergman is quoted in his autobiography *The Magic Lantern: An Autobiography* (New York: Penguin Books, 1988), 16.

23. Wassily Kandinsky is quoted in Heinz Werner, *Comparative Psychology of Mental Development* (New York: International Universities Press, 1973), 71–72.

24. Mark Chagall is quoted from his memoir *My Life* (London: Peter Owen Publishers, 2011), 170.

25. Maria Montessori is quoted from her book *The Discovery of Childhood* (New Delhi, India: Aakar Books, 2004), 255.

26. The benefits of intrinsic motivation are noted in John Mark Froiland and Frank C. Worrell, "Intrinsic Motivation, Learning Goals, Engagement, and Achievement in a Diverse High School," *Psychology in the Schools* 53, no. 3 (March 2016), https://www.researchgate.net/profile/Frank_Worrell /publication/292185199_Intrinsic_motivation_learning_goals_engagement _and_achievement_in_a_diverse_high_school/links/56af770f08ae9c1968b 45230.pdf.

27. Teresa Amabile is quoted in Beth A. Hennessey and Teresa M. Amabile, *Creativity and Learning* (Washington, DC: National Education Association, 1987), 12.

28. Teresa Amabile's study offering an instant camera to children either as a reward or not, is described in T. Amabile, B. Hennessey, and B. Grossman, "Social Influences on Creativity: The Effects of Contracted-For Reward," *Journal of Personality and Social Psychology* 50 (1986): 14–23.

29. For examples of teaching tricks to engage students, see Robert Marzano, Debra J. Pickering, and Tammy Heflebower, *The Highly Engaged Classroom: The Classroom Strategies Series* (Bloomington, MN: Marzano Research Laboratory, 2011).

30. Some of my own teaching tricks are described in Thomas Armstrong, *Multiple Intelligences in the Classroom*, 4th ed. (Alexandria, VA: ASCD, 2017). Note that the book is primarily concerned with applying Howard Gardner's theory of multiple intelligences to the classroom.

31. One area of educational research that seems promising in capturing the vitality and excitement of learning is the study of *flow*. This term, originated by Claremont Graduate School professor Mihaly Csikszentmihalyi, refers to a mental state of intense absorption in an activity that leaves the person involved, exhilarated, and inspired. Csikszentmihalyi studied professional artists, rock climbers, surgeons, and other highly trained individuals, all of whom reported entering into what appeared to be a meditative-like state while they were totally engaged in their work. For a good introduction to flow, see Mihaly Csikszentmihalyi, *Flow: The Psychology of Optimal Experience* (New York: Harper Perennial, 2008). Csikszentmihalyi has investigated flow in educational contexts, and many of his studies appear in his book *Applications of Flow in Human Development and Education: The Collected Works of Mihaly Csikszentmihalyi* (New York: Springer, 2014). Unfortunately, most of the scholarly research devoted to flow in recent years has been limited to computer-based applications, not to interactions in the real world.

32. The chalkboard "engagement" strategy is given in "Student Engagement," from the website Glossary of Educational Reform (created by the Great Schools Partnership), February 18, 2016, http://edglossary.org/student-engagement.

33. An example of a book that uses the word "content" in its title is Sharon Kane, *Literacy and Learning in the Content Areas* (New York: Routledge, 2017).

CHAPTER FOUR. CREATIVITY: TEACHING OUTSIDE THE BOX

1. Albert Einstein is quoted in *The Ultimate Quotable Einstein*, 100.

2. Leo Tolstoy is quoted from his article, "Are the Peasant Children to Learn to Write from Us, or Are We to Learn from the Peasant Children?" in *Tolstoy as Teacher: Leo Tolstoy's Writings on Education*, ed. Bob Blaisdell (New York: Teachers and Writers Collaborative, 2000), 3.

3. The idea of creative "micro-moments" in the classroom is taken up in Ronald A. Beghetto, "Nurturing Creativity in the Micro-Moments of the Classroom," in *Creatively Gifted Students Are Not Like Other Gifted Students: Research, Theory, and Practice*, eds. Kyung Hee Kim et al. (Rotterdam, the Netherlands: Sense Publishers, 2013), 3–16.

4. The example of Emily and the ant is given in Karen Gallas, "'Look, Karen, I'm Running Like Jell-O': Imagination as a Question, a Topic, a Tool for Literacy Research and Learning," *Research in the Teaching of English* 35 (May 2001): 457.

5. Lev Vygotsky is quoted from his 1930 book *Imagination and Creativity in Childhood*, published in the *Journal of Russian and European Psychology* 42, no. 1 (January–February 2004): 7.

6. Vygotsky is quoted in *Imagination and Creativity in Childhood*, 8.

7. For an account of recent discoveries regarding neuroplasticity, see Norman Doidge, *The Brain That Changes Itself: Stories of Personal Triumph from the Frontiers of Brain Science* (New York: Penguin, 2007).

8. For an account of developmental changes in the child and adolescent brain, see Jay N. Giedd et al., "Brain Development During Childhood and Adolescence: A Longitudinal MRI Study," *Nature Neuroscience* 2, no. 10 (October 1999): 861–63.

9. Jules Henry is quoted from his book, *Culture against Man* (New York: Random House, 1963), 286.

10. The report to the U.S. Congress, "Education of the Gifted and Talented" (the Marland Report), is available for viewing at https://www.valdosta.edu/colleges/education/pcft/document%20/marland-report.pdf. For an article dealing with the impact of this report on segregating creativity from the regular education curriculum, see Beghetto, "Nurturing Creativity in the Micro-Moments of the Classroom."

11. The Torrance Tests of Creative Thinking are currently published by Scholastic Testing Services Inc., accessed March 29, 2019, https://www.ststesting.com/gift.

12. Kaufman and Beghetto are quoted from their article "Creativity in the Schools: A Rapidly Developing Area of Positive Psychology," in *Handbook of Positive Psychology in Schools*, eds. R. Gilman, E. S. Huebner, and M. J. Furlong (New York: Routledge/Taylor & Francis Group, 2009), 175–88.

13. The study showing that a majority of teachers do not use creative approaches in their teaching despite the fact that it leads to academic gains is in John Schacter, Yeow Meng Thum, and David Zifkin, "How Much Does Creative Teaching Enhance Elementary School Students' Achievement?" *Journal of Creative Behavior* 40, no. 1 (2006): 47–72.

14. Studies demonstrating that the qualities of creative students are at odds with what teachers prefer to see in students are summarized in Abdullah Aljughaiman and Elizabeth Mowrer-Reynolds, "Teachers' Conceptions of Creativity and Creative Students," *Journal of Creative Behavior* 39, no. 1 (March 2005): 17–34.

15. For studies linking creative behavior with attention deficit hyperactivity disorder, see Bonnie Cramond, "Attention-Deficit Hyperactivity Disorder and Creativity: What is the Connection?" *Journal of Creative Behavior* 28, no. 3 (September 1994): 193–210; and Bonnie Cramond, "The Coincidence of Attention Deficit Hyperactivity Disorder and Creativity," ERIC, March 1995, https://eric.ed.gov/?id=ED388016.

16. For a study that documents the decline in student creativity since 1990, see Kyung Hee Kim, "The Creativity Crisis: The Decrease in Creative Thinking Scores on the Torrance Tests of Creative Thinking," *Creativity Research Journal* 23, no. 4 (2011): 285–95.

17. The statistic on teacher effectiveness ratings being determined by student test scores is taken from Jack Schneider, "The High Stakes of Teacher Evaluations," *Education Week*, June 5, 2012, https://www.edweek.org/ew/articles/2012/06/06/33schneider.h31.html.

18. The term "creaticide" and a discussion of its meaning are given in David Berliner, 'Narrowing Curriculum, Assessments, and Conceptions of What It Means to Be Smart in the U.S. Schools: Creaticide by Design," in *How Dogmatic Beliefs Harm Creativity and Higher-Level Thinking*, eds. Don Ambrose and Robert J. Sternberg (New York: Routledge, 2011), 79–93.

19. Stephen Hawking is quoted in Emma Brockes, "Return of the Time Lord," *Guardian*, September 27, 2005, https://www.theguardian.com/science/2005/sep/27/scienceandnature.highereducationprofile.

20. Jamie Highfill is quoted in "Common Core Nonfiction Reading Standards Mark The End Of Literature, English Teachers Say," *Huffington Post*, December 14, 2012, https://www.huffingtonpost.com/2012/12/10/common-core-nonfiction-reading-standards_n_2271229.html.

21. Haley Curfman's "white dress" project is described in Chrissy Callahan, "Why this 2nd Grade Teacher Let Her Students Draw All Over Her White Dress," *Today*, February 23, 2018, https://www.today.com/style/teacher-let-her-students-write-her-white-dress-t123729.

22. David Rufo's maze project is described in his article, "Building Forts and Drawing on Walls: Fostering Student-Initiated Creativity Inside and Outside the Elementary Classroom," *Art Education* (May 2012): 45, http://www3.kutztown.edu/arteducation/PDF/BuildingForts.pdf.

23. Rufo, "Building Forts and Drawing on Walls," 45.

24. Luke Perry's novel-writing project is described in Carol Pogash, "A School-for-Scribes Program Turns Kids into Novelists," *Edutopia*, January 28, 2009, https://www.edutopia.org/arts-national-novel-writing-month.

25. Isaac's video game project is described in Kelly Gallagher-Mackay and Nancy Steinhauer, "How Schools Can Stop Killing Creativity," *Walrus*, September 12, 2017, https://thewalrus.ca/how-schools-can-stop-killing-creativity.

26. The Analy High School maker room is described in Dianne Reber Hart, "Analy High School Program a National Model for Hands-On Learning," *Press Democrat*, February 12, 2016, https://www.pressdemocrat.com/news/5001548-181/analy-program-in-sebastopol-a.

27. The Catlin Gabel School shoe design-thinking project was described in Suzie Boss, "Shoe Design Offers a Trojan Horse for Problem Solving with Design Thinking," *Edutopia*, April 4, 2013, https://www.edutopia.org/blog/design-thinking-opportunity-problem-solving-suzie-boss.

28. For information about the work of Yong Zhao, see his book *World Class Learners: Educating Creative and Entrepreneurial Students* (Thousand Oaks, CA: Corwin Press, 2012). For information about Ken Robinson's work, see his book *Creative Schools: The Grassroots Revolution That's Transforming Education* (New York: Penguin, 2016).

29. Ken Robinson is quoted in Bob Morrison, "How Creativity, Education, and the Arts Shape a Modern Economy," *Arts and Minds: Conversations about the Arts in Education*, April 2005, https://www.ecs.org/clearinghouse/60/51/6051.pdf.

30. Martha Graham is quoted in Agnes de Mille, *Martha: The Life and Work of Martha Graham* (New York: Random House, 1991), 264.

CHAPTER FIVE. PLAYFULNESS: RESTORING CHILDHOOD TO PRESCHOOL AND KINDERGARTEN

1. Albert Einstein is quoted in Jacques Hadamard, *An Essay on the Psychology of Invention in the Mathematical Field* (Princeton, NJ: Princeton University Press, 1945), 142.

2. For an excellent book chronicling the cognitive, emotional, and imaginative benefits of children's play, see Jerome Singer, *The House of Make-Believe: Children's Play and the Developing Imagination* (Cambridge, MA: Harvard University Press, 1992).

3. The observation of children's language use at play is quoted from Rachel Cummings, "Language Play in the Classroom: Encouraging Children's Intuitive Creativity with Words through Poetry," *Literacy* 41, no. 2 (July 2007): 93–94.

4. D. W. Winnicott is quoted from his book *Playing and Reality* (London: Routledge, 1982), 14.

5. Isaac Newton is quoted in Sir David Brewster, *Memoirs of the Life, Writings, and Discoveries of Sir Isaac Newton, Volume 2* (Chestnut Hill, MA: Adamant Media Corporation, 2001), 407.

6. Alexander Fleming is quoted in K. C. Cole, "Play, by Definition, Suspends the Rules," *New York Times*, November 30, 1988, C16.

7. Frank Lloyd Wright is quoted in *Frank Lloyd Wright: An Autobiography* (San Francisco: Pomegranate Communications Inc., 2005), 13. For a fascinating look at how the original kindergarten movement influenced twentieth- century art and design, see Norman Brosterman, *Inventing Kindergarten* (New York: Harry N. Abrams, 1997).

8. Buckminster Fuller's kindergarten model is noted in Lydia Brosnahan, "Bucky Fuller Night: A Quirky Guy with a Dymaxion Sphere of Influence," *Walker Art Museum*, October 11, 2013, https://walkerart.org/magazine/bucky-fuller-night-a-quirky-guy-with-a-dymaxion-sphere-of-influence.

9. Mahler compares composing to building with blocks in Jonathan Carr, *Mahler: A Biography* (New York: Overlook Press, 1999), 10.

10. Johan Huizinga is quoted from his book *Homo Ludens* (Boston: Beacon Press, 1986), 173.

11. Evolutionary psychologists are quoted in Warner Greve, Tamara Thomsen, and Cornelia Dehio, "Does Playing Pay? The Fitness-Effect of Free Play During Childhood," *Evolutionary Psychology* 12, no. 2 (2014): 434–47.

12. A discussion of how areas of the brain are refined by play is from H. C. Bell, S. M. Pellis, and B. Kolb, "Juvenile Peer Play Experience and the Development of the Orbitofrontal and Media Prefrontal Cortices," *Behavioral Brain Research* 207, no. 1 (February 2010): 7–13.

13. The role of BDNF in play is described in T. J. Burgdorf et al., "Uncovering the Molecular Basis of Positive Affect Using Rough-and-Tumble Play in Rats: A Role for Insulin-Like Growth Factor I," *Neuroscience* 168, no. 3 (July 14, 2010): 769–77.

14. The expression of genes within an hour after a thirty-minute play session is discussed in N.S. Gordon et al., "Expression of C-Fos Gene Activation during Rough and Tumble Play in Juvenile Rats," *Brain Research Bulletin* 57, no. 5 (March 2002): 651–59.

15. Research on how play deprivation affects brain synaptogenesis and pruning is described in Sergio M. Pellis, Vivien C. Pellis, and Brett T. Himmler, "How Play Makes for a More Adaptable Brain: A Comparative and Neural Perspective," *American Journal of Play* 7, no. 1 (Fall 2014): 73–98.

16. How play deprivation affects the prefrontal cortices is described in Michael Yogman et al., "The Power of Play: A Pediatric Role in Enhancing Development in Young Children," *Pediatrics* 142, no. 3 (September 2018), http://pediatrics.aappublications.org/content/142/3/e20182058.

17. The role of play in stress management is described in Stephen M. Siviy, "Play and Adversity: How the Playful Mammalian Brain Withstands Threats and Anxieties," *American Journal of Play* 2, no. 3 (Winter 2010): 297–314.

18. Research with hamsters on the role of play deprivation in generating social stress is described in Cody A. Burleson et al., "Social Play in Juvenile Hamsters Alters Dendritic Morphology in the Medial Prefrontal Cortex and Attenuates Effects of Social Stress in Adulthood," *Behavioral Neuroscience* 130, no. 4 (August, 2016): 437–47.

19. For information about ADHD and the rise of technology and the decline of play, see Thomas Armstrong, "Attention Deficit Hyperactivity Disorder in Children: One Consequence of the Rise of Technologies and Demise of Play?" in *All Work and No Play: How Educational Reforms Are Harming Our Preschoolers*, ed. Sharna Olfman (Westport, Ct: Praeger, 2003), 161–76.

20. Statistics on preschool children's outdoor play behavior is from P. S. Tandon, C. Zhou, and D. A. Christakis, "Frequency of Parent-Supervised Outdoor Play of US Preschool-Aged Children," *Archives of Pediatric and Adolescent Medicine* 166, no. 8 (August 2012): 707–12.

21. The percentage decrease in children's play behavior is given in Sandra Hofferth and John F. Sandberg, "Changes in American Children's Time, 1981–1997," *Advances in Life Course Research* 6 (2001): 193–229.

22. The percentage decrease in children's play behavior between 1997 and 2003 is given in Sandra Hofferth, "Changes in American Children's Time: 1997 to 2003," *International Journal of Time Use Research* 6, no. 1 (2009): 26–47.

23. Statistics on the sedentary nature of day care are provided in Kristen A. Copeland et al., "Societal Values and Policies May Curtail Preschool Children's Physical Activity in Child Care Centers," *Pediatrics* 129, no. 2 (2012): 265–74.

24. Recommendations for daily physical activity in children and teens are given in *Physical Activity Guidelines for Americans*, 2nd ed. (Washington, DC: U.S. Department of Health and Human Services, 2018), https://health.gov/paguidelines/second-edition/pdf/Physical_Activity_Guidelines_2nd_edition.pdf.

25. Links between lack of physical activity, on the one hand, and obesity and type 2 diabetes, on the other, are described in Terrence Dwyer et al., "Decline in Physical Fitness from Childhood to Adulthood Associated with Increased Obesity and Insulin Resistance in Adults," *Diabetes Care* 32, no. 4 (April 2009): 683–87.

26. Statistics on states requiring daily recess in schools are from Sandy J. Slater et al., "The Impact of State Laws and District Policies on Physical Education and Recess Practices in a Nationally-Representative Sample of U.S. Public Elementary Schools," *Archives of Pediatric and Adolescent Medicine* 166, no. 4 (April 2012): 311–16.

27. The fact that only one state requires classroom-based physical activity breaks is from Society of Health and Physical Educators, *Shape of the Nation: Status of Physical Education in the USA*, 2016, 20, https://www.shapeamerica.org//advocacy/son/2016/upload/Shape-of-the-Nation-2016_web.pdf.

28. Declines in time devoted to drama and art in kindergarten are noted in Daphna Bassok, Scott Latham, and Anna Rorem," Is Kindergarten the New First Grade?" *AERA Open* 1, no. 4 (January–March 2016): 1–31.

29. The kindergarten teacher's comments on the restrictiveness in today's kindergartens is from Diane Ravitch, "Teachers: Common Core in Kindergarten Class," *Diane Ravitch's Blog*, December 22, 2013, https://dianeravitch.net/2013/12/22/25602.

30. Kindergarten teachers' encounters with their principals are quoted in Meghan Lynch, "More Play Please: The Perspective of Kindergarten Teachers on Play in the Classroom," *American Journal of Play* 7, no. 3 (Spring 2015): 357.

31. The Arkansas teacher is quoted in Timothy D. Walker," The Joyful Illiterate Kindergartners of Finland," *Atlantic*, October 1, 2015, https://www.theatlantic.com/education/archive/2015/10/the-joyful-illiterate-kindergartners-of-finland/408325.

32. Examples of Common Core reading and writing standards for kindergartners are given in *Common Core State Standards for English Language Arts & Literacy in History/Social Studies, Science, and Technical Subjects*, Common Core State Standards Initiative, 2010, 16, 19, http://www.corestandards.org/wp-content/uploads/ELA_Standards1.pdf.

33. The example of a Common Core math standard for kindergarten is given in *Common Core State Standards for Mathematics*," Common Core State Standards Initiative, 11, accessed March 29, 2019, http://www.corestandards.org/wp-content/uploads/Math_Standards1.pdf.

34. The statistic that 30 percent of kindergartens don't have a recess time is from Sandra Hofferth and John F. Sandberg, "Changes in American Children's Time, 1981–1997."

35. The advantages of play-based and academic preschools for later school success are from Rebecca A. Marcon, "Moving up the Grades: Relationship between Preschool Model and Later School Success," *Early Childhood Research & Practice* 4, no. 1 (2002), http://ecrp.uiuc.edu/v4n1/marcon.html.

36. For more information about the Reggio Emilia schools, see Carolyn Edwards, Lella Gandini, and George Foreman, eds., *The Hundred Languages of Children: The Reggio Emilia Experience in Transformation*, 3rd ed. (Santa Barbara, CA: Praeger/ABC-CLIO, 2011).

37. Sara Baldwin is quoted in "A Day in the Life of a Waldorf Kindergarten," *Simple Homeschool*, January 16, 2014, https://simplehomeschool.net/a-day-in-the-life-of-a-waldorf-kindergarten. For more information about Waldorf education, see Jack Petrash, *Understanding Waldorf Education: Teaching from the Inside Out* (Lewisville, NC: Gryphon House, 2002).

38. School rules for the Roseville Community Preschool are from Bev Bos and Jenny Chapman, *Tumbling over the Edge: A Rant for Children's Play* (Roseville, CA: Turn the Page Press, 2005), xv.

39. Bos and Chapman, *Tumbling over the Edge*, 7.

40. Habibis Hutch is described in Claire Osborne, "South Austin Preschool Doesn't Make Children Learn Their ABCs," *Austin American-Statesman*, January 22, 2007, http://www.freerepublic.com/focus/news/1771605/posts.

41. The quote is from Habibis Hutch's website, accessed March 29, 2019, https://www.habibishutch.com/curriculum-2.

CHAPTER SIX. CURIOSITY: FEEDING OUR CHILDREN'S HUNGER FOR KNOWLEDGE

1. Albert Einstein is quoted in "Death of a Genius—Old Man's Advice to Youth: 'Never Lose a Holy Curiosity,'" *Life* 38, no. 18 (May 2, 1955): 64.

2. Sugata Mitra is quoted in his article, "The Hole in the Wall Project and the Power of Self-Organized Learning," *Edutopia*, February 3, 2012, https://www.edutopia.org/blog/self-organized-learning-sugata-mitra.

3. For a skeptical look at the "hole in the wall" phenomenon, see Donald Clark, "Sugata Mitra: Slum Chic? 7 Reasons for Doubt," *Donald Clark Plan B*, March 4, 2013, http://donaldclarkplanb.blogspot.com/search?q=mitra.

4. William James is quoted from his book, *Talks to Teachers on Psychology: And to Students on Some of Life's Ideals* (South Yarra, Australia: Leopold Classic Library, 2016), 31.

5. For information about the evolutionary basis of curiosity, see Celeste Kidd and Benjamin Y. Hayden, "The Psychology and Neuroscience of Curiosity," *Neuron* 88, no. 3 (November 4, 2015): 449–60.

6. Research on the curiosity of newborns is provided in Alan Slater, Victoria Morrison, and David Rose, "Habituation in the Newborn," *Infant Behavior and Development* 7, no. 2 (April–June 1984): 183–200.

7. Michele Chouinard's research was described in Susan Engel, *The Hungry Mind: The Origins of Curiosity in Childhood* (Cambridge, MA: Harvard University Press, 2018), 47.

8. William Wordsworth's excerpt is from his poem "Ode: Intimations of Immortality from Recollections of Early Childhood," *Wordsworth's Poetry and Prose* (New York: W. W. Norton, 2013), 436.

9. Barbara Tizard and Martin Hughes's research on children's questions asked at home and school is provided in their book *Young Children Learning* (Cambridge, MA: Harvard University Press, 1984), 271.

10. Neil Postman is quoted from his book *The End of Education: Redefining the Value of School* (New York: Knopf, 1995), 68.

11. The Gallup poll of teens is summarized in Linda Lyons, "Most Teens Associate School with Boredom, Fatigue," Gallup, June 8, 2004, https://news.gallup.com/poll/11893/most-teens-associate-school-boredom-fatigue.aspx.

12. Ronald Beghetto is quoted in his "Creativity in the Classroom," in *The Cambridge Handbook of Creativity*, eds. James Kaufmann and Robert A. Sternberg (Cambridge: Cambridge University Press, 2010), 450.

13. The experiment with the multitube toy was described in Elizabeth Bonawitz et al., "The Double-Edged Sword of Pedagogy: Instruction Limits Exploration and Discovery," *Cognition* 120, no. 3 (September 2011): 322–30.

14. Susan Engel is quoted from her article "Open Pandora's Box: Curiosity and Imagination in the Classroom," Thomas H. Wright Lecture, Occasional Paper Series. Child Development Institute, Sarah Lawrence College, Summer 2006, http://citeseerx.ist.psu.edu/viewdoc/download?doi=10.1.1.456.3302&rep=rep1&type=pdf.

15. Reflections on teachers' reluctance to field questions from students are from Tim Post and Juliette H. Walma van der Molen, "Do Children Express Curiosity in School? Exploring Children's Experiences of Curiosity inside and outside the School Context," *Learning, Culture, and Social Interaction* 18 (2018–2019): 60–71.

16. George Loewenstein is quoted in Erik Shonstrom, "How Can Teachers Foster Curiosity?" *Education Week* 33, no. 33 (June 4, 2014), https://www.edweek.org/ew/articles/2014/06/04/33shonstrom.h33.html.

17. Wendy Ostroff is quoted from her book *Cultivating Curiosity in K-12 Classrooms* (Alexandria, VA: ASCD, 2016), 6.

18. The anonymous teacher's statements are from Valerie Strauss, "Teacher Slams Scripted Common Core Lessons that Must Be Taught Word for Word," *Washington Post*, November 30, 2013, https://www.washingtonpost.com/news/answer-sheet/wp/2013/11/30/teacher-slams-scripted-common-core-lessons-that-must-be-taught-word-for-word.

19. Strauss, "Teacher Slams Scripted Common Core Lessons that Must Be Taught Word for Word."

20. Colin Blakemore is quoted in S. Pincock, "Francis Harry Compton Crick: Co-Discoverer of the Structure of DNA and Nobel Prize Winner," *Lancet* 364, no. 9434 (2004): 576.

21. Stephen Hawking's quote on curiosity is taken from *Stephen Hawking: A Life from Beginning to End* (Hourly History, 2019).

22. Richard Feynman's experiments with ants are described in James Glieck, *Genius: The Life and Science of Richard Feynman* (New York: Pantheon, 1992).

23. The reference to the wobbling plate is from Richard Feynman, *Surely You're Joking, Mr. Feynman: Adventures of a Curious Character* (New York: W. W. Norton, 2018).

24. The fMRI experiment with blurry and clear pictures was described in Marieke Jepma et al., "Neural Mechanisms Underlying the Induction and Relief of Perceptual Curiosity," *Frontiers in Behavioral Neuroscience* 6, no. 5 (February 2012): 5.

25. Matthias Gruber is quoted in Matthias Gruber, Bernard D. Gelman, and Charan Ranganath, "States of Curiosity Modulate Hippocampus-Dependent Learning via the Dopaminergic Circuit," *Neuron* 84, no. 2 (October 22, 2014): 486–96.

26. The study linking curiosity with high math and reading achievement is in Prachi E. Shah et al., "Early Childhood Curiosity and Kindergarten Reading and Math Achievement," *Pediatric Research* 84 (2018): 380–86.

27. The study associating curiosity at age three with intelligence at age eleven is given in A. Raine et al., "Stimulation Seeking and Intelligence: A Prospective Longitudinal Study," *Journal of Personality and Social Psychology* 82, no. 4 (April 2002): 663–74.

28. The meta-analysis of more than two hundred studies on curiosity and academic achievement is described in S. Stumm, B. Hell, and T. Chamorro-Premuzik, "The Hungry Mind: Intellectual Curiosity Is the Third Pillar of Academic Performance," *Perspectives on Psychological Science* 6, no. 6 (2011): 574–88.

29. Sophie von Stumm is quoted in "Curiosity is Critical to Academic Performance," *Science Daily*, October 28, 2011, https://www.sciencedaily.com/releases/2011/10/111027150211.htm.

30. The independence of curiosity and self-control in children is related in Shah et al., "Early Childhood Curiosity and Kindergarten Reading and Math Achievement."

31. Kristen Wideen's science table is described in "A Classroom for Discovery and Curiosity—Part 1," *Mrs. Wideen's Blog*, October 1, 2013, http://www.mrswideen.com/2013/10/a-classroom-for-discovery-and-curiosity.html.

32. Liz DesLauriers's French classroom geography project is described in Bill Hudson, "Cultivating a Curious Mindset," Mounds Park Academy, November 29, 2018, https://www.moundsparkacademy.org/news/2018/11/29/cultivating-a-curious-mindset.

33. Courtney Couvreur is quoted in her article "Curiosity in a High School Classroom," Agency by Design Oakland, November 15, 2018, http://www.abdoakland.org/news/2018/6/25/curiosity-in-a-high-school-classroom.

34. Couvreur, "Curiosity in a High School Classroom."

35. For a historical look at curiosity cabinets, see Patrick Mauriès, *Cabinets of Curiosities* (New York: Thames and Hudson, 2011).

36. The Long Beach School District's project on curiosity cabinets is highlighted in Alex Chan, "Students Make Something of Themselves," *Orange County Register*, March 3, 2014, http://www.ocregister.com/2014/03/03/students-make-something-of-themselves.

37. Chan, "Students Make Something of Themselves."

38. Susan Engel is quoted in her article "The Case for Curiosity," *Educational Leadership* 70, no. 5 (February 2013): 36–40.

CHAPTER SEVEN. WONDER: REAWAKENING OUR CHILDREN'S SENSE OF AWE FOR THE MYSTERY OF LIFE

1. Albert Einstein is quoted in Isaacson, *Einstein*, 387.

2. Albert Einstein is quoted in his book *Autobiographical Notes* (Chicago: Open Court Publishing, 1999), 9.

3. Aristotle is quoted in *The Metaphysics* (New York: Penguin, 1999), 9.

4. Socrates is quoted in Plato, *Theaetetus* (Oxford: Oxford University Press, 2014), 23.

5. William Wordsworth's poem is from "Auguries of Innocence," in *The Complete Poetry and Prose of William Blake*, ed. David V. Erdman (New York: Anchor, 1982), 493.

6. For Richard Dawkins's musings about the importance of wonder in science, see his book *Unweaving the Rainbow: Science, Delusion and the Appetite for Wonder* (New York: Mariner Books, 2000).

7. For Rene Descartes's thinking about wonder, see his book *The Passions of the Soul* (Cambridge, MA: Hackett Publishing Co., 1989).

8. The adult's memory of a child experience of wonder in the "moors" was in Robinson, *Original Vision*, 32–33.

9. The adult's memory of a childhood encounter with himself as "ancient" is recounted in Robinson, *Original Vision*, 115.

10. Rachel Carson is quoted from her book *The Sense of Wonder* (New York: Harper and Row, 1987), 42–43.

11. For a study on the impact of virtual reality on the sense of wonder, see Alice Chirico et al., "The Potential of Virtual Reality for the Investigation of Awe," *Frontiers of Psychology* 7 (November 2016), https://doi.org/10.3389/fpsyg.2016.01766.

12. This particular Common Core State Standard is coded as CCSS. ELA-LITERACY.RI.3.3 and is available for viewing at the Common Core website, accessed March 29, 2019, http://www.corestandards.org/ELA-Literacy/RI/3/#CCSS.ELA-Literacy.RI.3.10.

13. G. K. Chesterton used Lewis Carroll's classic story of *Alice in Wonderland* to satirize the shortcomings of traditional schooling methods, including testing: "Poor, poor, little Alice! She has not only been caught and made to do lessons: she has been forced to inflict lessons on others. Alice is not only a schoolgirl but a schoolmistress . . . there will be lots and lots of examination papers, with questions like: (1) What do you know of the following: mimsy, gimble, haddocks' eyes, treacle-wells, beautiful soup? (2) Record all the moves in the chess game in 'Through the Looking -Glass', and give diagram. (3) Outline the practical policy of the White Knight for dealing with the social problem of green whiskers. (4) Distinguish between Tweedledum and Tweedledee." This discussion appears in the introduction to Lewis Carroll, *The Annotated Alice: Alice's Adventures in Wonderland and Through the Looking-Glass* (Harmondsworth, UK: Penguin, 1970), xiii.

14. Philip W. Jackson is quoted in Todd B. Rowen, "A Retrieval of Awe: Examining Disruption and Apprehension in Transformative Education," *Philosophy of Education* (2006): 212–20, https://ojs.education.illinois.edu/index.php/pes/article/view/1541/279. For more information about Jackson's dichotomy between the mimetic and transformative styles of learning, see Philip W. Jackson, *The Mimetic and the Transformative: Alternative Outlooks on Teaching* (New York: Teachers College Press, 1986).

15. One seminal research paper that defined awe in part as an inability to assimilate an experience into current mental structures is Dachar Keltner and Jonathan Heidt, "Approaching Awe, a Moral, Spiritual, and Aesthetic Emotion," *Cognition and Emotion* 17, no. 2 (2003): 297–314.

16. The research study on awe and altruism is described in Paul A. Piff, et al., "Awe, the Small Self, and Prosocial Behavior," *Journal of Personality and Social Psychology* 108, no. 6 (2015): 883–99.

17. The study linking experiences of awe to less aggressive behavior is described in Ying Yang et al., "Elicited Awe Decreases Aggression," *Journal of Pacific Rim Psychology* 10 (2016), https://doi.org/10.1017/prp.2016.8.

18. The study connecting awe to parasympathetic activation of the nervous system is described in Alice Chirico et al., "Effectiveness of Immersive Videos in Inducing Awe: An Experimental Study," *Scientific Reports* 7, no. 1 (April 27, 2017), doi:10.1038/s41598-017-01242-0.

19. The research linking awe to lower interleukin-6 levels is described in Jennifer E. Stellar et al., "Positive Affect and Markers of Inflammation: Discrete Positive Emotions Predict Lower Levels of Inflammatory Cytokines," *Emotion* 15, no. 2 (January 19, 2015): 129–33.

20. The study showing more question generation and better memory in a wonder-filled classroom is given in Yannnis Hadzigeorgiou, "Fostering a Sense of Wonder in the Science Classroom," *Research in Science Education* (October 2011), doi 10.1007/s11165-011-9225-6.

21. The study linking awe to more creative thinking is discussed in Alice Chirico et al., "Awe Enhances Creative Thinking: An Experimental Study," *Creativity Research Journal* 30, no. 2 (2018): 123–31.

22. Marisa Musaio is quoted from her article "Rediscovering Wonder in Education: Foundations, Approaching Methods, Feelings," *Estudios Sobre Educación* 23 (2012): 10.

23. The Waldorf English class's project is described in Betty Staley, "Wish, Wonder, Surprise," *Education as an Art* 32, no. 2 (Spring/Summer 1974), https://www.waldorflibrary.org/articles/25-wish-wonder-surprise.

24. Julie Mann is quoted in Paula Spencer, "Feeling Awe May Be the Secret to Health and Happiness," *Parade Magazine*, October, 7, 2016, https://parade.com/513786/paulaspencer/feeling-awe-may-be-the-secret-to-health-and-happiness.

25. Maria Montessori is quoted from a lecture given in Amsterdam in 1950, in Margaret E. Stephenson, "Cosmic Education," *NAMTA Journal* 38, no. 1 (Winter 2013): 199–210. For more information about cosmic education, see Michael Duffy and D'Neil Duffy, *Children of the Universe: Cosmic Education in the Montessori Elementary Classroom* (Santa Rosa, CA: Parent Child Press, 2002).

26. "The Powers of Ten" video was written and directed by designers Charles and Ray Eames, and is available on YouTube, accessed March 29, 2019, https://www.youtube.com/watch?v=0fKBhvDjuy0.

27. Pam Schmidt's classroom of fifty snakes is described in "Spangler Salutes Pam Schmidt," *Steve Spangler Science*, accessed March 29, 2019, https://www.stevespanglerscience.com/lab/experiments/pam-schmidt.

28. Greg Levoy is quoted in his article "7 Ways to Spark Your Sense of Wonder," *Psychology Today*, September 10, 2015, https://www.psychologytoday.com/us/blog/passion/201509/7-ways-spark-your-sense-wonder.

29. Rachel Carson is quoted from her book *The Sense of Wonder: A Celebration of Nature for Parents and Children* (New York: HarperPerennial), 44.

CHAPTER EIGHT. INDIVIDUALITY: RESISTING STANDARDIZATION, DATAFICATION, AND DEPERSONALIZATION IN EDUCATION

1. Albert Einstein is quoted in *Ideas and Opinions*, New York: Broadway Books, 1995, 64.

2. Albert Einstein is quoted in *Ideas and Opinions*, 56.

3. Einstein's teacher at the Luitpold Gymnasium is quoted in Isaacson, *Einstein*, 22.

4. Albert Einstein is quoted in *Ideas and Opinions*, 60.

5. Albert Einstein is quoted his *The World as I See It*, trans. Alan Harris (San Diego, CA: Book Tree, 2011), 9.

6. For scientific evidence that identical twins do not have exactly the same genes, see Adahad O'Connor, "The Claim: Identical Twins Have Identical DNA," *New York Times*, March 11, 2008, https://www.nytimes.com/2008/03/11/health/11real.html.

7. Pablo Casals is quoted from his autobiography *Joys and Sorrows*, assisted by Albert Eugene Kahn (New York: Simon and Schuster, 1970), 295.

8. Doris Lessing is quoted from the introduction to her novel *The Golden Notebook* (New York: Bantam Books, 1973), xv.

9. Ralph Waldo Emerson is quoted from his essay "Self-Reliance," in *The Portable Emerson* (New York: Penguin, 1981), 160.

10. Henry David Thoreau is quoted from his essay "Civil Disobedience," in *Henry David Thoreau: Collected Essays and Poems* (New York: Library of America, 2001), 217.

11. For a history of the factory model of American education, see Joel H. Spring, *Education and the Rise of the Corporate State* (Boston: Beacon Press, 1972).

12. Diane Ravitch is quoted in Elizabeth Weil, "American Schools Are Failing Nonconformist Kids: Here's How," *New Republic*, September 2, 2013, https://newrepublic.com/article/114527/self-regulation-american-schools-are-failing-nonconformist-kids.

13. The statistic on mandatory school-uniform use in public schools is given in Marc Bain, "More U.S. School Kids than Ever Are Wearing Uniforms This Fall," *Quartzy*, September 11, 2018, https://qz.com/quartzy/1382336/school-uniforms-are-rapidly-on-the-rise-at-us-public-schools.

14. Val Gillies is quoted in Weil, "American Schools Are Failing Nonconformist Kids."

15. The fifth grade standard is taken from the English Language Arts section of the Common Core State Standards official website, 28, accessed

June 19, 2019, http://www.corestandards.org/wp-content/uploads/ELA _Standards1.pdf. The high school math standard is taken from the Mathematics section of the Common Core State Standards official website, 71, accessed June 19, 2019, http://www.corestandards.org/wp-content/uploads /Math_Standards1.pdf.

16. Jack Hassard is quoted in his guest post "Common Core Values: Do They Include Authoritarianism?" *Education Week Teacher*, May 8, 2012, https://blogs.edweek.org/teachers/living-in-dialogue/2012/05/common _core_values_do_they_inc.html.

17. Justin Tarte is quoted in Rae Pica, "Debunking the Belief that All Children Are the Same," *Parent Toolkit*, August 15, 2016, https://www .parenttoolkit.com/general/news/general-parenting/debunking-the-belief -that-all-children-are-the-same.

18. The high school student who criticizes the lack of individuality in the schools is quoted in "Do Public Schools Hinder Individuality?" Debate. org, accessed March 29, 2019, https://www.debate.org/opinions/do-public -schools-hinder-individuality.

19. *New York Times* reporter Natasha Singer has followed the trend of high-tech businesses entering the school computer market in a series of articles. See, for example, her article, "How Google Took Over the Classroom," *New York Times*, May 13, 2017, https://www.nytimes.com/2017/05/13 /technology/google-education-chromebooks-schools.html.

20. Anthony Cody is quoted in his article, "Is Robo-Grading Driving the Design of Common Core Tests?" *Education Week Teacher*, November 25, 2013, http://blogs.edweek.org/teachers/living-in-dialogue/2013/11/is_robo -grading_driving_the_de.html.

21. The anonymous teacher who spoke against "robo-grading" is quoted in Paul Horton, "Common Core and the Gettysburg Address," *Education Week Teacher*, November 21, 2013, https://blogs.edweek.org/teachers/living -in-dialogue/2013/11/paul_horton_common_core_and_th.html.

22. Columbus Public Schools third-grade testing results are reported in Shannon Gilchrist, "Robo-Scoring of Essays Does Not Compute, Some Educators Say," *Columbus Dispatch*, February 10, 2018, https://www.dispatch .com/news/20180210/robo-scoring-of-essays-does-not-compute-some -educators-say.

23. The example of the student who looked for shoes online and then saw an ad for shoes pop up in her SparkNotes chapter summary is from Anya Kamenetz, "5 Doubts about Data-Driven Schools," *nprEd*, June 3, 2016, https://www.npr.org/sections/ed/2016/06/03/480029234/5-doubts-about -data-driven-schools.

24. Kamenetz, "5 Doubts about Data-Driven Schools."

25. For information on the use of "predictive analysis" to ascertain a student's likely future in school, see Vasukki Rethinam, "Predictive

Analytics in K-12: Advantages, Limitations & Implementation," *The Journal*, June 12, 2014, https://thejournal.com/articles/2014/06/12/predictive-analytics-in-k-12-advantages-limitations-implementation.aspx.

26. For a critical article on "data walls," see Valerie Strauss, "How 'Data Walls' in Classrooms Humiliate Kids," *Washington Post*, February 14, 2014, https://www.washingtonpost.com/news/answer-sheet/wp/2014/02/14/how-data-walls-in-classrooms-can-humiliate-young-kids.

27. John Hattie's effect sizes for hundreds of teaching strategies can be found in his books *Visible Learning for Teachers: Maximizing Impact on Learning* (New York: Routledge, 2012), and *Visible Learning: A Synthesis of Over 800 Meta-Analyses Relating to Achievement* (New York: Routledge, 2008).

28. Albert Einstein is quoted from *Ideas and Opinions*, 63.

29. The students' rock project is described in L. Rokas, "Every Student from This Elementary School Had to Paint One Rock in His Own Style, and Here's the Result." *Bored Panda*, accessed March 29, 2019, https://www.boredpanda.com/painted-rocks-art-project-only-one-you-sharon-elementary-jessica-moyes.

30. For information about differentiated instruction, see Carol Ann Tomlinson, *The Differentiated Classroom: Responding to the Needs of All Learners*, 2nd ed. (Alexandria, VA: ASCD, 2014). To learn about universal design for learning, see David Rose and Anne Meyer, *Teaching Every Student in the Digital Age: Universal Design for Learning* (Alexandria, VA: ASCD, 2002).

31. The Avalon School experience is related in K. Traphagen and T. Zorich, "Time for Deeper Learning: Lessons from Five High Schools," National Center on Time & Learning, Spring, 2013, https://timeandlearning.org/sites/default/files/resources/deeperlearninges.pdf.

32. Monument Mountain Regional High School's Independent Project is cited in L. Vangelova, "This Is What a Student-Designed School Looks Like," *Mind/Shift–KQED News*, July 14, 2014, http://ww2.kqed.org/mindshift/2014/07/14/this-is-what-a-student-designed-school-looks-like.

33. Debra Sivia Sadofsky was quoted in "Playing for an Education," Sudbury Valley School, accessed March 28, 2019, https://sudburyvalley.org/essays/playing-education. Also see Roza A. Valeevaa and Ramilya Sh. Kasimova, "Alternative Educational System Sudbury Valley as a Model for Reforming School," *Procedia: Social and Behavioral Sciences* 182 (2015): 274–78.

34. For a book that describes Sudbury's ideals and practices, see Daniel Greenberg, *Free at Last: The Sudbury Valley School* (Framingham, MA: Sudbury Valley School Press, 1995).

35. Lawrence Baines's comparison of American schooling with Russia's 1930s nationalization of the schools is from his article "Stalinizing

American Education," *Teachers College Record*, September 16, 2011, http://www.lawrencebaines.com/stalinizing-american-education.html.

36. Baines, "Stalinizing American Education."

37. Wilhelm Frick was quoted in Lisa Pine, *Education in Nazi Germany* (New York: Berg, 2010), 22.

CHAPTER NINE. NEURODIVERSITY: EMPHASIZING THE STRENGTHS OF KIDS WITH SPECIAL NEEDS

1. Albert Einstein Jr. is quoted in Victor Goertzel and Mildred G. Goertzel, *Cradles of Eminence*, Tucson, Arizona: Gifted Psychology Press, 2004, 248.

2. Thomas Edison is quoted in Goertzel and Goertzel, *Cradles of Eminence*, 248.

3. Marcel Proust's teachers' evaluation of his writing is given in Goertzel and Goertzel, *Cradles of Eminence*, 247.

4. Edvard Grieg is quoted in Goertzel and Goertzel, *Cradles of Eminence*, 243.

5. Sigrid Unset is quoted in Goertzel and Goertzel, *Cradles of Eminence*, 243.

6. Figures on the number of special education students in the United States are from, "The Condition of Education: Children and Youth with Disabilities," National Center for Education Statistics, April 2018, https://nces.ed.gov/programs/coe/indicator_cgg.asp.

7. For information about Henry Goddard and the eugenics movement, see Gould, *Mismeasure of Man*, and James W. Trent, *Inventing the Feeble Mind: A History of Mental Retardation in the United States* (Berkeley: University of California Press, 1995). For information about the work of Samuel Orton and Alfred Strauss, see Daniel P. Hallahan and Cecil D. Mercer, "Learning Disabilities: Historical Perspectives" (paper, Learning Disabilities Summit, "Building a Foundation for the Future," Washington, DC, August 27–28, 2001), https://doi.org/10.2307/1511118. For Samuel Kirk's account of "learning disabilities," see his "Learning Disabilities: A Historical Note," *Academic Therapy* 17, no. 1 (September 1981): 7.

8. The letter by eight New York principals to parents about standardized testing for their kids with special needs is reprinted in Valerie Strauss, "N. Y. School Principals Write Letter of Concern about Common Core Tests," *Washington Post*, November 21, 2013, https://www.washingtonpost.com/news/answer-sheet/wp/2013/11/21/n-y-school-principals-write-letter-of-concern-about-common-core-tests.

9. Katharine Beals is quoted in her article, "The Common Core Is Tough on Kids with Special Needs," *Atlantic*, February 21, 2014, https://www.theatlantic.com/education/archive/2014/02/the-common-core-is-tough-on-kids-with-special-needs/283973.

10. Harvey Blume is quoted in "Neurodiversity: On the Neurological Underpinnings of Geekdom," *Atlantic*, September 1998, https://www.the atlantic.com/magazine/archive/1998/09/neurodiversity/305909. An earlier use of the term in an academic setting was by autism rights activist Judy Blume, "Odd People In: The Birth of Community Amongst People on the Autistic Spectrum" (undergraduate thesis, University of Technology, Sydney, Australia, 1998). The thesis is available on Kindle as *Neurodiversity: The Birth of an Idea*, https://www.amazon.com/NeuroDiversity-Birth -Idea-Judy-Singer-ebook/dp/B01HY0QTEE. The conceptual beginnings of the neurodiversity movement within the autism rights community have been traced to a speech given by autism rights activist Jim Sinclair at the 1993 International Conference on Autism in Toronto. It was reprinted in the Autism Network International newsletter, *Our Voice* 1, no. 3 (1993), https://www.autreat.com/dont_mourn.html.

11. For a look at how the concept of neurodiversity can positively transform special education, see Thomas Armstrong, "Neurodiversity: The Future of Special Education?" *Educational Leadership* 74, no. 7 (April 2017): 10–16.

12. For information about the link between autism, detecting details, and systemizing capabilities, see Simon Baron-Cohen et al., "Talent in Autism: Hyper-Systemizing, Hyper-Attention to Detail, and Sensory Hypersensitivity," *Philosophical Transactions of the Royal Society* 364, no. 1522 (2009): 1377–83. For information on the higher IQ scores of people with autism who take the Raven's Progressive Matrices, see Laurent Mottron, "The Power of Autism," *Nature* 479 (November 2, 2011): 33–35.

13. For more on the abilities of dyslexics with three-dimensional spatial abilities, see Catya von Károlyi et al., "Dyslexia Linked to Talent: Global Visual-Spatial Ability," *Brain and Language* 85, no. 3 (June 2003): 426–31. For research on the ability of dyslexics to perceive images with low spatial frequencies, see Matthew H. Schneps et al., "History of Reading Struggles Linked to Enhanced Learning in Low Spatial Frequency Scenes," *PloS One* 7, no. 1 (2012), https://journals.plos.org/plosone/article?id=10.1371/journal .pone.0035724; and Geiger G. Cattaneo et al., "Wide and Diffuse Perceptual Modes Characterize Dyslexics in Vision and Audition," *Perception* 37, no. 11 (2008): 1745–64. For information about the link between dyslexia and entrepreneurship, see Judy Logan, "Dyslexic Entrepreneurs: The Incidence, Their Coping Strategies, and Their Business Skills," *Dyslexia* 15, no. 4 (November 2009): 328–46.

14. For information on the creative behaviors of people with ADHD, see Holly A. White and Priti Shah, "Creative Style and Achievement in Adults with Attention-Deficit/Hyperactivity Disorder," *Personality and Individual Differences* 50, no. 5 (April 2011): 673–77. For the link between novelty-seeking and ADHD, see Deborah E. Lynn et al., "Temperament and

Character Profiles and the Dopamine D4 Receptor Gene in ADHD," *American Journal of Psychiatry* 162 (2005): 906–14.

15. For information about the social and emotional expressiveness of individuals with intellectual disabilities such as Down syndrome, see Elizabeth Dyckens, "Toward a Positive Psychology of Mental Retardation," *American Journal of Orthopsychiatry* 76, no. 2 (April 2006): 185–93. For more about the link between Williams syndrome and musical capability, see Howard M. Lenhoff et al., "Williams Syndrome and the Brain," *Scientific American* 277, no. 6 (December 1997): 68–73.

16. For more information about the link between bipolar disorder and artistic achievement, see Kay Redfield Jamison, *Touched with Fire: Manic-Depressive Illness and the Artistic Temperament* (New York: Free Press, 1996). For links between bipolar disorder and creativity, see Diana I. Simeonova et al., "Creativity in Familial Bipolar Disorder," *Journal of Psychiatric Research* 39, no. 6 (November 2005): 623–31.

17. For information about the enhanced visual imagery capabilities of deaf individuals, see Karen Emmorey, Stephen M. Kosslyn, and Ursula Bellugi, "Visual Imagery and Visual-Spatial Language: Enhanced Imagery Abilities in Deaf and Hearing ASL Signers," *Cognition* 46, no. 2 (February, 1993): 139–81.

18. Blind individuals with above-normal auditory abilities are discussed in Patrice Voss et al., "Early- and Late-Onset Blind Individuals Show Supra-Normal Auditory Abilities in Far-Space," *Current Biology* 14, no. 19 (October 2004): 1734–38.

19. For information on ADHD conferring advantages in a hunting-and-gathering society, see Henry Harpending and Gregory Cochran, "In Our Genes," *Proceedings of the National Academy of Science* 99, no. 1 (January 8, 2002): 10–12.

20. Temple Grandin is quoted in Andrew Solomon, "The Autism Rights Movement," *New York Magazine*, May 25, 2008, http://nymag.com/news /features/47225.

21. The evolutionary advantages of bipolar disorder are discussed in Kareen K. Akiskala and Hagop S. Akiskal, "The Theoretical Underpinnings of Affective Temperaments: Implications for Evolutionary Foundations of Bipolar Disorder and Human Nature," *Journal of Affective Disorders* 85, no. 1–2 (March 2005): 231–39.

22. For information about the evolutionary advantages of dyslexia, see K. Ehardt, "Dyslexia, Not Disorder," *Dyslexia* 15, no. 4 (November 2009): 363–66.

23. For an explanatory model of ADHD using a machine metaphor, see Matthew R. Galvin, *Otto Learns about His Medicine* (Washington, DC: Magination Press, 2001). For a children's book on the ability of the brain to change in response to experience (neuroplasticity), see JoAnn Deak, *Your*

Fantastic Elastic Brain (San Francisco: Little Pickle Press, 2010). The metaphor of the brain as a rain forest has been discussed in my book, *The Myth of the ADHD Child: 101 Ways to Improve Your Child's Behavior and Attention Span without Drugs, Labels, or Coercion* (New York: TarcherPerigee, 2017), and originally comes from the work of Nobel Prize–winning biologist Gerald Edelman. See, for example, his book *Neural Darwinism: The Theory of Neuronal Group Selection* (New York: Basic Books, 1987).

24. For a description of the concept of niche construction in evolutionary biology, see John F. Odling-Smee, Kevin N. Laland, and Marcus W. Feldman. *Niche Construction: The Neglected Process in Evolution* (Princeton, NJ: Princeton University Press, 2013).

25. For more information on the process of applying niche construction to special education, see Thomas Armstrong, *Neurodiversity in the Classroom: Strength-Based Strategies for Helping Students with Special Needs Succeed in School and Life* (Alexandria, VA: ASCD, 2012).

26. Patrick Waters is quoted from his article "Encouraging Neurodiversity in Your Makerspace or Classroom," *Edutopia*, December 24, 2015, https://www.edutopia.org/blog/encouraging-neurodiversity-in-makerspace -classroom-patrick-waters.

27. Stevenson School's position on equity is quoted in Eric Herro and Molly Bozzo, "Neurodiversity and Differentiation," *Independent Teacher* (National Association of Independent Schools), Spring 2017, https://www .nais.org/magazine/independent-teacher/spring-2017/neurodiversity-and -differentiation.

28. William Henderson is quoted in his article, "Champions of Inclusion: Making the Extraordinary Ordinary," *International Journal of Whole Schooling* 3, no. 1 (2006): 7. For more information about the William W. Henderson Inclusion Elementary School, see William Henderson, *The Blind Advantage: How Going Blind Made Me a Stronger Principal and How Including Children with Disabilities Made Our School Better for Everyone* (Cambridge, MA: Harvard Education Press, 2011).

29. For information about the bright job prospects available in the IT field for people on the autism spectrum, see Shirley S. Wang, "How Autism Can Help Land You a Job," *Wall Street Journal*, March 27, 2014, https:// www.wsj.com/articles/companies-find-autism-can-be-a-job-skill-13959 63209.

30. For more information about the gifts of dyslexia in the workplace, see Brock Eide and Fernette Eide, *The Dyslexic Advantage: Unlocking the Hidden Potential of the Dyslexic Brain* (New York: Plume, 2012).

31. For more about the career possibilities of people diagnosed with ADHD, see Kathleen Nadeau, *The ADHD Guide to Career Success*, 2nd ed. (New York: Routledge, 2015).

CHAPTER TEN. COMPASSION: EDUCATING THE HEART IN THE "SELFIE" GENERATION

1. Albert Einstein is quoted in Walter Sullivan, "The Einstein Papers: A Man of Many Parts," *New York Times*, March 29, 1972, 20, https://www.nytimes.com/1972/03/29/archives/the-einstein-papers-a-man-of-many-parts-the-einstein-papers-man-of.html.

2. The story of Ryan Hreljac's well project is reported in Vicki Zakrzewski, "Put the Awe Back in 'Awesome': Helping Students Develop Purpose," *Edutopia*, June 10, 2013, https://www.edutopia.org/blog/awe-helping-students-develop-purpose-vicki-zakrzewski. Ryan tells his own story at https://www.ryanswell.ca/about-ryans-well/ryans-story.

3. The Dalai Lama is quoted from "Education Matters Says His Holiness the Dalai Lama in Sydney," June 13, 2013, https://www.dalailama.com/news/2013/education-matters-says-his-holiness-the-dalai-lama-in-sydney.

4. The Dalai Lama is quoted from his book (with Howard Cutler) *The Art of Happiness, 10th Anniversary Edition: A Handbook for Living* (New York: Riverside, 2009), 50–51.

5. Paul Bloom is quoted in his article, "The Moral Life of Babies," *New York Times*, May 5, 2010, https://www.nytimes.com/2010/05/09/magazine/09babies-t.html.

6. The altruism of chimpanzees is discussed in Martin Schmelz et al., "Chimpanzees Return Favors at a Personal Cost," *Proceedings of the National Academy of Sciences* 114, no. 28 (July 11, 2017): 7462–67.

7. The Harvard Graduate School of Education's survey of students' perceptions of parents is in the executive summary of their report, "The Children We Mean to Raise: The Real Messages Adults Are Sending about Values," Making Caring Common Project, July 2014, https://static1.squarespace.com/static/5b7c56e255b02c683659fe43/t/5bae774424a694b5feb2b05f/1538160453604/report-children-raise.pdf.

8. The statistics cited by *Highlights* magazine were from "Highlights—The State of the Kid—2017," accessed March 28, 2019, https://www.highlightskids.com/stateofthekid2017.

9. The percentage of parents who want their kids to be kind is taken from a University of Wisconsin press release, Marianne Spoon, "Sesame Street Brings UW Center's Kindness Curriculum to Kids," January 19, 2017, https://news.wisc.edu/sesame-street-brings-uw-centers-kindness-curriculum-to-kids.

10. The two studies on narcissism in college students are described in Jean M. Twenge and Joshua D. Foster, "Birth Cohort Increases in Narcissistic Personality Traits among American College Students, 1982–2009," *Social Psychological and Personality Science* 1, no. 1 (January 1, 2010): 99–106.

11. The study on "empathic concern" and "perspective taking" among college students is in Sara H. Konrath, Edward H. O'Brien, and Courtney Hsing, "Changes in Dispositional Empathy in American College Students over Time: A Meta-Analysis," *Personality and Social Psychology Review* 15, no. 2 (May, 2011): 180–98.

12. Figures on bullying in schools were taken from "Youth Risk Behavior Survey—Data Summary and Trends Report—2007–2017," Centers for Disease Control and Prevention, accessed March 28, 2019, https://www.cdc.gov/healthyyouth/data/yrbs/pdf/trendsreport.pdf.

13. Figures on students' viewing of cyberbullying are from Amanda Lenhard et al., "Teens, Kindness, and Cruelty on Social Network Sites," Pew Research Center, November 9, 2011, http://www.pewinternet.org/2011/11/09/teens-kindness-and-cruelty-on-social-network-sites.

14. Susan Engel and Marlene Sandstrom are quoted from their article "There's Only One Way to Stop a Bully," *New York Times*, July 22, 2010, https://www.nytimes.com/2010/07/23/opinion/23engel.html.

15. The study comparing nine- to eleven-year-old kids who either performed acts of kindness or mapped places they had visited is from Kristin S. Layous et al., "Kindness Counts: Prompting Prosocial Behavior in Preadolescents Boosts Peer Acceptance and Well-Being," *PloS One* 7, no. 12 (December 26, 2012), https://doi.org/10.1371/journal.pone.0051380.

16. The study of at-risk adolescents and CBCT is in Sheethal D. Reddy et al., "Cognitive-Based Compassion Training: A Promising Prevention Strategy for At-Risk Adolescents," *Journal of Child and Family Studies* 22, no. 2 (February, 2013): 219–30.

17. The researchers' statement on the benefits of acts of kindness is from Shelly L. Kerr, Analise O'Donovan, and Chris Pepping, "Can Gratitude and Kindness Interventions Enhance Well-Being in a Clinical Sample?" *Journal of Happiness Studies* 16, no. 1 (March 2015): 20.

18. For the study on the link between literary fiction and empathy, see David Comer Kidd and Emanuele Castano, "Reading Literary Fiction Improves Theory of Mind," *Science* 342, no. 6156 (October 18, 2013): 377–89. See also a related article, Pam Belluck, "For Better Social Skills, Researchers Recommend a Little Chekhov," *New York Times*, October 3, 2013, https://well.blogs.nytimes.com/2013/10/03/i-know-how-youre-feeling-i-read-chekhov.

19. To read about noncognitive skills and their impact on success in school and life, see Leslie Morrison Gutman and Ingrid Schoon, "The Impact of Non-Cognitive Skills on Outcomes for Young People," London: Institute of Education, November 21, 2013, https://pdfs.semanticscholar.org/f4a5/2db3001fb6fb22eef5dc20267b5b807fd8ff.pdf.

20. The Compassionate Schools Project is quoted from its website, accessed March 28, 2019, https://www.compassionschools.org/program.

21. Lisa Flook and Laura Pinger are quoted from their article, "Lessons from Creating a Kindness Curriculum," Center for Healthy Minds, University of Wisconsin, Madison, accessed March 28, 2019, https://center healthyminds.org/join-the-movement/lessons-from-creating-a-kindness -curriculum.

22. Lisa Flook is quoted in Marianne Spoon, "Sesame Street Brings UW Center's Kindness Curriculum to Kids," January 19, 2017, University of Wisconsin, Madison press release, https://news.wisc.edu/sesame-street-brings -uw-centers-kindness-curriculum-to-kids.

23. The study of the benefits of a preschool kindness curriculum is reported in Lisa Flook et al., "Promoting Prosocial Behavior and Self-Regulatory Skills in Preschool Children through a Mindfulness-Based Kindness Curriculum," *Developmental Psychology* 51, no. 1 (January 2015): 44–51.

24. Frank Wagner Elementary School's observance of Kindness Week is described in Kelly Sullivan, "Kindness Rocks at Frank Wagner Elementary," *Monroe Monitor*, February 20, 2018, https://www.monroe.wednet .edu/fwe/about/wildcat-news/news-post/~post/kindness-rocks-at-frank -wagner-elementary-20180220.

25. Reed Intermediate School's "kindness carts" are described in Eliza Hallabeck, "Reed Sixth Graders Run 'Kindness Carts,'" *Newtown Bee*, June 22, 2018, https://www.newtownbee.com/reed-sixth-graders-run-kindness -carts.

26. Erin Dobson is quoted in John Monfredo, "The Buddy Bench: A Symbol of Kindness in Our Schools," *Go Local Worcester*, May 6, 2018, http://www.golocalworcester.com/news/monfredo-the-buddy-bench-a -symbol-of-kindness-in-our-schools.

27. Kristin Neff is quoted from her article "Why Self-Compassion Trumps Self-Esteem," *Greater Good Magazine*, May 27, 2011, https:// greatergood.berkeley.edu/article/item/try_selfcompassion.

28. Neff, "Why Self-Compassion Trumps Self-Esteem."

29. Rachel Simmons's self-compassion activities for kindergartners and first graders are described in her article "The Promise of Self-Compassion for Stressed-Out Teens," *New York Times*, February 20, 2018, https://www .nytimes.com/2018/02/20/well/family/self-compassion-stressed-out-teens .html.

30. Xavier Zamarron is quoted in Ki Sung, "Learning Mindfulness Centered on Kindness to Oneself and Others," *KQED News Mind/Shift*, June 18, 2018, https://www.kqed.org/mindshift/51308/learning-mindfulness -centered-on-kindness-to-oneself-and-others.

31. The meta-analysis on the positive impact of self-compassion on adolescent distress is described in Imogen C. Marsh, Stella W. Y. Chan, and Angus MacBeth, "Self-Compassion and Psychological Distress in Adolescents—A Meta-Analysis," *Mindfulness* 9, no. 2 (August 2018): 1011–27.

32. The study on self-compassion overriding the negative impact of low-esteem is in Sarah L. Marshall et al., "Self-Compassion Protects Against the Negative Effects of Low Self-Esteem: A Longitudinal Study in a Large Adolescent Sample," *Personality and Individual Differences* 74 (February 2015): 116–21.

33. The positive impact of self-compassion on the immune system is described in Juliana G. Breines et al., "Self-Compassion as a Predictor of Interleukin-6 Response to Acute Psychosocial Stress," *Brain, Behavior, and Immunity* 37 (March 2014): 109–14.

34. Evie Blad is quoted in her article, "Adults Send Children Mixed Messages about Kindness. Here's Why That Matters to Schools," *Education Week*, November 21, 2017, http://blogs.edweek.org/edweek/rulesforengagement/2017/11/adults_send_children_mixed_messages_about_kindness_heres_why_that_matters_to_schools.html.

35. For research on the contagion of acts for the social good, see James H. Fowler and Nicholas A. Christakis, "Cooperative Behavior Cascades in Human Social Networks," *Proceedings of the National Academy of Sciences* 107, no. 12 (March 23, 2010): 5334–38.

36. The little boy's comment was cited in Erin Canty, "When Kindness Is in the Curriculum," *Good Education*, September 1, 2017, https://education.good.is/articles/kindness-in-the-curriculum.

CHAPTER ELEVEN. CARE FOR NATURE: CULTIVATING A REVERENCE FOR ALL LIVING THINGS

1. Albert Einstein is quoted in *The Ultimate Quotable Einstein*, 32.

2. Tagore's short story "The Parrot's Training" is available online, accessed March 28, 2019, https://www.fortlewis.edu/Portals/137/tagore%20parrot%20education.pdf.

3. Tagore is quoted in *A Tagore Reader* (New York: Macmillan, 1961), 214.

4. Tagore is quoted in "My School" (a lecture delivered in America) in R. Tagore, *Personality* (London: Macmillan & Co., 1917), http://www.swaraj.org/shikshantar/tagore_myschool.html.

5. Tagore is quoted in "My School."

6. The decline by half of animals on Earth is reported in Damian Carrington, "What Is Biodiversity and Why Does It Matter to Us?" *Guardian*, March 12, 2018, https://www.theguardian.com/news/2018/mar/12/what-is-biodiversity-and-why-does-it-matter-to-us.

7. The loss of biodiversity in the last forty years is cited in Megan Ray Nichols, "What Is Biodiversity Loss and Why Is It a Problem?" *Interesting Engineering*, June 4, 2018, https://interestingengineering.com/what-is-biodiversity-loss-and-why-is-it-a-problem.

8. The $125 trillion figure in free services provided by nature is cited by the World Wildlife Federation, in *Living Planet Report—2018: Aiming Higher,* eds. M. Grooten and R. E. A. Almond (Gland, Switzerland: World Wildlife Federation, 2018), https://wwf.panda.org/knowledge_hub/all_publications/living_planet_report_2018.

9. For more about the potential "sixth extinction," see Elizabeth Kolbert, *The Sixth Extinction: An Unnatural History* (New York: Picador, 2015).

10. The U.S. consumption rate is cited in WWF, *Living Planet Report.*

11. The UN Report citing 2040 as a make-or-break year for climate change is discussed in Coral Davenport, "Major Climate Report Describes a Strong Risk of Crisis as Early as 2040," *New York Times,* October 7, 2018, https://www.nytimes.com/2018/10/07/climate/ipcc-climate-report-2040.html.

12. For E. O. Wilson's views on "biophilia" see his book *Biophilia* (Cambridge, MA: Harvard University Press, 1984).

13. For more information about "nature-deficit disorder," see Richard Louv's book *Last Child in the Woods: Saving Our Children from Nature-Deficit Disorder* (Chapel Hill, NC: Algonquin Books, 2008).

14. The figures on time spent outdoors and with electronic media are given in "Children in Nature: Improving Health by Reconnecting Youth with the Outdoors," National Recreation and Park Association, accessed March 28, 2019, https://www.nrpa.org/uploadedFiles/nrpa.org/Advocacy/Children-in-Nature.pdf.

15. The fifth grader who prefers the indoors is quoted in Richard Louv, "Leave No Child Inside," *Orion Magazine,* accessed March 28, 2019, https://orionmagazine.org/article/leave-no-child-inside.

16. Information about the rise in childhood obesity is from Ashley Cockrell Skinner et al., "Prevalence of Obesity and Severe Obesity in US Children, 1999–2016," *Pediatrics* 141, no. 3 (March 2018), http://pediatrics.aappublications.org/content/141/3/e20173459.

17. For research on the link between less time spent in "green" environments and childhood obesity, see Inga Petraviciene et al., "Impact of the Social and Natural Environment on Preschool-Age Children Weight," *International Journal of Environmental Research and Public Health* 15, no. 3 (March 2018): 449.

18. The number of children and adolescents diagnosed with ADHD in 2016 is from "Data and Statistics About ADHD," Centers for Disease Control and Prevention, September 21, 2018, https://www.cdc.gov/ncbddd/adhd/data.html.

19. For research on the decrease in symptoms of ADHD in green environments, see Frances E. Kuo and Andrea Faber Taylor, "A Potential Natural Treatment for Attention-Deficit/Hyperactivity Disorder: Evidence

from a National Study," *American Journal of Public Health* 94, no. 9 (September 2004): 1580–86.

20. Statistics on the epidemic of mood disorders among adolescents are given in "Any Mood Disorder," National Institute of Mental Health, accessed March 28, 2019, https://www.nimh.nih.gov/health/statistics/any-mood-disorder.shtml#part_155961. Research on the positive effects of nature on adolescent emotional well-being is discussed in Li Dongying et al., "Moving Beyond the Neighborhood: Daily Exposure to Nature and Adolescents' Mood," *Landscape and Urban Planning* 172 (May 2018): 33–43.

21. The list of benefits that accrue to children who spent time in nature is provided in Collin O'Mara, "Kids Do Not Spend Nearly Enough Time Outside: Here's How (and Why) to Change That," *Washington Post*, May 29, 2018, https://www.washingtonpost.com/news/parenting/wp/2018/05/30/kids-dont-spend-nearly-enough-time-outside-heres-how-and-why-to-change-that. See also Sylvia Collado and Henk Staats, "Contact with Nature and Children's Restorative Experiences: An Eye to the Future," *Frontiers in Psychology* 7 (2016): 1885.

22. The practice of cutting recess to make more time for language arts and math is cited in Catherine Ramstetter, Robert Murray, and Andrew S. Garner. "The Crucial Role of Recess in School," *Journal of School Health* 80 (2010): 517–26.

23. The decline in recess and figures for daily recess are given in Catherine Ramstetter and Robert Murray, "Time to Play: Recognizing the Benefits of Recess," *American Educator*, Spring 2017, https://www.aft.org/sites/default/files/ae_spring2017ramstetter_and_murray.pdf.

24. Research findings on student engagement and attention in the classroom after time spent outdoors are provided in Erin Largo-Wight et al., "Nature Contact at School: The Impact of an Outdoor Classroom on Children's Well-Being," *International Journal of Environmental Health Research* 28, no. 6 (December 2018): 653–66, and Ming Kuo, Matthew H. E. M. Browning, and Milbert L. Penner, "Do Lessons in Nature Boost Subsequent Classroom Engagement? Refueling Students in Flight," *Frontiers in Psychology* 4, no. 8 (January 2018): 2253.

25. For information on the overly academic nature of environmental education in schools, see Michelle Nijhuis, "Green Failure: What's Wrong with Environmental Education?" *Yale Environment 360*, May 26, 2011, https://e360.yale.edu/features/green_failure_whats_wrong_with_environmental_education. See also Charles Saylan and Daniel Blumstein, *The Failure of Environmental Education (And How We Can Fix It)* (Berkeley: University of California Press, 2011).

26. Fiddlehead Forest Preschool is described in Lillian Mongeau, "Preschool without Walls," *New York Times*, December 29, 2015, https://www.nytimes.com/2015/12/31/fashion/outdoor-preschool-in-nature.html.

27. Kit Harrington is quoted in Mongeau, "Preschool without Walls."

28. Brad Rumble is quoted in Louis Sahagun, "Just Attracting, Naturally," *Los Angeles Times*, April 16, 2012, http://articles.latimes.com/2012/apr/16/local/la-me-bird-school-20120416.

29. Oak Forest Elementary School's nature projects are described in Susan Brenna, "Take a Hike: How to Make Being Outdoors In," *Edutopia*, March 1, 2006, https://www.edutopia.org/outdoor-education-nature-deficit-disorder.

30. Antonella Bassini is quoted in Andy Newman, "School's Out for the Animals, Too," *New York Times*, June 24, 2016, https://www.nytimes.com/2016/06/26/nyregion/summer-is-here-and-schools-out-for-the-animals-too.html.

31. The wetlands laboratory project at Christ Church Episcopal School is described in Andrew Moore, "Science Teacher Transforms Detention Pond Into 'Wetlands Laboratory' for Environmental Education," *Greenville Journal*, October 3, 2018, https://greenvillejournal.com/2018/10/03/science-teacher-transforms-detention-pond-into-wetlands-laboratory-for-environmental-education.

32. The aquaponics program in Leavenworth, Kansas, is described in Mark Rountree, "Educator Develops Aquaponics Program in His Classroom," *Leavenworth Times*, February 14, 2019, https://www.leavenworthtimes.com/news/20190214/educator-develops-aquaponics-program-in-his-classroom.

33. The Seattle and Maine high school projects are described in Evantheia Schibsted, "Kids Count: Young Citizen Scientists Learn Environmental Activism," *Edutopia*, October 2, 2007, https://www.edutopia.org/service-learning-citizen-science.

34. Jane Goodall is quoted from her keynote address at the September 21, 2013, Humane Education Conference, "Educating for a Just, Peaceful and Sustainable Future," hosted by New York University's Animal Studies Initiative in the NYU Global Center for Academic and Spiritual Life, accessed March 28, 2019, https://www.youtube.com/watch?v=bd9m-wrll5c.

35. Roots & Shoots projects are described at Jane Goodall's Roots & Shoots website, accessed March 28, 2019, https://rootsandshoots.org/projects/search.

36. Research on the connection between environmental attitudes and a feeling of being part of nature is given in Wesley P. Schultz et al., "Implicit Connections with Nature," *Journal of Environmental Psychology* 24, no. 1 (March 2004): 31–42.

37. The study that linked schools close to urban green sites with empathy and concern for other life forms is from M. Giusti, S. Barthel, and L. Marcus, "Nature Routines and Affinity with the Biosphere," *Children, Youth and Environments* 24, no. 3 (2014): 16–42.

38. The study emphasizing the connection between self-choice explorations of nature, environmental literacy, and ecological citizenship is described in Stanley T. Asah et al., "Mechanisms of Children's Exposure to Nature: Predicting Adulthood Environmental Citizenship and Commitment to Nature-Based Activities," *Environment and Behavior* 50 (July 2017), http://dx.doi.org/10.1177/0013916517718021.

39. The study concluding that nature education needs to be open-ended and immersive is described in Randy White and Vicki L. Stoeklin, "Nurturing Children's Biophilia: Developmentally Appropriate Environmental Education for Young Children," White Hutchinson Leisure and Learning Group, November 9, 2008, https://www.whitehutchinson.com/children/articles/nurturing.shtml.

40. Mary Oliver is quoted from her book *Upstream: Selected Essays* (New York: Penguin, 2016).

CHAPTER TWELVE. TOLERANCE: NURTURING A DEEP RESPECT FOR HUMAN DIFFERENCES

1. Albert Einstein is quoted in *The Ultimate Quotable Einstein*, 297.

2. Martin Luther King Jr. is quoted from his article "The Purpose of Education," first published in *Maroon Tiger*, January–February, 1947, 10, King Institute, accessed May 31, 2019, https://kinginstitute.stanford.edu/king-papers/documents/purpose-education.

3. Martin Luther King, Jr., quoted in "Purpose of Education."

4. Statistics on hate groups are provided in "Hate Groups Reach Record High," Southern Poverty Law Center, February 19, 2019, https://www.splcenter.org/news/2019/02/19/hate-groups-reach-record-high.

5. Gun-related deaths are reported in Kate Smith, "Gun Death Statistics: CDC Study Says Gun Deaths Are on the Rise After Years of Decline," CBS News, November 9, 2018, https://www.cbsnews.com/news/gun-death-statistics-cdc-study-says-gun-deaths-are-on-the-rise-after-years-of-decline.

6. Figures on numbers of children and teens shot every day are from "Key Gun Violence Statistics," Brady Campaign to End Gun Violence, accessed March 28, 2019, http://www.bradycampaign.org/key-gun-violence-statistics.

7. Figures on detained immigrant children are from Shefali Luthra and Marisa Taylor, "1 in 5 Immigrant Children Detained during 'Zero Tolerance' Border Policy Are Under 13," *Washington Post*, June 20, 2018, https://www.washingtonpost.com/national/health-science/1-in-5-immigrant-children-detained-during-zero-tolerance-border-policy-are-under-13/2018/06/20/c98e0d42-74b3-11e8-bda1-18e53a448a14_story.html.

8. Figures on bullied and threatened gay youth are from Rebecca Damante, "Can Education Reduce Prejudice against LGBT People?" *Century*

Foundation, June 16, 2016, https://tcf.org/content/commentary/can-edu cation-reduce-prejudice-lgbt-people.

9. Figures on students who've seen hate-related graffiti in their schools are from Francisco Vara-Orta, "Hate in Schools," *Education Week*, August 6, 2018, https://www.edweek.org/ew/projects/hate-in-schools.html.

10. Robert Trestan is quoted in Eli Sherman, "Hate 'Mainstream' in Massachusetts Schools," *Patriot Ledger*, December 6, 2018, https://www .patriotledger.com/news/20181204/hate-mainstream-in-massachusetts -schools.

11. For a discussion of the evolutionary origins of prejudice, see Steven L. Neuberg and Catherine A. Cottrell, "Evolutionary Basis of Prejudice," in *Evolution and Social Psychology*, eds. Mark Schaller, Jeffrey Simpson, and Douglas T. Kenrick (New York: Psychology Press, 2006), 162–88.

12. Research on prejudice in infants is described in Neha Mahajan and Karen Wynn, "Origins of 'Us' versus 'Them:' Prelinguistic Infants Prefer Similar Others," *Cognition* 124, no. 2 (August 2012): 227–33.

13. For information about the neuroscience of prejudice, see David M. Amodio, "The Neuroscience of Prejudice and Stereotyping," *Nature Reviews Neuroscience* 15, no. 10 (October 2014): 670–82.

14. The child asking about what name she is supposed to hate is from Gordon Allport, *The Nature of Prejudice: 25th Anniversary Edition* (New York: Basic Books, 1979), 307.

15. Mahzarin Banaji is quoted in James H. Burnett III, "Racism Learned," *Boston Globe*, June 10, 2012, https://www.bostonglobe.com/business/2012 /06/09/harvard-researcher-says-children-learn-racism-quickly/gWuN1Z G3M40WihER2kAfdK/story.html.

16. Research on the divergence of implicit and explicit racism at age ten is described in Andrew Scott Baron and Mahzarin R. Banaji, "The Development of Implicit Attitudes: Evidence of Race Evaluations from Ages 6 and 10 and Adulthood," *Psychological Science* 17, no. 1 (2006): 53–58. The automatization of racist attitudes around the age of twelve or thirteen is given in Juliane Degner and Dick Wentera, "Automatic Prejudice in Childhood and Early Adolescence," *Journal of Personality and Social Psychology* 98, no. 3 (2010): 356–74.

17. The disproportionate number of black students suspended or expelled from school is reported in Tom Loveless, "2017 Brown Center Report on American Education: Race and School Suspensions," Brookings Institution, March 22, 2017, https://www.brookings.edu/research/2017 -brown-center-report-part-iii-race-and-school-suspensions. See also Laura R. McNeal, "Managing Our Blind Spot: The Role of Bias in the School-to-Prison Pipeline," *Arizona State Law Journal* 48, no. 2 (2016): 285–311.

18. Statistics on the disproportionate number of black prisoners in state prisons are given in Ashley Nellis, "The Color of Justice: Racial and Ethnic

Disparity in State Prisons," *Sentencing Project*, June 14, 2016, http://www
.sentencingproject.org/publications/color-of-justice-racial-and-ethnic
-disparity-in-state-prisons.

19. Information about the lack of civil rights protections for LGBTQ
students and limited-English proficiency students in voucher programs is
from Kevin G. Welner and Preston C. Green, "Private School Vouchers:
Legal Challenges and Civil Rights Protections," *Civil Rights Project*, March
5, 2018, https://www.civilrightsproject.ucla.edu/research/k-12-education
/integration-and-diversity/private-school-vouchers-legal-challenges-and
-civil-rights-protections.

20. The statistic on how only 8 percent of high school seniors knew that
slavery was the central cause of the Civil War is from "Teaching Hard
History: American Slavery," Southern Poverty Law Center, 2018, https://
www.splcenter.org/sites/default/files/tt_hard_history_american_slavery.pdf.

21. The example of a classroom simulation where students attempted to
reproduce life in a slave ship is taken from Ingrid Drake, "Classroom Simulations: Proceed With Caution," *Teaching Tolerance* 33 (Spring 2008),
https://www.tolerance.org/magazine/spring-2008/classroom-simulations
-proceed-with-caution.

22. For Mica Pollock's thoughts about being "colormute," see her book
Colormute: Race Talk Dilemmas in an American School (Princeton, NJ:
Princeton University Press, 2005).

23. The high school teacher who used democratic deliberation in his
classroom is quoted in Paula McAvoy and Diana Hess, "Classroom Deliberation in an Era of Political Polarization," *Curriculum Inquiry* 43, no. 1
(2013): 15.

24. Steve Caudill's approaches for creating civil discourse in the classroom are given in Catherine Gewertz, "Students Learn to Put the 'Civil' in
Civil Discourse," *Education Week*, November 27, 2018, https://www.edweek
.org/ew/articles/2018/11/28/students-learn-to-put-the-civil-in.html.

25. The study using diversity education to reduce antiblack bias is
described in Laurie A. Rudman, Richard D. Ashmore, and Melvin L. Gary,
"Unlearning Automatic Biases: The Malleability of Implicit Prejudice and
Stereotypes," *Journal of Personality and Social Psychology* 81, no. 5 (2001):
856–68.

26. Principal Don Vu is quoted in his article, "Passport to Tolerance,"
Edutopia, October 19, 2018, https://www.edutopia.org/article/passport
-tolerance.

27. Aeriale Johnson is quoted in Heather Cichowski, "This Multi-Colored
Stack of Paint Is Actually Each Student's Unique Skin Color," *A Plus*, August
31, 2018, https://aplus.com/a/teacher-aeriale-johnson-skin-color-paint-diver
sity-project-twitter?no_monetization=true.

28. Molly Barker's classroom empathy project is described in Kristin Miller, "Teaching Compassion: Changing the World through Empathy and Education," *ParentMap*, August 28, 2012, https://www.parentmap.com/article/compassion-changing-the-world-through-empathy-and-education.

29. Antoinette Dempsey-Waters is quoted in Melinda D. Anderson, "What Kids Are Really Learning about Slavery," *Atlantic*, February 2, 2018, https://www.theatlantic.com/education/archive/2018/02/what-kids-are-really-learning-about-slavery/552098.

30. The use of virtual reality in combating racial prejudice is discussed in Donna Banakou, Parasuram D. Hanumanthu, and Mel Slater," Virtual Embodiment of White People in a Black Virtual Body Leads to a Sustained Reduction in Their Implicit Racial Bias," *Frontiers in Human Neuroscience*, 10 (2016): 601.

31. Research on the importance of cross-group friendships is discussed in Dominic Abrams, "Processes of Prejudice: Theory, Evidence, and Intervention," Equality of Human Rights Commission, Spring 2010, https://www.equalityhumanrights.com/sites/default/files/research-report-56-processes-of-prejudice-theory-evidence-and-intervention.pdf.

32. The "Mix It Up Day" at Wilson Middle School is described in Drew C. Wilson, "Mixing It Up with New Friends: Springfield Middle Lunch Table Switch Teaches Life Lessons," *Wilson Times*, February 27, 2019, http://wilsontimes.com/stories/mixing-it-up-with-new-friends,162688.

33. For more on the importance of school-community connections in fostering tolerance in students, see *Education Policies and Practice to Foster Tolerance, Respect for Diversity, and Civic Responsibility in Children and Young People in the EU: Examining the Evidence* (Luxembourg: Publications Office of the European Union, 2016), accessed March 28, 2019, http://nesetweb.eu/wp-content/uploads/2015/08/NESET2_AR3.pdf.

34. The story of student journalists covering the Michael Brown murder in St. Louis is described in Michael Bragg, "High School Journalists Cover Michael Brown's Funeral after Addressing Legal, Safety Concerns," Student Press Law Center, August 27, 2014, http://www.splc.org/article/2014/08/high-school-journalists-cover-michael-browns-funeral-after-addressing-legal-safety-concerns.

35. Cheryl Maayan is quoted in her article "Middle School Social Justice Trips Bring Meaning to Young Teens," *Prizmah Journal*, accessed March 29, 2019, https://prizmah.org/middle-school-social-justice-trips-bring-meaning-young-teens.

36. The importance of teaching tolerance through internal motivation rather than external control is discussed in Lisa Legault, Jennifer N. Gutsell, and Michael Inzlicht, "Ironic Effects of Antiprejudice Messages: How

Motivational Interventions Can Reduce (but Also Increase) Prejudice," *Psychological Science* 22, no. 12 (2011): 1472–77.

CHAPTER THIRTEEN. BEAUTY: SENSITIZING KIDS TO AN AESTHETIC APPRECIATION OF THE WORLD

1. Albert Einstein is quoted in Isaacson, *Einstein*, 387.

2. Albert Einstein is quoted in Isaacson, 223.

3. Albert Einstein is quoted in *Ideas and Opinions*, 66.

4. John Dewey is quoted from his book *Art as Experience* (New York: Tarcher/Perigee, 2005), 38.

5. The brain scan study that dealt with visual and musical beauty is described in Tomohiro Ishizu and Semir Zeki, "Toward a Brain-Based Theory of Beauty," *PLoS One* 6, no. 7 (2011), https://doi.org/10.1371/journal .pone.0021852.

6. The brain scan study that focused on mathematical beauty was described in Semir Zeki et al., "The Experience of Mathematical Beauty and Its Neural Correlates," *Frontiers of Human Neuroscience* 13, no. 8 (February 2014): 68.

7. The common basis for both aesthetic and moral judgments in the medial orbitofrontal cortex is discussed in Mihai Avram et al., "Neuro-functional Correlates of Esthetic and Moral Judgments," *Neuroscience Letters* 8, no. 534 (February 2013): 128–32.

8. Matsuo Bashō's aesthetic is described by Cor van den Heuvel, in *Bashō's Narrow Road: Spring & Autumn Passages* (Berkeley, CA: Stone Bridge Press, 1996), 18–19.

9. Friedrich Schiller is quoted in *Modern History Sourcebook: J. C. Friedrich Von Schiller (1759–1805): Letters upon the Aesthetic Education of Man, 1794* (New York: Fordham University, 1998), https://sourcebooks. fordham.edu/mod/schiller-education.asp.

10. Patricia Tarr is quoted from "Aesthetic Codes in Early Childhood Classrooms: What Art Educators Can Learn from Reggio Emilia," *Art Education* 54, no. 3 (May 2001): 33.

11. The quote from the President's Committee on the Arts and Humanities is taken from Ellen Winner, Thalia R. Goldstein, and Stéphan Vincent-Lancrin, *Educational Research and Innovation. Art for Art's Sake?: The Impact of Arts Education* (Paris: OECD Publishing, 2013), 29.

12. Andrew Simmons is quoted from his article "Why Teaching Poetry is So Important," *Atlantic*, April 8, 2014, https://www.theatlantic.com /education/archive/2014/04/why-teaching-poetry-is-so-important/360346.

13. For studies linking art education to academic achievement, see Daniel H. Bowen and Brian Kisida, "Investigating Causal Effects of Arts Education Experiences: Experimental Evidence from Houston's Arts Access

Initiative," *Research Brief for the Houston Independent School District* 7, no. 3 (February, 2019), https://kinder.rice.edu/sites/g/files/bxs1676/f/down loads/Brief%20-%20Investigating%20Causal%20Effects%20of%20Arts%20 Education%20Experiences.pdf; and Mariale M. Hardiman et al., "The Effects of Arts-Integrated Instruction on Memory for Science Content," *Trends in Neuroscience and Education* 14 (March 2019): 25–32.

14. For an article critical of the integration of the arts into academic subjects, see Jay P. Greene, "Arts Integration Is a Sucker's Game," *Education Week,* October 2, 2017, https://www.edweek.org/ew/articles/2017/10/04 /arts-integration-is-a-suckers-game.html.

15. Ellen Winner and Lois Hetland are quoted from their article, "The Arts and Academic Achievement: What the Evidence Shows," *Arts Education Policy Review* 102, no. 5 (2001): 3–6.

16. For information about the Monart method of art instruction, go to the website of the Monart School of the Arts, accessed March 29, 2019, https://monart.com; or see Mona Brookes, *Drawing with Children: A Creative Method for Adult Beginners, Too* (New York: Tarcher, 1996).

17. The Getty art skills are listed in "Grade-by-Grade Guide to Building Visual Arts Lessons—Grades 5 & 6." J. Paul Getty Museum, accessed March 29, 2019, http://www.getty.edu/education/teachers/building_lessons /grades_5_6.html.

18. The 2016 music and visual art scores of American students are reported in Hayley Miller, "U.S. Students Are Struggling in the Arts. Donald Trump's Budget Would Make the Problem Worse," *Huffington Post,* April 30, 2017, https://www.huffingtonpost.com/entry/us-students-strug gling-arts-and-donald-trump_us_58ff678be4b0c46f0782711b.

19. Rudolf Steiner is quoted from his lecture "Truth, Beauty, and Goodness," given in Dornach, Switzerland, on January 19, 1923, Rudolf Steiner Archive & e.Lib, accessed March 29, 2019, https://wn.rsarchive.org/Lec tures/19230119p01.html.

20. The fifth-grade teacher's aesthetic lesson on the atmosphere is described in Mark Girod, Todd Twyman, and Steve Wojcikiewicz, "Teaching and Learning Science for Transformative, Aesthetic Experience," *Journal of Science Teacher Education* 21, no. 7 (November 2010): 801–24, https://www.researchgate.net/publication/225646442_Teaching_and _Learning_Science_for_Transformative_Aesthetic_Experience.

21. The teacher's aesthetic lesson on molecular motion was given in Kevin J. Pugh and Mark Girod, "Science, Art, and Experience: Constructing a Science Pedagogy from Dewey's Aesthetics," *Journal of Science Teacher Education* 18, no. 1 (February 2007): 9–27.

22. Carl Connelly's description of a museum art piece is given in Tracie Costantino, "Articulating Aesthetic Understanding through Art Making," *International Journal of Education & the Arts* 8, no. 1 (February 6, 2007),

https://www.researchgate.net/publication/234747515_Articulating_Aes
thetic_Understanding_through_Art_Making.

23. Maxine Greene is quoted from her book *Variations on a Blue Gui-
tar: The Lincoln Center Institute Lectures on Aesthetic Education* (New
York: Teachers College Press, 2018), 54.

24. The potter's art making at an elementary school was described in
Dustin Fox, "Artist Shows How Ceramics Are Made at Donehoo," *Gadsden
Times,* February 15, 2019, https://www.gadsdentimes.com/news/20190215
/artist-shows-how-ceramics-are-made-at-donehoo.

25. Composer and musician Andrew Lipke is quoted in Brandon Baker,
"Local Composer Looks to Instill Lifelong Confidence in Mt. Airy Middle
Schoolers," *Philly Voice,* June 8, 2016, https://www.phillyvoice.com/henry
-h-houston-students-andrew-lipke-recognized-harrisburg-classroom
-recorded-album.

26. The fourth-grade art teacher's comments on "art as struggle" are in
Amanda Karioth Thompson, "Sealey Fourth-Graders Learn to Analyze
Art, Emotion," *Tallahassee Democrat,* January 29, 2019, https://www.tal
lahassee.com/story/life/wellness/2019/01/29/sealey-fourth-graders-ana
lyze-art-emotion/2704594002.

27. Elliot Eisner and Herbert Read's vision of education as the preparation of artists is given in Elliot W. Eisner, "Artistry in Education," *Scandi-
navian Journal of Educational Research* 47, no. 3 (July 2003): 373–84.

28. Howard Gardner is quoted in Sandra L. Bryan and Marsha M. Sprague,
"Educating the Spirit for Beauty," *Classroom Leadership* 2, no. 4 (December
1998/January 1999), http://www.ascd.org/publications/classroom-leadership
/dec1998/Educating-the-Spirit-for-Beauty.aspx.

29. Frank Lloyd Wright is quoted in John Rattenbury, *A Living Architecture: Frank Lloyd Wright and Taliesin Architects* (Portland, OR: Pomegranate Communications, 2000), 67.

CHAPTER FOURTEEN. THE EINSTEIN CLASSROOM: EDUCATION FOR OUR CHILDREN'S FUTURE

1. Albert Einstein is quoted in *Ideas and Opinions,* 63.

2. Goethe is quoted from his book *Wilhelm Meister's Apprenticeship*
(Princeton, NJ: Princeton University Press, 1989), 326.

3. See Chapter 9, note 1.

4. Balzac's teacher is quoted in Illingworth and Illingworth, *Lessons
from Childhood,* 86.

5. Johann Georg Albrechtsberger is quoted in Amanda Karioth Fischer,
Beethoven: A Character Study (New York: Dodd, Mead, and Company,
1905), 21.

6. John Gurdon's teacher is quoted in Nicholas Wade, "Cloning and Stem Cell Work Earns Nobel," *New York Times*, October 8, 2012, https://www .nytimes.com/2012/10/09/health/research/cloning-and-stem-cell-discoveries -earn-nobel-prize-in-medicine.html.

7. The Gallup poll of teacher engagement is summarized in *State of America's Schools Report: The Path to Winning Again in Education*, Gallup, 2014, https://www.gallup.com/services/178769/state-america-schools-report .aspx.

8. Jane Goodall is quoted in her keynote address at the September 21, 2013, Humane Education Conference, "Educating for a Just, Peaceful and Sustainable Future."

9. H. L. Mencken is quoted from his book *A Mencken Chrestomathy* (New York: Vintage, 1982), 303.

10. For a look at how the now defunct and discredited No Child Left Behind law stifled learning, see Deborah Meier and George Wood, eds., *Many Children Left Behind: How the No Child Left Behind Act Is Damaging Our Children and Our Schools* (Boston: Beacon Press, 2004).

11. Nietzsche's phrase is taken from his essay *The Use and Abuse of History* (New York: Cosimo Classics, 2005), 23.

12. For information about the use of bribes to gain students college admissions and scholarships, see Jennifer Medina, Katie Benner, and Kate Taylor, "Actresses, Business Leaders and Other Wealthy Parents Charged in U.S. College Entry Fraud," *New York Times*, March 12, 2019, https://www .nytimes.com/2019/03/12/us/college-admissions-cheating-scandal.html.

13. Edward Thorndike's statement appeared in his article "The Contribution of Psychology to Education," *Journal of Educational Psychology* 1, no. 1 (1910), at Classics in the History of Psychology, accessed March 29, 2019, https://psychclassics.yorku.ca/Thorndike/education.htm.

14. For information about how school-ranking websites influence real estate values, see Valerie Strauss, "What To Know before Using School Ratings Tools from Real Estate Companies," *Washington Post*, June 14, 2017, https://www.washingtonpost.com/news/answer-sheet/wp/2017/06/14 /what-to-know-before-using-school-ratings-tools-from-real-estate-companies.

15. For a British take on the problems with educational acronyms, see "Secret Teacher: WALT, WILF, EBI—We're Awash with Useless Acronyms," *Guardian*, December 26, 2015, https://www.theguardian.com /teacher-network/2015/dec/26/secret-teacher-awash-with-useless-acronyms.

16. For information about the vagaries of textbook adoption committees, see *The Mad, Mad World of Textbook Adoption* (Washington, DC: Thomas B. Fordham Institute, September 2004), https://edex.s3-us-west-2. amazonaws.com/publication/pdfs/Mad%20World_Test2_8.pdf.

17. For an excellent critical view of for-profit schools and privatization in general, see Diane Ravitch, *Reign of Error: The Hoax of the Privatization*

Movement and the Danger to America's Public Schools (New York: Vintage, 2014).

18. For a description of the opt-out movement, see "Just Say No to Standardized Tests: Why and How to Opt Out," FairTest, April 2018, http://www.fairtest.org/get-involved/opting-out; and Oren Pizmony-Levy, "Opinion: The Opt-Out Movement is Gaining Ground, Quietly." *Hechinger Report*, October 18, 2018, https://hechingerreport.org/opinion-the-opt-out-move ment-is-gaining-ground-quietly. For a report on a Chicago teachers' strike that sought to eliminate value-added assessment of teachers, see Richard Rothstein, "Teacher Accountability and the Chicago Teachers Strike," *Working Economics*, Economic Policy Institute, September 14, 2012, https://www.epi.org/blog/teacher-accountability-chicago-teachers.

19. One book that provides practical guidelines for initiating substantive school change is Harvey Alvey's *Fighting for Change in Your School: How to Avoid Fads and Focus on Substance* (Alexandria, VA: ASCD, 2017).

APPENDIX A. WEAPONS OF MASS INSTRUCTION: FIFTEEN REASONS STANDARDIZED TESTS ARE WORTHLESS

1. Donald McCabe of Rutgers University surveyed twenty-five thousand high school students from 2001 to 2008 and found that more than 90 percent said they had cheated in some way. See Maura J. Casey, "Digging Out Roots of Cheating in High School," *New York Times*, October 12, 2008, https://www.nytimes.com/2008/10/13/opinion/13mon4.html. Misuse of psychostimulants like Adderall for studying purposes is discussed in Shaheen E. Lakhan and Annette Kirchgessner, "Prescription Stimulants in Individuals with and without Attention Deficit Hyperactivity Disorder: Misuse, Cognitive Impact, and Adverse Effects," *Brain and Behavior* 2, no. 5 (September 2012): 661–77.

2. Cheating by teachers in the Chicago Public Schools is discussed in Steven D. Leavitt and Stephen J. Dubner, *Freakonomics: A Rogue Economist Explores the Hidden Side of Everything* (New York: William Morrow, 2009). For information on the teacher cheating scandal in the Atlanta Public Schools, see Valerie Strauss, "How and Why Convicted Atlanta Teachers Cheated on Standardized Tests," *Washington Post*, April 1, 2015, https://www.washingtonpost.com/news/answer-sheet/wp/2015/04/01/how-and-why-convicted-atlanta-teachers-cheated-on-standardized-tests.

3. For information on the impact of standardized testing on creativity, see Don Batt, "Standardized Tests are Killing Our Students' Creativity, Desire to Learn," *Denver Post*, March 7, 2013, https://www.denverpost.com/2013/03/07/standardized-tests-are-killing-our-students-creativity-desire-to-learn.

4. For information on the inequities in standardized testing, see Zachary A. Goldfarb, "These Four Charts Show How the SAT Favors, Rich, Educated Families," *Washington Post*, March 5, 2014, https://www.washingtonpost .com/news/wonk/wp/2014/03/05/these-four-charts-show-how-the-sat -favors-the-rich-educated-families; and for information about socioeconomic inequities in American schools, see Jonathan Kozol, *Savage Inequalities: Children in America's Schools* (New York: Broadway Books, 2012).

5. For a teacher's personal perspective on teaching to the test, see Kelly Gallagher, "Why I Will Not Teach to the Test," *Education Week*, November 12, 2010, https://www.edweek.org/ew/articles/2010/11/17/12gallagher _ep.h30.html.

6. For the relationship between standardized testing and stress, see Christina Simpson, "Effects of Standardized Testing on Students' Well-Being," Harvard Graduate School of Education, May 2016, https://projects .iq.harvard.edu/files/eap/files/c._simpson_effects_of_testing_on_well _being_5_16.pdf.

7. For a look at alternative assessments that provide different ways for students to demonstrate their knowledge, see Deborah Meier and Matthew Knoester, *Beyond Testing: Seven Assessments of Students and Schools More Effective Than Standardized Tests* (New York: Teachers College Press, 2017).

8. See Gould, *Mismeasure of Man*.

9. For information about the study of Harvard graduates who could not give an accurate account of why it's cold in winter and warmer in summer, see Howard Gardner, *The Disciplined Mind: Beyond Facts and Standardized Tests, the K-12 Education that Every Child Deserves* (New York: Penguin, 2000).

10. For a look at how expectations affect standardized test results, see Robert Rosenthal and Lenore Jacobson, *Pygmalion in the Classroom: Teacher Expectation and Pupils' Intellectual Development* (Carmarthen, UK: Crown House Publishing, 2003).

Index

About the Author

Thomas Armstrong, PhD, is the executive director of the American Institute for Learning and Human Development (www.institute4learning.com) and an award-winning author and speaker who has been an educator for more than forty-five years. Over 1.3 million copies of his books are in print in English on issues related to learning and human development. He is the author of nineteen books, including *Multiple Intelligences in the Classroom, Mindfulness in the Classroom, Neurodiversity in the Classroom, The Human Odyssey* and *The Power of the Adolescent Brain.* His books have been translated into twenty-eight languages. Dr. Armstrong has given more than one thousand keynotes, workshop presentations, and lectures on six continents in twenty-nine countries and forty-four states in the past thirty-two years. His clients have included *Sesame Street,* the Bureau of Indian Affairs, the European Council of International Schools, the Republic of Singapore, and several state departments of education. He can be reached by emailing him at thomas@institute4learning.com.

Twitter: @Dr_Armstrong